FLORIDA'S
FINEST
COOKBOOK

A Cookbook
from
The Junior League of South Brevard

"Recipes from America's Space Coast"

The Junior League of South Brevard, Inc. is an organization of women committed to promoting volunteerism and to improving the community through the effective action and leadership of trained volunteers. Its purpose is exclusively educational and charitable.

The Junior League reaches out to women of all races, religions, or national origins who demonstrate an interest in and commitment to volunteerism.

Money raised in the community furthers The Junior League's purpose and programs.

	First Edition	
First Printing	October 1984	10,000 copies
Second Printing	October 1988	5,000 copies
Third Printing	May 1992	10,000 copies

Additional copies may be obtained by addressing:

Florida's Finest
Junior League of South Brevard, Inc.
Post Office Box 361905
Melbourne, Florida 32936
(407) 255-9545

Cover Illustration by Fred Daunno
Cover Design by Bob Haydon

ISBN-0-9613261-0-7

Printed in the USA by
WIMMER BROTHERS
A Wimmer Company
Memphis • Dallas

Introduction

The vastness of this area is breathtaking. A glance brings miles of uninterrupted pastureland, dotted only by a few hammocks, scrubs, or a single palm standing at the horizon. The sky is a watercolor painting — fading from azure to periwinkle to pale red and disappearing beyond a line of pinetrees. A sweeping view finds the rising of an interstate highway carrying its population to a certain destination. Swamplands and tropical wilderness have given way to high-tech industry and the Space Age.

Yet the charm and loveliness that is Brevard remains today. The Indian River Lagoon sparkles in a mid-morning sun. In the early days of settlement, the river carried many pioneering families to their new homes and served as a main artery for transporting goods. Now as part of the Intracoastal Waterway, the rich land along the river produces world-renown citrus. Some seventy miles of white sand beaches have made Brevard an attractive vacation destination for decades. The beach is a haven in itself, the ocean a panacea. A few hours of quiet solitude or a day building sandcastles and chasing waves renews even the weariest spirit. The sand is warm, the salt air inviting, the ocean soothing. It's true: once you get sand in your shoes, it's hard to leave.

The Junior League of South Brevard invites you to enjoy the delights of the area through its cookbook, **Florida's Finest**. Some recipes are family traditions, passed from grandmother to granddaughter over a mixing bowl. Some are more current creations intended to become family treasures. We have seasoned our collection with regional favorites such as Mullet Dip, Mud Pie, and Mango Ice Cream as well as the old standards of Conch Fritters, Key Lime Pie, and Florida Orange Cake. Here's to sand in your shoes ... and a pleasant taste in your mouth!

—*Noretta D'Albora Huff*
A Native Brevardian

Junior League
of South Brevard, Inc.

1500 W. Eau Gallie Blvd., Suite 3B, Melbourne, FL 32935, (407) 255-9545

Community Projects

- **Immunization:** Public awareness campaign focusing on early immunization of young children.
- **Mini Grant Program:** Funding assistance for eligible non-profit agencies.
- **Space Coast Science Center:** Supporting the Center through research and development of exhibits.
- **Elderly Care/Ventures in Living:** Funding and fellowship for field trips and activities in conjunction with the Easter Seal Adult Day Care Program.
- **The Haven for Children:** Founded by the JLSB in 1987, a temporary, emergency shelter for abused and neglected infants and children up to 6 years of age.
- **Parent Educators:** Classes based on the STEP program (Systematic Training for Effective Parenting) in preparation for the challenges and responsibilities of parenting.
- **Teen Yellow Pages:** A pocket size referral guide distributed to 25,000 Brevard County teens.
- **Teen Parents Education Program:** Education for teens about pregnancy prevention, educating teen mothers about babies and nutrition.
- **Home Management Development:** A program consisting of classes on budget skills, basic home repair, nutrition and care (in conjunction with Habitat for Humanity and the Salvation Army).
- **Life Skills:** Combination program featuring Parent Education classes, Home Management classes and workshops on Elderly Care.
- **Fire Safety House:** Mobile unit used to teach fire and home safety.
- **Habitat for Humanity House:** Building a house in conjunction with South Brevard Habitat for Humanity.

4

Junior League of South Brevard Membership

Hollis Adams
Lisa Adams
Beverly Addicott
Sylvia Alford
Mary Allen
Janelle Alward
Colleen Amgott
Margo Angleton
Nancy Ankney
Barbara Armstrong
Tracey Armstrong
Deana Austin
Julie Austin
Chevon Baccus
Diane Baccus Horsley
Ronda Banner
Becky Barkley
Carolyn Basile
Wendy Becker
Patricia Beckman
Kennie Kay Bender
Ann Bettin
Sandy Bockman
Joanne Bolivar
June Bordelon
Catherine Bostwick McGee
Nancy Boyd
Suzanne Boyd
Margaret Boyer
Penny Brandt
Sarah Brewer
Pat Briel
Sharlee Brittingham
Terry Brown
Marty Brownell
Cynthia Brubaker
Lynda Brutz
Sandra Bryan
Dee Burner
Miriam Burns
Elaine Butts
Deedie Calhoun
Sandee Cameron
Siclinda Canty-Elliott
Donna Capps
Barbara Carnichael
Mimi Carter
Dianne Caylor
Joan Cerow
Marion Cheney
Gail Chiles
Jane Cislo
Carol Clark
Maria Clark
Cathleen Clarke

Joan Clements
Janine Cleveland
Katherine Cobb
Roslyn Cobb
Sandra Coe
Barbara Cofer
Judith Coleman
Linda Coleman
Louanne Coll
Carol Collins
Marion Collins
Ann Corcoran
Dianne Creel
Connie Crouch
Linda Crouch
Sarah Crytzer
Kelly Cunningham
Phyllis Curry
Valerie Davis
Laurie DeBoer
Pam Dettmer
Gladys Donovan
Ann Downey
Julia Dreyer
Sherrie Dugan
Mirna Dujovne
Amy Edgerton
Ellen Eells
Pam Egan
Stephany Eley
Elizabeth Evans
Kathy Eward
Lynn Ezelle
Sylvia Fain
Holly Fay
Laura Featherhoff
Linda Hallenbeck
Susan Finch
Sherri Finger-Gonzalez
Joan Flavin
Doris Floyd
Dorothy Foley
Catherine Ford
Karen Foreman
Eileen Franco
Pat Gachet
Peggy Gagnon
Kay Gardner
Debbie Gentry
Olivia Gillespie
Barbara Gillis
Larie Gleason
Vanessa Goldman
Penny Goode
Mary Jane Goodwin

Alice Graff
Yvonne Graham
Sally Gray
Tory Gray
Jamie Grofik
Lynda Hall
Nancy Hall
Jean Halloway
Patti Hamilton
Lanette Haney
Bobbi Hart
Mary Hartdegen
Judy Healy
Lydia Heatwole
Louisa Hedman
Tanya Herbert
Rhonda Hester
Barbara Higgins
Pam Hobson
Kelly Hoffman
Susan Hopkins
Leslie Hoppes
Leslie Howard
Yvonne Hoyman
Robin Huck
Retta Huff
Valree Hughes
Elna Humphrey
Antonia Hunt
Donna Inghram
Lu Lu Jane
Becky Johnson
Kaaren Johnson
Mary Kate Johnson
Shirley Johnson
Alexis Johnsten
Patricia Jones
Sharon Jones
Lisa Kahn
Pamela Kaminski
Henel Keehn
Barbara Keller
Janet Kemerait
Judi Kerr
Suzanne Kerr
Janice Kershaw
Jill Klucher
Paulette Kmoch
Sharon Knowles
Ann Knowlton
Althea Krasny
Annelle Krempely
Ann Krieger
Janet Kull
Sansi Landry

Junior League of South Brevard Membership

CeCee Lane
Mary Lou Lane
Anne Lange
Ann Law
Rochelle Lawandales
Smokey Leathers
Jil Lewis
Danielle Lightle
Bell Lilienfeld
Marcia Littlejohn
Nancy Livingston
Ann Lorelle
Barbara Losson
Lisa MacDonald
Sue Maguire
Mary Mallory
Sallie Manassah
Gloria Mandel
Ferne Mann
Peggy Marquette
Reedi Massey
Margie Matheson
Sandra McAllister
Donna McCain
Melba McCaslin
Kathleen McClelland
Delores McLaughlin
Beth McMullan
Teresa McNeight
Carol McQuagge
Cathleen Meeder
Lee Ann Meehan
Mary Meeks
Jackie Menzel
Liane Mihlebach
Melinda Miller
Dian Milligan
Dorothy Mitterling
Lettie Mizell
Dureene Moore
Rita Moreno
Susie Morris
Shirley Ann Moss
Sara Moule
Meredith Mullins
Catherine Murtha
Gail Nace
Pat Nason
Sharon Neilson
Grace Nelson
Sherry Nelson
Maxine Nohrr
Christine O'Connor
Robbin O'Neal

Sheila Olson
Ginny Osman
Kathy Osman
Patricia Ottesen
Norma Padgett
Cinda Parker
Ruth Anne Parker
Joni Paulson
Marilyn Penn
Nancy Pepple
Pamela Peters
Carol Platt
Dottie Ports
Wendy Potter
Mary Carol Poynter
Katie Prestwood
Patricia Puritt
Anne Randall
Bonnie Ranzino
Kathy Rathmann
Jan Reed
Kim Register
Marty Remark
Dianne Rhodes
Judy Roach
Mary Roberts
Joy Robertson
Judith Robinson
Gloria Rochelle
Sherry Rogers
Michele Romandetti
Denise Rotolante
Clara Roy
Sunny Rudloff
Barbara Rudolph-Smith
Kathleen Ruff
Pamela Rufo
Sno-Ann Russell
Monica Russo
Sherry Ryals
Charlotte Sandberg
Dixie Sansom
Diane Scheuerer
Kela Schram
Kate Setterbo
Barbara Shaw
Mona Ann Shumake
Martha Sinclair
Janeille Sisserson
Roslyn Smedberg
Constance Smith
Joyce Smith
Rhanda Smith
LeAnn Smithson

Loan Sorensen
Carmen Spector
Carol Stewart
Julie Storms
Marlene Stroop
Lisa Stump
Lori Sutherland
Susan Suttles
Janice Teegen
Maryellyn Thomas
Mona Thompson
Mary Lu Tombleson
Marcie Tomcykoski
Carolyn Tooley
Lorraine Totty
Carol Tumser
Kathy Turner
Marcia Turner
Sherry Tydor
Rosemary Ubinger
Judy Ufferman
Sharon Underill
Janice Unger
Susie Van Meter
Elaine Vicari
Rosie Vita
Laurie Walker
Mary Wallis
Susan Walters
Ann Warden
Kimberly Warden
Robbie Watkins
Mimi Wells
Holly Wesche Zeiters
Betsy West
Mary Westerfield
Kimberly Wetzel
Terri White
Barbara Whittington
Penny Wilkie
Terrie Wilkowske
Joy Willard-Williford
Ann Williams
Theresa Williams
Dorn Williamson
Barbara Wilson
Regina Wilson
Gay Winters
Karen Witt
Lorraine Woodley
Lisa Wright
Debra Kaplan Young
Patty Ziegler
Mary Zizzo

Table of Contents

Original Cookbook Committee

CHAIRMAN	Anne Fuller
CO-CHAIRMAN	Pat Briel
	Margo Angleton
	Pattie Bowman
	Ann Downey
	Jeanne Duce
	Sylvia Fain
	Pam Fitzgerald
	Bobbi Hart
	Alden Jacobus
	Alexis Johnsten
	Darci Jones-Francey
	Sharon Knowles
	Mary Lou Lane
	Jane Madry
	Gloria Mandel
	Jenifer Marx
	Melba McCaslin
	Pat Pruitt
	Clara Roy
	Charlotte Sandberg
	Pat Scafati
	Gwen Van Landingham

Cookbook Committee

CHAIRMAN	Dureene Moore
TREASURER	Donna Capps
COMMITTEE MEMBERS	Pat Gachet
	Jean Halloway
	Ann Krieger
	Lisa Stump

SPACE COAST TRADITIONS

Pineapple I, By Mari M. Conneen. Original Watercolor.

HOLIDAY BRUNCH

Syllabub
Eau Gallie Oyster Bisque
Quail Southern Style
Wild Rice Pilaf
Spinach Salad Mold
Holiday Ambrosia

Christmas In Old Brevard

From the late 1920's to the early 1950's, one of Brevard's pioneer families held an annual seated Christmas breakfast for their friends and neighbors. After presents had been opened and wrapping paper tossed away, the fire was rekindled and the family awaited the arrival of the first guests.

The party began on the front lawn overlooking the beautiful Indian River with guests sipping goblets of syllabub or eggnog. Everyone then adjourned indoors to be seated at banquet tables winding throughout the decorated first-floor rooms.

The highlight of the Christmas breakfast was the quail on toast. In the early years, the men hunted the week prior to Christmas for the quail, which were then so plentiful in the Brevard area. In later years, after refrigerated storage was introduced, the men hunted all fall to fill rented lockers with quail.

The breakfast ended with a delectable citrus ambrosia, using oranges and grapefruit freshly picked from the trees dotting the yard. At mid-afternoon the guests meandered on to another of several holiday parties along Brevard's riverfront. Christmas in old Brevard was truly a day of celebration.

PACKING HOUSE PARTY

Traditionally, grove families celebrated the close of a successful season by entertaining at a "packing house party."

Smoked Mullet Dip
Guacamole Dip
Cornish Hens a l' Orange
Artichoke Pasta Salad
Marinated Broccoli and Cauliflower
Biscuits
Orange Blossom Honey
Florida Orange Cake

Florida Gold

The Indian River is 150 miles long. The land that borders it produces some of the finest citrus products in the world. This land is rich and fertile; the climate is warmed by the ocean breezes. These are perfect conditions to grow, what is, by its own industry standards, the sweetest, juiciest, and richest fruit of all.

Indian River fruit includes ten varieties of oranges, four of grapefruit, two of tangerines, lemons, limes, kumquats, and calamondins. Other than citrus, the area has produced pineapples, coconuts, avocados, mangos, papaya, guava, bananas, sugar cane, and scuppernongs (a plum-flavored grape).

The citrus industry developed in the mid-1800's when, following the War Between the States, soldiers and their families were given land to homestead. These pioneers cleared their land by hand, while facing bears, panthers, alligators, rattlesnakes, a few unfriendly Indians, and swarms of mosquitoes. Having survived these hardships, the industry was nearly destroyed by hurricanes and freezes in the 1890's. But with great faith and determination, these hardy pioneers started over; and by 1910, millions of boxes of fruit were again being shipped to northern markets.

Today, fruit is usually picked by hand, then sent to packing houses, where it is washed, sorted, graded, and packed for shipment. The fruit may be sent to canneries or to retail or wholesale markets in the U.S. or overseas. It is often shipped in beautiful gift boxes to many parts of the world; but, wherever it goes, Indian River fruit is Florida Gold!

INDIAN RIVER BUFFET

Deviled Crab
Boiled Shrimp
Deviled Clams
Crab Salad
Ranch House Beans
Indian River Cole Slaw
Garlic Bread

Seafood Celebration

From the banks of the river and the ocean jetties, in freshwater lakes and in saltwater lagoons, almost everyone in Florida fishes. Offering some of the finest fishing grounds on the eastern seaboard, Brevard waters abound in hundreds of varieties of seafood — Florida lobster, shrimp, rock shrimp, oysters, scallops, crabs, clams, mullet, trout, grouper, snapper, pompano, kingfish, mackeral, redfish, catfish, and drum. An old tale tells of a fisherman who wore wide-necked, over-sized shirts fastened snugly at the waist and wrists. The enterprising man then dunked himself in the river until his shirt was teeming with fish.

At the turn of the century, the river residents celebrated their rich sea bounty with fish fry parties featuring mullet and hush puppies. In the 1920's an annual Washington's Birthday Fish Fry in Old Eau Gallie became such a widely anticipated event that folks traveled for miles to attend it.

Today, the fish-fry tradition is carried on in a tiny seaside community in South Brevard. Started in 1966 as a community effort, the Grant Seafood Festival called attention to the necessity of protecting the shell-fish industry and the Indian River's seafood resources. More than 50,000 people from nearly every state attend the two-day event, making it one of the largest and best-known seafood festivals in the country. The festival set a world record in 1984, when 17,600 frog legs were cooked and served!

BARBECUE BONFIRE

Ella's Old St. Augustine Chicken Perloo
Chicken and Ribs
Chicken Barbecue Sauce
Marna's Swamp Cabbage
Confetti Salad
Fresh Mint Tea

A Day At The Beach

Beach parties have always been popular entertainment in Brevard County. Decades ago, the main course of the beach picnic was perloo (pilaff or pilau), a thick stew made with shrimp, chicken, or ham, rice, tomatoes, and datil pepper. The perloo simmered for hours in large pots hanging over a fire. Other traditional picnic fare was swamp cabbage from freshly cut hearts of palm. Trees near the picnic site were chopped down, and the tenderest of the hearts were served raw with seasoned mayonnaise or dipped in a bowl of bacon drippings, according to an old Seminole Indian recipe. After dark, huge bonfires were built along the beach in an attempt to attract the rum-runners who cruised Brevard's coastline.

Today Space Coast residents and visitors enjoy the all-day beach party! Join in and spread your brightly colored blanket on the golden sand and watch the dazzling sun creep high over the blue horizon. While seagulls fly in perfect formation overhead, enjoy your sunrise breakfast of orange juice, hard-boiled eggs, and doughnuts. At lunchtime, pull out the citrus iced tea and cold crab sandwiches. Toss leftover crumbs to the scampering sand crabs as they scurry in and out of their hide-aways, eyeing you suspiciously.

After an afternoon of frisbee, volleyball, surfing, or sailboarding, you are ready for a quick sail along the coast in a colorful catamaran. Back on shore, it's time to sit back and relax before the beach barbecue. Build a sandcastle, comb the beach for shells, watch the hundreds of coquina, as they free themselves from the breaking waves and quickly disappear into the sand.

As the sun goes down and the breezes pick up, the smell of salty air and suntan lotion give way to the aroma of charcoal and sizzling meat. After a hearty feast of corn-on-the-cob, baked beans, Cole slaw, ribs and chicken, take a stroll down the beach. Search for turtle tracks and you may witness one of nature's phenomena — a mammoth mother loggerhead laying her eggs.

MOONLIGHT CRUISE

Seviche Balboa
General Clover's Cheese Spread
Crackers
Cold Avocado Soup
Curried Chicken Salad
Pineapple Muffins
Orange Blossom Special
Sharon's Caramel Pecan Bars

Brevard Waters

Centuries ago, bearded pirates prowled the high seas, ravaging small skiffs and sturdy galleons. They traded their stolen bounty for food and rum, telling tales of Indians and wealth along the Florida coast. When pirates or explorers attempted to go ashore, they were attacked by wild natives in fleets of dug-out canoes. But the greatest danger at sea was not the pirates or the Indians, it was the unforgiving natural elements — the devastating hurricanes, the gale-force winds, the swift currents, and the lashing tides.

Although there was blockade running and an occasional naval battle during the Civil War, the nineteenth century brought more tranquil times to Brevard waters. Boating was often the only available means of transportation and communication between the settlers. A floating dentist's office, a sailing mailboat that took three weeks to complete its route, and supply boats which served as traveling stores were the order of the day. The lone doctor for the region sailed up and down the river blowing a conch shell to announce his arrival. If a person needed medical treatment, he marked the end of his dock with a flag to signal the doctor to stop.

Drastic changes have taken place in Brevard County since the launching of the Space Age. Since the completion of the intracoastal waterway as a luxury cruise route, millions of dollars have been invested in marinas, yacht clubs, docks, waterfront shopping centers, restaurants, and a vast array of watercraft. Brevard boaters may choose the serene waters of the Indian or Banana Rivers — or they may opt to navigate Sebastian Inlet and challenge the Atlantic.

TENNIS BRUNCH

Mimosas
Romaine Soup
Sausage Cheese Bake
Cracker-style Grits
Rise 'n' Shine

Sports Scene

Gently swaying palm trees, live oak trees laced with Spanish moss, sweet-scented Confederate jasmine, and flaming hibiscus blossoms provide a perfect backdrop to the casual lifestyle that characterizes Brevard County. Add bright, sunny skies and cooling ocean breezes, and one has a haven for year-'round golf and tennis. It is not surprising that golf courses and tennis courts abound in this area.

Golf is a recent addition to the Brevard sports scene but its popularity is thriving. By contrast, tennis has been played in Central Florida for several decades and it continues to be a perennial favorite. In the early 1900's, residents spent their Sundays at one of the river plantations for a morning of lawn tennis, followed by an afternoon of sailing on the Indian River.

Today, tennis parties are a popular way of entertaining guests — providing both fun and exercise. After a morning of sizzling singles or friendly doubles matches, the tennis enthusiasts adjourn to the hostess' poolside patio for a brunch buffet. The tables are often covered with crisp white cloths, spring-green napkins, and baskets of red geraniums. On the buffet table one finds a green-checkered tablecloth adorned with an oversized basket of tropical flowers, accented with trailing ivy. Brevardians certainly have a courtship with the grand game of tennis.

GALA COCKTAIL PARTY

Gala Crabmeat Dip
Frosted Artichokes with Caviar
Florida Crackers
Miniature Chicken Drumsticks
Baked Ham with Dijon Mustard
Meatballs Caliente
Spicy Pineapple Jelly
served on cream cheese
Clara's Chocolate-Covered Cherries
Divine Divinity
Mini-cheesecake Cups
Monte Carlos
Baklava
Cinnamon-Sugared Pecans

Cultural Customs

Man cannot live on sand, surf, and sun alone — even in Florida! Fortunately, the natural attributes of Brevard County are well complemented by a myriad of fine cultural offerings. These include a symphony orchestra, an art museum, a community theater, a municipal band, a science center, dance groups, an historical museum, a concert series, and several sidewalk art festivals. In addition, the area boasts fine medical and social service facilities, as well as excellent schools and colleges.

To support and maintain the high quality of life on the Space Coast, many of Brevard's most important social happenings are fund-raising events: cocktail parties, receptions, dinners, and elegant balls hosted by non-profit organizations. From barbecues to black ties, all parties have the essential ingredients of sparkling drink, superb food, and enjoyable socializing.

For many years, one of the highlights of the social season was the annual Champagne Gala hosted by the Junior League of South Brevard. The party was well-known for its large silver platters laden with sumptuous hors d'oeuvres and desserts created by some of Brevard's best cooks. Around the beautifully decorated tables, the party guests sipped the chilled champagne, sampled the spicy dips and delicate meringues, and mingled with old and new friends for an evening replete with festivity and conviviality.

OUT OF THIS WORLD

Dried Apricots (IM)
Breakfast Roll (I) (NF)
Granola with Blueberries (R)
Vanilla Instant Breakfast (B)
Grapefruit Drink (B)

Ground Beef with Pickle Sauce (T)
Noodles and Chicken (R)
Stewed Tomatoes (T)
Pears (FD)
Almonds (NF)
Strawberry Drink (B)

Tuna (T)
Macaroni and Cheese (R)
Peas with Butter Sauce (R)
Peach Ambrosia (R)
Chocolate Pudding (T) (R)
Lemonade (B)

Foods Fit For An Astronaut

In 1513, the Spanish Royal Historian, Antonio de Herrera, accompanied Ponce de Leon on a mission to find a shorter route to the Far East. Instead, they discovered Cape Canaveral and the eastern coast of Central Florida. De Herrera wrote "And believing that this land was an island, they called it La Florida, because it has a very beautiful view of many cool woodlands, and it is level and uniform; moreover, they discovered it in the time of the feast of the flowers."

Over 400 years later, Cape Canaveral was rediscovered with the launching of the Space Age. Less than two hours south of the United States' oldest permanent settlement of St. Augustine stands the world's gateway to the stars, the Kennedy Space Center. A number of electronics firms have located in the Melbourne area, making Brevard a leader in high technology.

With the dawn of the space program arose new questions: "What on earth does an astronaut eat?" After the first manned orbit, experts found that swallowing food in weightless conditions was relatively easy, once the food reached the mouth! Because helmets could not be removed in the early days of the program, all foods were in bite-sized pieces, freeze-dried, or in toothpaste-type squeeze tubes.

Today, the astronaut in flight eats pretty much what everyone else eats, but the difference is still in the preparation and packaging. Space meals must be appealing and nutritious, light in weight, easily prepared, and safely and conveniently packaged. The food must be able to withstand the pressures, temperatures, and vibrations of a space flight. To meet these unique standards, the food is usually prepared in one of the following ways:

THERMOSTABILIZED (T) — heat-processed foods in aluminum tins.

IRRADIATED (I) — preserved by a radiation process; packaged in flexible foil pouches.

INTERMEDIATE MOISTURE (IM) — dried foods with a low moisture content; in flexible plastic pouches.

FREEZE-DRIED (FD) — foods prepared to the ready-to-eat stage, frozen, then dried in a freeze dryer to remove water. Some may be eaten as is (freeze-dried ice cream), others require addition of moisture.

REHYDRATABLE (R) — dried foods that are rehydrated with water in a semi-rigid plastic container.

BEVERAGES (B) — dry powder mix packed in rehydratable containers.

NATURAL FORM (NF) — foods that are naturally low in moisture, such as nuts, cookies, and candy bars; can be eaten in the same form that they are purchased at the supermarket.

In all likelihood, Ponce de Leon introduced oranges to the North American mainland when he discovered Florida in 1513. However, there is evidence of the orange tree much earlier in history.

"In the full of spring on the banks of a river —
Two big gardens planted with thousands of orange trees.
Their thick leaves are putting the clouds to shame."
                                                    First Century Chinese Poet
                                                                Tu Fu

APPETIZERS

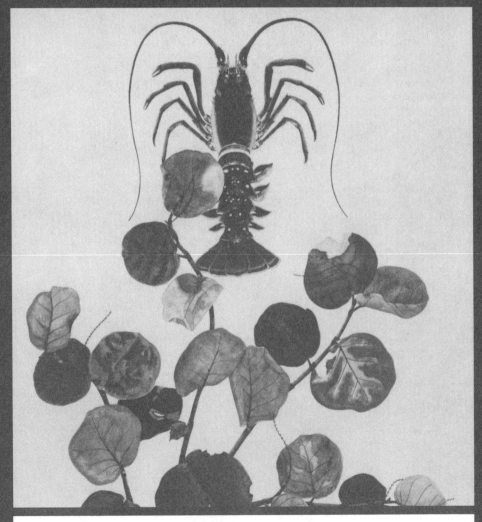

Lobster with Sea Grapes, By Mari M. Conneen.
Original Watercolor. Collection of Mr. & Mrs. Kurt Gsteiger.

Appetizers

* Denotes Quick and Easy Recipes

Seviche Balboa

Yields 1 gallon

2 pounds firm white fresh
    fish, such as grouper
2-3 cups chopped onions
2 hot red peppers, finely
    chopped
6 tablespoons salt
Juice of 24 limes
1 hot red pepper, quartered

*Variations: Use shrimp, scallops
    or conch.*

- Cut fish into ½-inch chunks.
- Place fish and onions in glass jar
  or large ceramic bowl.
- Add chopped peppers, salt and
  lime juice. Stir well.
- Be sure there is enough juice to
  completely cover fish. If not, add
  more.
- Place peppers on top and
  marinate for 4-6 hours. Test for
  hot taste.
- Remove quartered peppers when
  hot enough.
- Refrigerate 24 hours and serve in
  cocktail bowls as appetizers or
  partially drain and serve in large
  bowl with crackers.

Chili Con Queso

Yields ½ gallon

4 pounds Velveeta cheese
2 onions, chopped
8 cloves garlic, minced
1 (16-ounce) can tomatoes,
    drained
2 cups chopped green
    peppers
2 tablespoons
    Worcestershire sauce
3 green chilies, chopped

- Melt cheese, being careful not to
  burn. Add remaining ingredients.
  Mix well.
- Serve hot in chafing dish with
  corn chips.
- Recipe may be halved to serve a
  smaller number.

Guacamole

Serves 6-8

2 ripe avocados
2 tablespoons picante sauce
2 teaspoons lime (or lemon)
   juice, freshly squeezed
½ small onion, finely chopped
Seasoned salt to taste
Corn chips

- Peel and mash avocados.
- Combine with picante sauce, lime juice, onions and seasoned salt.
- Chill. Serve with corn chips.

Harbor Vegetable Dip

Yields 1½ cups

1 cup mayonnaise
2 tablespoons chili sauce
2 tablespoons chopped
   chives
2 tablespoons grated onion
2 teaspoons tarragon vinegar
⅛ teaspoon thyme
¼ teaspoon curry powder
¼ teaspoon salt
Raw vegetables

- Combine first 8 ingredients until well blended.
- Refrigerate until serving time.
- Good with raw vegetables or shrimp.

 To keep guacamole dip from turning dark, place an avocado seed in center of bowl until ready to serve.

Nacho Layered Dip

Serves 12-15

1 ripe avocado, mashed
Garlic salt, to taste
Tabasco, to taste
1 can bean dip
1 can chopped green chilies
1 chopped onion
1 chopped tomato
1 large can ripe olives,
    chopped
1 cup shredded cheese
    (Monterey Jack or
    mozzarella)
Sour cream (optional)

- Mash avocado. Add seasonings.
- Layer ingredients on serving tray
  and surround with nacho chips.

Nelson Family Curry Britton

Serves 4

1 cup mayonnaise
3 tablespoons catsup
1 tablespoon Worcestershire
    sauce
2 tablespoons grated onion
1 tablespoon curry powder
Salt to taste
½ teaspoon Tabasco

- Mix all ingredients and chill.
- Serve with raw vegetables.

*Note: Should be made several days
    ahead.*

Smoked Mullet Dip

Yields 1 cup

1 (3-ounce) plus 1 (8-ounce)
package cream cheese,
softened
2 tablespoons mayonnaise
2 tablespoons milk
1 tablespoon finely chopped
onion
2 tablespoons chopped
pimiento
½-¾ cup smoked mullet,
finely chopped

• Combine all ingredients. Chill.

Note: May substitute 2 tablespoons drained tuna and 2 teaspoons liquid smoke if smoked fish is not available.

Sombrero Dip

Serves 12-15

1 pound ground beef
½ cup chopped onion
¼-½ cup salsa brava
3 teaspoons chili powder
1 teaspoon salt
1 (15-ounce) can red kidney
beans
1 cup grated sharp cheddar
cheese
½ cup chopped onion
½ cup sliced green olives

• Brown meat and onion.
• Stir in salsa brava, chili powder
and salt.
• Mash in beans with liquid. Heat.
• Garnish with cheese, onion and
olives. Serve hot with chips.

Spinach Dip 'n' Rye

Serves 20

1 cup mayonnaise
1 cup sour cream
1 envelope Hidden Valley
  Ranch salad dressing
1 package chopped frozen
  spinach
Pinch dill weed
Pinch onion powder

- Thaw frozen spinach and drain well.
- Mix with all other ingredients.
- Dip should set in refrigerator 2 or 3 hours before serving.
- Serve with rye or pumpernickle bread squares.

Sunset Salsa

Yields 3-4 cups

2 firm ripe tomatoes, finely
  chopped
1 (3-ounce) can black olives,
  chopped
4-6 green onions, finely
  chopped
2 (4-ounce) cans chopped
  green chilies (do not drain)
1 envelope Italian salad
  dressing, prepared
Tabasco to taste

- Mix together well. Let sit several hours. Drain.
- Serve with dip-size Fritos.

Hot Beef Dip

Serves 8-10

1 (8-ounce) package cream
   cheese, softened
½ cup sour cream
1 (2½-ounce) jar dried beef,
   cut into pieces
1 small onion, finely diced
Dash Tabasco
3 tablespoons chopped green
   pepper
¼ cup chopped nuts
Parsley for garnish

- Blend cheese with sour cream.
- Add all other ingredients except nuts and parsley. Blend.
- Spread into baking dish. Add nuts.
- Bake at 350° for 15-20 minutes. Cool 20 minutes.
- Serve with crackers or deli-rye bread.
- Garnish with parsley.

Bacon-Tomato Spread

Serves 6-8

1 (8-ounce) package cream
   cheese, softened
2 tablespoons prepared
   mustard
½ teaspoon celery salt
6 slices bacon, crisply
   cooked, drained and
   crumbled
1 ripe tomato, peeled, seeded
   and finely chopped
¼ cup finely chopped green
   pepper

- Stir together cream cheese, mustard and celery salt.
- Fold in bacon, tomato and pepper.
- Pat into round ball. Wrap in foil or clear wrap. Chill at least 2 hours before serving.

Caviar Mousse

Serves 12

2 (4-ounce) cans lumpfish
  caviar
3 tablespoons chopped fresh
  parsley
2 tablespoons minced onion
1 cup sour cream
¼ teaspoon white pepper
1½ teaspoons unflavored
  gelatin
2 tablespoons water
½ cup whipping cream,
  whipped

- Set aside 2 tablespoons caviar, 2 tablespoons parsley and 1 tablespoon onion for garnish. Cover and refrigerate.
- Combine remaining caviar, parsley and onion with sour cream and pepper in non-metal bowl and blend well.
- Sprinkle gelatin over water in small saucepan. Stir over low heat until gelatin dissolves.
- Remove from heat and stir into caviar mixture.
- Fold in whipped cream.
- Turn into 2-cup non-metal mold.
- Cover and refrigerate until set.
- Unmold and let stand at room temperature 15 minutes before serving.
- Surround with cucumber slices and melba toast. Garnish with reserved caviar, parsley and onion.

Orange Sugared Pecans

Yields 3 cups

1½ cups sugar
½ cup orange juice
1 teaspoon grated orange
  rind
3 cups pecan halves

- Boil sugar and orange juice together until soft-ball stage, 238°.
- Remove from heat.
- Add grated orange rind and pecans.
- Beat until creamy.
- Pour out and separate into pecan halves.

Cold Salmon Mousse

Serves 6

1 tablespoon unflavored
  gelatin softened in ¼ cup
  water or chicken broth
1 cup hot sour cream (do not
  boil)
1 pound canned red salmon,
  drained
¼ cup mayonnaise
1 tablespoon grated onion
1 teaspoon onion powder
1 tablespoon finely chopped
  celery
1 tablespoon Worcestershire
  sauce
3 teaspoons lemon juice
3 drops Tabasco
1 teaspoon salt
¼ teaspoon white pepper
1 cup whipped cream
Capers for garnish
Ripe olives for garnish

- Add softened gelatin to hot sour cream.
- Stir to mix thoroughly and let cool.
- Add salmon broken into pieces, mayonnaise, onion, celery and seasonings.
- Mix all in food processor. Refrigerate.
- When mixture begins to congeal, fold in whipped cream.
- Pour into greased mold and decorate with capers and ripe olives. Serve cold with horseradish mayonnaise.

Watercress Sandwiches

Serves 12

½ cup butter, softened
½ cup finely chopped
  watercress
1 teaspoon grated onion
¾ teaspoon Worcestershire
  sauce
½ teaspoon salt
⅛ teaspoon pepper
1 loaf sandwich bread, crusts
  removed

- Cream butter. Add remaining ingredients.
- Spread on ½ of bread.
- Top with other half of bread.
- Cut sandwiches into quarters.
- Serve on platter garnished with parsley.

Crowned Crab

Serves 20

1 teaspoon gelatin
¼ cup cold water
2 (8-ounce) packages cream cheese
2 tablespoons sherry
¾ teaspoon seasoned salt
1 (2-ounce) jar pimiento
1 (6-ounce) package frozen king crab (thaw, drain and cut up)
⅛ teaspoon black pepper
¼ cup chopped parsley
Fresh parsley for garnish

- Soften gelatin in water. Stir over hot water to dissolve.
- Beat into cream cheese until smooth.
- Add remaining ingredients and pour into 3-cup mold.
- Refrigerate until set.
- Unmold and garnish with parsley.

Fancy Chicken Log

Yields 3 cups

2 (8-ounce) packages cream cheese
1 tablespoon bottled steak sauce
½ teaspoon curry powder
1½ cups minced cooked chicken
¼ cup minced celery
¼ cup chopped fresh parsley
¼ cup chopped toasted almonds

- Blend together cream cheese, steak sauce and curry powder.
- Add chicken, celery, and 2 tablespoons parsley.
- Shape into a 9-inch log.
- Roll in remaining parsley and almonds.
- Wrap in plastic and chill 4 hours or overnight.
- Serve with a variety of crackers. Garnish with parsley sprigs.

General Clover Cheese Spread

Serves 25-30

3 ounces cream cheese
¼ cup butter
3 (10-ounce) packages
  cheddar cheese
1 teaspoon horseradish
1 teaspoon Worcestershire
  sauce
1 ounce dry sherry wine, or
  more, if desired
4-6 drops Tabasco

- Have first 3 ingredients at room temperature for easy mixing.
- Blend cream cheese and butter.
- Add small amounts of cheddar cheese.
- Add remaining ingredients and continue blending until mixture is smooth.
- Fill attractive dishes or storage containers with cheese. Cover tightly. Refrigerate.

Liverwurst Pâte´

Serves 12-16

1 pound liverwurst, mashed
  with fork
1 clove garlic, pressed
½ teaspoon sweet basil
3 tablespoons minced onions

Topping
1 (8-ounce) package cream
  cheese
1 clove garlic, pressed
⅛ teaspoon Tabasco
1 tablespoon mayonnaise
1 (4-ounce) jar caviar
Minced parsley

- Blend first 4 ingredients thoroughly. Pat into igloo shape. Chill several hours.
- Make topping of cream cheese, garlic, Tabasco and mayonnaise. Spread topping over liverwurst. Chill overnight.
- Add caviar just before serving. Garnish with minced parsley, if desired.

Pâte' de Maman

Serves 6

1 quart chicken stock
1 stalk celery, diced
3 sprigs parsley, minced
6 whole peppercorns
12 ounces duck or chicken
  livers, diced
½ medium onion, minced
2 cloves garlic, minced
½ teaspoon ground nutmeg
Pinch cayenne
2 teaspoons dry mustard
¼ teaspoon ground cloves
1 tablespoon cognac
1 pound sweet butter,
  softened
Boston or romaine lettuce
  leaves
Small gherkins

- Heat stock to boiling.
- Add celery, parsley and pepper-corns. Simmer for 10 minutes.
- Add livers, onion and garlic. Simmer for 5 minutes.
- Strain and reserve stock.
- Blend vegetables and liver in food processor or blender, making a paste.
- Add nutmeg, cayenne, mustard, cloves and cognac. Mix well. Add a little reserved stock, if necessary.
- Blend butter with liver paste. When all butter is absorbed, place in a buttered 6-cup mold and chill.
- Serve sliced, on lettuce leaf, garnished with small gherkins and French bread.

Oyster Mousse

Serves 6-8

2 envelopes unflavored gelatin
½ cup water
1 (8-ounce) package cream
  cheese, softened
1 cup mayonnaise
2 (4-ounce) cans smoked
  oysters, drained and minced
2 tablespoons chopped parsley
1 tablespoon Worcestershire
  sauce
½ teaspoon garlic powder
Tabasco to taste

- Soften gelatin in water and set aside. Combine cream cheese and mayonnaise in saucepan. Cook over low heat until cream cheese melts and is smooth.
- Fold in next 5 ingredients and softened gelatin.
- Spoon into a well-greased 3½-cup mold.
- Cover and chill. Unmold and serve with crackers.

Smoked Oyster Spread

Yields 1 cup

1 (8-ounce) package cream
  cheese
1 teaspoon lemon juice
2 teaspoons Worcestershire
  sauce
1 teaspoon soy sauce
½ teaspoon minced garlic
1 (3½-ounce) tin smoked
  oysters, drained

- Mix first 5 ingredients.
- Chop oysters and stir into mixture.
- Refrigerate at least 2 hours before serving.
- Serve at room temperature with crackers.

Pineda Shrimp Spread

Serves 12

1 tablespoon unflavored
  gelatin
¼ cup water
1 can tomato soup
2 (8-ounce) packages cream
  cheese, softened
1 cup mayonnaise
¾ cup chopped celery
½ cup chopped onion
12 ounces cooked shrimp,
  chopped
Lemon slices for garnish
Watercress for garnish

- Soak gelatin in cold water.
- Heat soup to boiling. Add gelatin and cool.
- Add cream cheese and mayonnaise, mixing well.
- Stir in remaining ingredients.
- Pour into greased 6-cup mold and cover tightly. Chill.
- Unmold onto serving tray.
- Garnish with lemon slices dipped in paprika and fresh watercress. Surround with crackers.

Rumaki Spread

Serves 25-35

½ pound chicken livers
1 tablespoon soy sauce
½ cup soft butter
½ teaspoon onion salt
½ teaspoon dry mustard
¼ teaspoon ground nutmeg
Dash or two cayenne pepper
1 (5-ounce) can water chestnuts, drained and minced
6 slices crisp cooked bacon,
  crumbled
1-2 tablespoons Courvoisier
  or whiskey (optional)
Thinly sliced green onions for
  garnish

• Cook seasoned chicken livers in
  butter.
• Place in blender or food
  processor with soy sauce,
  butter, onion salt, mustard,
  nutmeg and cayenne pepper.
• Blend until mixture is smooth,
  stirring with spatula as needed.
• Remove. Stir in water chestnuts
  and bacon. Garnish with onions.

Russian Egg Salad

Serves 10

1 dozen hard-boiled eggs,
  chopped
3 tablespoons finely chopped
  green pepper
3 tablespoons finely chopped
  green onions
3 tablespoons finely chopped
  celery (optional)
Salt and pepper to taste
¼ cup mayonnaise
1 (3-ounce) jar caviar
½ cup sour cream

• Mix together eggs, green pepper,
  onions, celery, salt, pepper and
  mayonnaise. Refrigerate.
• When ready to serve, mound egg
  salad mixture on platter. Frost
  with sour cream, then layer of
  caviar.
• Serve with party rye.

Steak Tartare

Serves 20

2 pounds finely ground steak
½ small jar capers
1 onion, chopped
1 tablespoon garlic powder
2 tablespoons
   Worcestershire sauce
1 tablespoon soy sauce
Fresh ground black pepper to
   taste
4 egg yolks
Parsley for garnish

- Mix all ingredients. Mold in desired shape. Refrigerate.
- Sprinkle parsley on top. Serve with rye bread squares.

Vegetable Spread

Serves 15-20

2 medium tomatoes, seeded,
   drained and finely chopped
1 cup finely chopped celery
1 small onion, finely chopped
1 cucumber, seeded and
   finely chopped
1 envelope plain gelatin
¼ cup cold water
¼ cup boiling water
1 pint mayonnaise
1 teaspoon salt

- Combine vegetables and drain well on paper towels.
- Soften gelatin in cold water. Add boiling water. Cool.
- Fold in mayonnaise and salt. Add vegetables.
- Pour into lightly oiled mold. Chill until firm. Serve with crackers.

Pepper Jelly

Yields 7 pints

1 (4-ounce) can green chilies
1 (10-ounce) can jalapeño
  peppers
½ cup pepper juice, add
  water if needed
6½ cups sugar
1 cup cider vinegar
1 bottle Certo
Green food coloring

*Variation: May use 4 large green
  peppers and ¼ cup chopped
  fresh jalapeños in place of
  canned peppers. If using
  fresh, add an additional ½
  cup vinegar.*

- Drain peppers, saving juice.
- Chop and seed peppers.
- Quickly blend peppers and juice in blender. Pour in large pot.
- Add sugar and vinegar, bring to boil, stirring constantly.
- Skim foam from top. Add Certo and boil 7 minutes. Remove from heat. Add food coloring.
- Let stand 5 minutes. Skim top again.
- Pour into hot, sterile jelly jars.

Spicy Pineapple Jelly

Serves 15-20

2 (12-ounce) jars pineapple
  preserves
1 (18-ounce) jar apple jelly
1 (1½-ounce) can dry mustard
1 (12-ounce) jar horseradish

- Mix all ingredients together in large bowl. Refrigerate until ready to use.
- May be stored for months in jar in refrigerator.
- Pour over top of cream cheese. Serve with crackers.

Artichoke Squares

Yields 30 squares

2 (6-ounce) jars marinated
  artichokes
1 onion, chopped
1 clove garlic, minced
4 eggs
¼ cup bread crumbs
Dash Tabasco
½ teaspoon oregano
Salt and pepper to taste
2 cups shredded cheddar
  cheese

- Drain juice from 1 jar of artichokes into a skillet.
- Sauté onion and garlic in juice.
- Drain other jar and chop all artichokes.
- Beat eggs. Add bread crumbs, Tabasco, oregano, salt and pepper.
- Stir in the onion, garlic, cheese and artichokes. Mix well.
- Bake in a well-greased 9 x 13-inch pan for ½ hour at 325°. Cut into squares and serve hot.

Asparagus Rolls

Yields 125 rolls

2 (8-ounce) packages cream
  cheese
½ jar Marie's Blue Cheese
  Dressing
2 long loaves white bread,
  thinly sliced
3 cans asparagus spears
1¼ sticks butter, melted

- Mix cream cheese and dressing until smooth.
- Remove crust from bread. Roll bread with a rolling pin.
- Spread bread with mixture.
- Roll asparagus in bread.
- Dip rolled asparagus in melted butter.
- Bake at 450° until golden brown.

Black Olive Bites

Serves 28

1½ cups chopped black olives
1½ cups sharp cheddar
   cheese, grated
1 cup mayonnaise
1 teaspoon curry powder
1 cup chopped scallions
18 English muffins

- Mix all ingredients together, except muffins.
- Split, lightly butter and toast muffins.
- Spread mixture on muffins. Brown under broiler. Quarter before serving. May use melba or toast rounds.

Cheese and Jalapeño Squares

Yields 54 small pieces

1 pound sharp cheddar
   cheese
1 pound Monterey Jack
   cheese with jalapeño
   peppers
6 eggs
1 (13-ounce) can evaporated
   milk

- Grate cheeses separately.
- Butter well a 13½ x 8¾-inch baking dish.
- Place a layer of cheddar on bottom of baking dish.
- Add layer of Monterey Jack cheese.
- Top layer with remaining cheddar cheese.
- Beat eggs well. Add milk, blend well, pour over cheeses.
- Bake 40-45 minutes in 350° oven.
- Cool. Cut into bite-sized pieces.

 To keep cheese from sticking, rub grater with a dab of butter.

Cheese Strips

Yields 36

1 loaf white bread
½ pound sharp cheddar
  cheese, grated
6 slices crisp bacon,
  crumbled
1 small onion, minced
1 cup mayonnaise
Salt and pepper to taste

Variation:
3 sticks butter
¼ teaspoon garlic powder
1½-2 cups Parmesan cheese

- Cut off crusts and slice bread in 1/3-inch strips.
- Mix all ingredients and spread on bread.
- Lay on cookie sheet and freeze. Store in plastic bag until needed.
- Bake on cookie sheet at 350° 10-15 minutes or until bubbly. Serve immediately.

- Cut crusts from bread and cut into 1/3-inch strips.
- Bake on baking sheet at 350° for 5 minutes.
- Melt butter and garlic. Cool. Dip bread strips into butter and roll in Parmesan.
- Follow directions for above recipe.

Miniature Chicken Drumsticks

20 chicken wings or
  drumettes
2 tablespoons salad oil
½ cup soy sauce
¼ cup dry sherry
¼ cup catsup
2 tablespoons sugar
¼ teaspoon ground ginger

- Cut wingtips at joint.
- In 5-quart Dutch oven or sauce-pan, cook chicken wings in hot salad oil over high heat, stirring constantly, about 7 minutes.
- Reduce heat to medium.
- Add remaining ingredients, stirring to blend.
- Cover and cook about 25 minutes, stirring occasionally.
- Uncover. Cook 10 minutes longer, stirring frequently, until almost all liquid is absorbed and chicken is tender.

Conch Fritters

Serves 4-6

1 egg
2 tablespoons water
1½-2 pounds ground conch
3 tablespoons chopped onion
2 small hot red peppers,
   finely chopped
½ teaspoon pepper
1 teaspoon salt
¼ teaspoon thyme
1 cup sifted all-purpose flour
1 teaspoon baking powder

- Beat egg and water together. Add to ground conch.
- Combine with onion, peppers and seasonings.
- Sift in flour and baking powder. Mix well. If runny, add small amount of flour.
- Drop by small teaspoon into hot oil (375°) and fry until golden brown. (May also make flat cakes and fry until brown.)
- Drain and serve, using toothpicks. Dip in cocktail sauce appetizer.

Corn Onion Puffs

Yields 4 dozen small, 8 large

1 cup water
½ cup vegetable oil
¾ cup flour
¼ cup cornmeal
1 envelope onion soup mix
4 eggs
Tuna or chicken salad

- In medium saucepan, bring water and oil to a boil.
- Add flour, cornmeal and onion soup mix.
- Cook and stir over medium heat until mixture leaves sides of pan.
- Remove from heat. Add eggs, one at a time, beating well after each.
- Drop by teaspoons onto greased cookie sheet. Bake at 375° for 25-30 minutes.
- Cool. Split and fill with chicken or tuna salad just before serving.
- Makes 4 dozen appetizers or 8 for a main course.

Cream Puffs

Yields 30

1 cup water
½ cup butter
1 cup flour
⅛ teaspoon salt
4 eggs

- Heat water to near boiling. Remove from heat.
- Add butter.
- When butter has melted, return to heat and bring to a boil.
- Stir in flour, stirring well until it forms a ball.
- Remove from heat.
- Beat in eggs, one at a time, beating until smooth.
- Drop from teaspoon onto ungreased cookie sheet.
- Bake at 400° for 25-30 minutes.
- Fill with your favorite meat or seafood salad.

Dockside Dip

Yields 1½-quart casserole

2 (14-ounce) cans artichoke hearts, drained & chopped
2 cups mayonnaise
2 cups grated Parmesan cheese
2 (6-ounce) packages frozen crabmeat with shrimp, thawed, drained and flaked
½ cup dry seasoned bread crumbs

- Combine first 4 ingredients, mixing well.
- Spoon into lightly greased 1½-quart casserole. Top with bread crumbs.
- Bake at 325° for 15-20 minutes.

48

Fiesta Bean Dip

Yields 1½-quarts

1 (15-ounce) can Garcia's
  Black Bean Soup
2 cloves garlic
1 tablespoon vinegar
1 (10½-ounce) can bean and
  bacon soup
½ cup sour cream
1 can jalapeño pepper
½ teaspoon cayenne pepper
½ teaspoon dry mustard
½ teaspoon chili powder
4-5 drops Tabasco

- Place black bean soup, garlic and vinegar in blender. Blend until smooth.
- Pour into 1½-quart heatproof container.
- Place bean and bacon soup, sour cream and jalapeño pepper in blender. Blend until smooth.
- Add 2 soup mixtures together. Blend well.
- Add seasonings. Blend well.
- Refrigerate overnight.
- Before serving, heat slowly to avoid burning.
- Serve with corn chips.

Florida Crackers

Serves 50

1 box Waverly crackers
2 pounds sliced bacon
Parmesan cheese (optional)

- Cut each slice bacon in half. Stretching bacon diagonally, wrap around each cracker.
- If using Parmesan cheese, sprinkle over each cracker.
- Place on rack in baking pan. Broil in oven until brown.
- Serve hot or at room temperature.

 Keep crackers crisp in humid weather by wrapping securely and storing in refrigerator.

Frosted Artichokes With Caviar

Yields 2 cups

1 (8-ounce) package cream
   cheese, softened
2 tablespoons sour cream
2 teaspoons mayonnaise
1 teaspoon lemon juice
2 teaspoons grated onion
1 teaspoon garlic salt
1 (8½-ounce) can artichokes,
   drained
1 (3-ounce) jar caviar

- Combine first 6 ingredients.
- Chop artichokes and pack into a mound on a serving plate.
- Spread cream cheese mixture over artichokes.
- Spread caviar over top.
- Serve with mild crackers.

Lobster Bites

Yields 80-100

48 slices bread
½ pound Velveeta cheese
½ stick butter
1 pound or more lobster
   meat, cooked and chopped

- Trim crusts from bread. Roll thin with rolling pin.
- Melt cheese and butter. Add lobster.
- Spread mixture on bread. Roll into fingers.
- Place seam down on cookie sheet and freeze. Store in plastic bags.
- When ready to serve, slice each in half. Brush with melted butter and bake at 350° for 10 minutes.

 Garlic bulbs stay fresher when kept uncovered in pantry.

Lobster Thermidor

Serves 50 for cocktails

3-6 pounds lobster meat,
    cooked, trimmed and
    chopped
¾ cup butter plus 3
    tablespoons
½ cup flour
1½ cups half and half
½ pound fresh, chopped
    mushrooms
3 tablespoons fresh, chopped
    parsley
½ teaspoon Dijon mustard
1 cup sherry

- Melt ¾ cup butter in a large
  Dutch oven.
- Add flour and stir until smooth.
- Add cream and stir until sauce is
  thickened. Remove from heat.
- Saute' lobster meat and mush-
  rooms in 3 tablespoons butter
  for 5 minutes.
- Add to cream sauce with remain-
  ing ingredients, except sherry.
- Heat, stirring constantly for 5
  minutes.
- Add sherry.
- Serve in chafing dish with toast
  points for cocktails or in a pastry
  shell for dinner.

Neptune Nibblers

Serves 20

1 cup grated sharp cheese
1 (6-ounce) package
    crabmeat
2 egg whites, stiffly beaten
20 (2-inch) toast rounds,
    buttered (may use Melba
    rounds)
6 strips crisp bacon, finely
    crumbled

- Fold cheese, crabmeat and egg
  whites together.
- Pile on toast rounds; sprinkle
  with bacon.
- May make 2-3 hours ahead. Put
  on cookie sheets, cover with
  plastic wrap and refrigerate.
- Before serving, broil until cheese
  melts.

Meatballs Caliente

Serves 10

¾ pound ground beef
¾ cup fine dry bread crumbs
1½ tablespoons minced onion
½ teaspoon prepared
  horseradish
3 drops Tabasco sauce
2 eggs, beaten
1 teaspoon salt
½ teaspoon pepper

Sauce
¾ cup catsup
½ cup water
¼ cup vinegar
1 tablespoon minced onion
2 tablespoons brown sugar
2 teaspoons Worcestershire
  sauce
1 teaspoon dry mustard
¼ teaspoon pepper
1½ teaspoons salt
3 drops Tabasco sauce

- Combine first 8 ingredients and form into ¾-inch meatballs. Brown on all sides.
- Mix sauce ingredients.
- Pour over browned meatballs, which have been drained.
- Simmer 15 minutes, covered.

Gala Crabmeat Dip

Serves 25

1 pound crabmeat
2 (8 ounce) packages cream
  cheese
2 cloves garlic, crushed
½ cup mayonnaise
2 teaspoons mustard
¼ cup white wine
2 tablespoons powdered sugar
Salt and pepper to taste

- Mix ingredients well.
- Serve warm with crackers.

Parmesan Meatballs

Yields 20-25

1 pound ground beef
½ pound ground veal
½ pound ground pork
1 cup bread crumbs soaked
  in 2 cups milk
2 eggs
3 tablespoons freshly grated
  Parmesan cheese
¼ teaspoon dried tarragon,
  crushed
Salt and pepper to taste
5 tablespoons finely chopped
  onion
1 small clove garlic, minced
2 tablespoons butter
4-6 tablespoons butter
2 tablespoons flour
2 cups heavy cream

- Mix together meats, bread crumbs, eggs, Parmesan cheese, salt, pepper and tarragon.
- Saute' onion and garlic in butter. Add to meat mixture.
- Shape mixture into tiny balls, walnut-sized. Saute' in butter until browned.
- Place browned meatballs in casserole or chafing dish to keep warm.
- Add flour to remaining juices and meat bits. Whisk in heavy cream. Stir constantly over low heat for 5 minutes.
- Pour sauce over meatballs and serve warm.

Italian Mushrooms

Serves 10-15

30 large whole mushrooms
1 pint pizza sauce
1 pound pre-cooked Italian
  hot sausage, sliced
1 pound mozzarella cheese

- Break stems off mushrooms. Wash caps.
- Saute' in butter, open end first. Flip over and saute' until limp.
- Remove and drain liquid.
- Transfer caps to 9 x 11-inch baking pan.
- Fill each cap with pizza sauce. Place slice of sausage on each cap. Cover with piece of cheese.
- Bake for 5 minutes at 350°. Serve immediately.

Stuffed Mushrooms

Serves 12

2 tablespoons butter
½ cup bread crumbs
Garlic juice to taste
1 teaspoon fresh chopped
  parsley
Salt and pepper, to taste
2 cans crabmeat
1 pound large fresh
  mushrooms, cleaned with
  stems removed
Grated Parmesan cheese

- Melt butter. Add bread crumbs. Mix thoroughly.
- Add seasonings and crabmeat, mixing gently.
- Let set for a few minutes to blend seasonings.
- Stuff mushroom cavity with crabmeat mixture.
- Sprinkle with cheese. Bake 15 minutes at 350°.
- Serve hot.

Note: May substitute minced clams for crabmeat.

Mushroom Canapés

Yields 6 dozen

½ pound fresh mushrooms,
  finely chopped
1 (8-ounce) package cream
  cheese
2 teaspoons minced onion
Salt and pepper, to taste
1-inch bread rounds

- Sauté chopped mushrooms in 1-2 tablespoons butter. Add onion.
- Stir in cream cheese, salt and pepper.
- Toast bread rounds on one side.
- Spread toasted side with margarine and mound with mushroom mixture.
- Cover and refrigerate up to 2 days or freeze.
- Heat until hot at 350°.

Mushroom Turnovers

Serves 30

1 cup butter
1 (8-ounce) package cream
  cheese
½ teaspoon salt
2 cups regular flour
1 egg yolk
2 teaspoons cream

Filling
2 (4-ounce) cans mushrooms,
  drained and sliced
½ cup minced onion
2 tablespoons butter
½ teaspoon salt
½ teaspoon pepper
1 teaspoon lemon juice
1 tablespoon flour
½ cup cream
1 tablespoon sherry

*Variation: ½ cup grated cheddar
or Monterey Jack cheese
may be added to enhance the
flavor of the filling.*

- Mix first 3 ingredients until smooth.
- Add flour and continue to mix.
- Flatten dough into 8 x 6-inch pan.
- Chill for 3 hours or overnight.
- Knead once. Roll to ⅛-inch thickness.
- Cut into 2½-inch rounds.
- Place 1 teaspoon filling in center of each round. Fold over, moisten edges and seal with fork.
- Place on greased cookie sheet.
- Mix cream and yolk. Brush each round.
- Chill rounds 1 hour or freeze before baking.
- Bake 350° for 25-30 minutes.
- Saute' mushrooms and onions in butter for 5 minutes. Add salt, pepper, lemon juice. Stir. Simmer 2 minutes.
- Add flour and cream. Simmer and stir until smooth.
- Stir in sherry. Chill 2 hours or more.

To wash mushrooms, put a handful of flour in sink of water, swish and remove. Mushrooms come clean immediately and don't get soggy or slimy.

Hot Oyster Spinach Dip

Serves 20

2 cans oysters
2 (10-ounce) packages frozen
    chopped spinach
1½ cups Italian bread crumbs
1 tablespoon garlic powder
Salt and pepper to taste
Pinch tarragon

- Drain oysters and chop.
- Cook spinach, drain.
- Mix with remaining ingredients.
- Heat thoroughly.
- Serve in chafing dish with fresh vegetables or crackers.

Pye's Pickled Shrimp

Serves 15

2½ pounds shrimp
7-8 bay leaves
2-3 large onions, sliced
1¼ cups salad oil
¾ cup white vinegar
1½ teaspoons salt
2½ teaspoons celery seeds
2½ teaspoons capers and
    juice
Tabasco sauce to taste

- Boil shrimp with a little lemon juice or crab boil and salt and pepper. Cool.
- Peel and devein.
- Alternate layers of shrimp and sliced onions in shallow dish. Add bay leaves.
- Mix all other ingredients. Pour over shrimp and onions.
- Store in covered dish in refrigerator for 24 hours before serving.

 To store onions for long periods, hang in panty hose, knotted between each onion.

Shrimp In Snail Butter

Yields 30

½ cup butter
2 tablespoons minced
  shallots or green onions
3 large fresh garlic cloves,
  crushed
2 tablespoons fresh parsley,
  finely minced
Salt and pepper to taste
1 loaf homemade-style white
  bread
1 package frozen tiny shrimp

- Allow butter to come to room temperature. Cream well.
- Mix onions, garlic and parsley.
- Add butter and blend well, seasoning with salt and pepper.
- Cut 30 rounds from bread with cookie cutter.
- Spread about ½ teaspoon butter mixture on each bread round.
- Place 4 or 5 shrimp on each round and top with another dab of butter.
- Arrange rounds on a cookie sheet. Bake on middle shelf at 350° 10 minutes or until butter bubbles and shrimp are hot.

Shrimp Toast
from Basin Street, Palm Bay
Yields 48

Cooking oil for deep frying
1½ pounds uncooked, peeled
  and deveined shrimp
½ cup water chestnuts
1 small onion
1½ teaspoons peanut oil
1½ teaspoons dry white wine
½ teaspoon salt
½ teaspoon ground pepper
Dash Tabasco
½ teaspoon lemon juice
½ teaspoon Worcestershire
  sauce
12 slices firm white sandwich
  bread, crusts trimmed

- Pour 2-inches cooking oil in deep fryer or skillet and heat to 250°.
- Mix shrimp, water chestnuts and onion in food processor until very fine.
- Add wine, peanut oil, salt, pepper, Tabasco, lemon juice and Worcestershire sauce. Mix well.
- Spread mixture evenly over trimmed bread slices.
- Fry bread slices until brown, about 4 minutes. Drain on paper towel and cut slices into 4 strips. Serve immediately.

Spinach Feta Strudel

Serves 16

1 box strudel Fillo dough
   leaves
1½ cup chopped onion
½ cup chopped scallions
2 sticks butter
5 eggs, beaten
½ pound feta cheese,
   chopped
½ cup fresh dill or 1
   tablespoon dried dill
2 (12-ounce) packages
   chopped spinach, cooked
   according to package
   directions
Salt and pepper to taste
1 cup melted butter

- Defrost dough, keeping sealed in bag until used.
- Saute' onions and scallions in 1 tablespoon butter. Mix them in bowl with beaten eggs, crumbled cheese and dill.
- Add cooled and drained spinach. Season with salt and pepper.
- Melt remaining butter. Brush butter on bottom of 14 x 10-inch pan.
- Put layer of dough in pan and butter.
- Repeat, using about ½ of the dough.
- Spread spinach and cheese filling and cover with remaining buttered dough.
- Bake at 350° for one hour or until light golden. Serve as hors d'oeuvres in small squares or as a vegetable cut in larger squares.

Oysters Champagne
from the Mango Tree, Cocoa Beach

Serves 4

24 oysters in shells
1½-2 cups champagne
2 cups fresh mushrooms,
   finely diced
4 tablespoons butter
1 cup chopped green onions
4 tablespoons instant beef
   bouillon granules
Hollandaise sauce

- Thoroughly clean shells. Remove oysters and retain shells.
- Poach oysters in champagne by boiling 1 minute. Set aside.
- Saute' mushrooms and onions in butter 7-8 minutes. Stir in bouillon and mix.
- Place 1 tablespoon mixture in each shell. Top with 1 poached oyster.
- Spoon hot hollandaise over top and serve.

Italian Spinach Squares

Yields 84 squares

2 (10-ounce) packages frozen
  chopped spinach
3 tablespoons butter
1 small onion, chopped
¼ pound mushrooms, sliced
4 eggs
¼ cup fine dry bread crumbs
1 (10¾-ounce) can condensed
  cream of mushroom soup
¼ cup grated Parmesan
  cheese
⅛ teaspoon pepper
⅛ teaspoon dried basil
⅛ teaspoon oregano

- Place spinach in a wire strainer. Rinse under hot water to thaw. Press out all water. Set aside.
- Melt butter in frying pan over medium heat. Add onion and mushrooms and cook, stirring until onion is limp.
- In a bowl, beat eggs with a fork. Stir in bread crumbs, mushroom soup, 2 tablespoons of cheese, pepper, basil and oregano.
- Mix drained spinach, onion mixture, and soup mixture; blend well.
- Place in a well-greased 9-inch square baking pan. Sprinkle with remaining cheese.
- Bake uncovered in a 325° oven for 35 minutes or until set when lightly touched.
- Cool slightly, then cover and refrigerate. Cut into 1-inch squares and serve cold or reheat in a 325° oven for 10 to 12 minutes.

 To clean burned and scorched pans, sprinkle liberally with baking soda, adding just enough water to moisten. Let stand for several hours. Then lift burned portion right out of the pan!

Swiss Sandwich Puffs

Serves 16

16 slices party rye bread
½ cup mayonnaise
¼ cup finely chopped onion
¼ cup finely chopped parsley
Salt and pepper to taste
8 slices Swiss cheese
Ripe olives, sliced and pitted
(optional)

- Toast bread on both sides.
- Combine mayonnaise, onion, parsley, salt and pepper.
- Spread on toast.
- Cut each cheese slice into quarters. Place a cheese square on each piece of toast, covering mayonnaise mixture.
- Broil 3-4 inches from heat until cheese melts and is puffy and golden, 2-3 minutes.
- Place sliced olives on top and serve hot.

Swiss Cheese Fondue

Serves 5-6

French bread or hard rolls
3 cups natural Swiss cheese
1 tablespoon all-purpose flour
1 clove garlic (optional)
1¼ cups white wine
Fresh ground pepper to taste
Dash nutmeg
3 tablespoons cooking sherry

Note: Guests spear a chunk of bread and dip into hot cheese mixture. If cheese mixture becomes too thick, thin with warmed white wine.

- Cut French bread into bite-sized pieces.
- Cut cheese in julienne strips.
- Toss cheese with flour to coat.
- Rub inside of fondue pot with garlic.
- Pour in white wine. Warm just until air bubbles start to rise. Do not cover. Do not boil.
- Stir constantly.
- Add a handful of cheese, continue stirring until melted.
- Continue adding all the cheese, stirring until well blended and mixture is gently bubbling.
- Stir in pepper and nutmeg. Add sherry. Blend well.

BEVERAGES & SOUPS

*Beach Encounter, Little Girl on Beach with Crab,
By Charles Velek. Original Oil, 20x24.*

BEVERAGES

Soups

* Denotes Quick and Easy Recipes

Orange Julius

Serves 4-6

1 (6-ounce) can frozen orange
    juice
6 ounces milk or vanilla ice
    cream
6 ounces water
2-3 tablespoons sugar
½ teaspoon vanilla
1 egg (optional)
10-12 small ice cubes

- Put all ingredients in blender.
- Blend on high speed until thick and creamy.

Mulled Cider

Serves 15-20

2 quarts apple cider
½ cup brown sugar
1 teaspoon allspice
½ teaspoon whole cloves
2 sticks cinnamon
1 medium orange, sliced

- Place all of the ingredients in slow cooker for 2-8 hours.
- Serve hot on a cold night.

Coffee Punch

Serves 50-60

4 quarts strong coffee
1 quart whipping cream
5 tablespoons sugar
5 teaspoons vanilla
2 gallons coffee or vanilla ice
    cream

- Make coffee and chill.
- Whip cream, adding sugar and vanilla.
- Spoon ice cream into large punch bowl.
- Add whipped cream.
- Pour cold coffee over. Mix well.

Variation: For mocha taste, add ½ cup chocolate syrup.

 Leftover coffee punch may be frozen and later used for coffee ice.

Sunny's Lemonade

Yields 4 quarts

6 large lemons
2 cups sugar
2 cups water

- Roll lemons on countertop to soften so they yield more juice. Peel.
- Heat sugar and water in heavy saucepan until syrup boils. Add peeling and boil gently for 3-4 minutes in covered pan. Strain.
- Squeeze lemons. Strain juice and add to syrup.
- When ready to use, mix 3 parts water with 1 part syrup. Will keep for weeks in refrigerator.

Rainbow Punch

Serves 30

1 (6-ounce) box strawberry gelatin
1 cup hot water
1 quart cold water
1 cup sugar
Juice of 6 lemons
2 (46-ounce) cans pineapple juice
1 quart vanilla ice cream
1 quart pineapple sherbet
3 (32-ounce) bottles ginger ale

- Dissolve gelatin in hot water.
- Add cold water and sugar.
- Dissolve sugar. Add other ingredients.

Cranapple Cooler

Serves 35-40

2 cups cranberry juice
1 (32-ounce) bottle Sprite or
  7-Up
½ (23-ounce) can pineapple-
  grapefruit juice
1 pint pineapple sherbet

- Mix in large punch bowl.
- Ice or ice ring may be added, if needed.

Fresh Mint Tea

Yields 2 quarts

1 quart water
13 tea bags
¼ cup fresh mint leaves,
  lightly packed
Juice of 2 lemons
1 (6-ounce) can frozen orange
  juice
1 cup sugar

- Combine tea, mint leaves and water. Cover. Bring to boil and remove from heat.
- Let steep 30 minutes.
- Add all other ingredients, plus more water to make 2 quarts liquid.
- Strain and chill.
- Serve over ice.

St. Bernard

Serves 1

1 ounce Amaretto
Black coffee
Fresh whipping cream
Freshly ground semi-sweet
  chocolate

- Into a tall stem glass, put 1 ounce Amaretto.
- Place knife in glass to prevent breakage. Pour ¾ full with black coffee. Remove knife.
- Spoon on whipped cream and ground chocolate.
- Wrap hot glass with linen napkin and serve.

Champagne Punch

Yields 3 quarts

1 (6-ounce) can frozen lemonade
1 (6-ounce) can frozen
  limeade
1 can water
½ fifth cognac
1 quart club soda
1 bottle champagne

- Mix all ingredients in punch
  bowl.
- Serve with lemon-lime ice ring.

Claret Punch

Serves 24

½ cup fresh or frozen lemon
  juice
1 (6-ounce) can frozen
  pineapple juice
1 cup sugar
1 (750 ml.) bottle claret wine
2 (28-ounce) bottles chilled
  ginger ale

- Combine fruit juices and sugar
  until sugar dissolves.
- Add wine and chill.
- Pour in ginger ale when ready to
  serve.

Tropical Refresher

Serves 50

1 (6-ounce) box strawberry-
  banana gelatin
2 cups boiling water
2 bananas, mashed
2 cups lemonade
5 cups orange juice
2 cups pineapple juice
4 quarts ginger ale

- Dissolve gelatin in boiling water.
- Add bananas and juices
- Chill until ready to serve. Add
  ginger ale.

Easy Wine Citrus Punch

Serves 20

2 cups orange juice
1 (6-ounce) can frozen
   lemonade
1 cup orange liqueur
1 (750 ml.) bottle dry white
   wine, chilled
1 (28-ounce) bottle
   carbonated water, chilled
Ice mold
Orange slices

- In punch bowl, stir together
  orange juice, lemonade, liqueur
  and wine.
- When ready to serve add
  carbonated water and ice mold.
- Garnish with orange slices.

Glee Wine

Serves 12

Juice and rind of two lemons
2 cups water
8-10 whole cloves
1 (2-inch) stick cinnamon
3 tablespoons sugar
1 quart red Bordeaux wine

- Strain lemon juice. Cut rind into
  fine slices.
- Place in enameled saucepan with
  water, spices and sugar.
- Bring slowly to boil.
- Add wine and heat thoroughly.
  Do not boil.
- Serve hot in heated punch cups.

Mimosa

Yields 1½ quarts

1 fifth champagne, chilled
25 ounces fresh orange juice,
   chilled

- Mix together. Serve over
  crushed ice in champagne glass.

Syllabub

Serves 16

1 quart light coffee cream
8 ounces fresh orange juice
Grated rind of one orange
Grated rind of one lemon
1 bottle dry white wine
8 ounces sugar
1 ounce triple sec

Topping:
1 cup whipping cream
¼ cup grated orange rind

- Whip together first 7 ingredients. Chill thoroughly for at least 4 hours.
- When ready to serve, pour into punch bowl. Top with whipped cream and sprinkle with orange rind.

Hot Buttered Rum

Serves 25-30

1 quart French vanilla ice cream
1 pound softened butter (not margarine)
1 pound powdered sugar
1 pound light brown sugar
1 tablespoon ground nutmeg
1 tablespoon ground cinnamon
1 ounce rum per serving
1 cinnamon stick per serving
Whipped cream for garnish

- Whip together ice cream, butter, both sugars, nutmeg and cinnamon. Store in refrigerator until ready to serve.
- Place 1 large tablespoon mix and 1 ounce rum in 1 cup hot water.
- Stir with cinnamon stick.
- Top with whipped cream.

B-52

from Eau Gallie Yacht Club, Indian Harbour Beach
Serves 3

3½ ounces Grand Marnier
3½ ounces Bailey's Irish Cream
3½ ounces Kahlua

- Shake ingredients together and serve.
- Sip slowly!

Frozen Margueritas

Serves 4

1 (6-ounce) can frozen
    limeade, thawed
¾ cup tequila
¼ cup triple sec or other
    orange liqueur
Crushed ice - about 15 ice
    cubes
Lime slices (optional)
Salt

- Mix together in blender until smooth.
- Use a lime wedge to wet the rim of glass and line rim with salt.
- Pour into glasses and serve immediately.

Peach Smash

Yields 4-6 drinks

1 (6-ounce) can frozen orange
    juice concentrate
4-6 ounces rum, vodka or gin
1 large peach, peeled and
    sliced, or 10-ounce
    package frozen peaches
½ ounce orange liqueur
4-5 ice cubes
Mint sprigs, dusted with
    powdered sugar

- Place orange juice, rum, peach slices, orange liqueur and ice in blender. Process at high speed until slushy and smooth.
- Immediately pour into wine or champagne glasses.
- Serve with sprigs of mint.

Toddy

Serves 1

1 teaspoon sugar or honey
1 cinnamon stick
¾ ounce Apple Jack
¾ ounce light rum
¼ ounce Myer's rum
Fresh cider

- In preheated mug (heat in hot water), place honey, cinnamon stick, rums and Apple Jack. Fill mug with hot cider.

Toss-Up Martini

from Eau Gallie Yacht Club, Indian Harbour Beach

Serves 1

¾ ounce gin
¾ ounce vodka
¼ ounce dry vermouth (for
   extra dry martini)
½ ounce dry vermouth (for
   dry martini)
1 ounce dry vermouth (for
   regular martini)
1 ounce sweet vermouth (for
   sweet martini)
Twist of lemon or olive

- Stir ingredients briskly over cracked (not crushed) ice until cold.
- Strain into frosty, 3-ounce stemmed cocktail glass.
- Serve with a twist of lemon or olive.
- For "on the rocks" use old fashioned glass and pour over ice.

Irish Coffee

Serves 1

Coffee
Sugar
1 lemon
Kahlua
Creme de cocoa
Bourbon
Cointreau
Whipped cream
Powdered sugar

- Make pot of coffee.
- Rub slice of lemon around edge of Irish coffee glass or wine glass.
- Dip glass into sugar. Allow to sit until ready to use.
- Place 1 heaping teaspoon sugar in glass.
- Add 1 shot each Kahlúa and Crème de cocoa.
- Add a little less than 1 shot bourbon per glass.
- Pour ¾ full with coffee.
- Top with sweetened whipped cream and add 1 teaspoon cointreau.

 For a perfect pot of coffee, one pinch of salt in the basket will remove some of acid taste, don't forget — always start with cold water.

Cold Avocado Soup

Serves 4

1 large avocado
½ cup grated onion
2 cups consomme'
3 tablespoons lemon juice
1 cup sour cream
Salt and pepper to taste

- Blend avocado, onion, consomme' and lemon juice in blender or processor until smooth.
- Add sour cream. Salt and pepper to taste. Blend briefly.
- Chill and serve very cold.

Cream of Cauliflower Soup

Serves 6

2 tablespoons butter
1½ cups chopped onions
2 cups chicken broth
1 head cauliflower (broken into small florets, cooked tender)
2 cups heavy cream
Salt to taste
White pepper to taste
Parsley or chives, chopped

- Heat butter. Add onions and saute' about 4 minutes.
- Add broth and cauliflower.
- Heat to boiling point.
- Add cream. Do not let boil.
- Season to taste. Garnish with parsley.

Garlic Soup

Serves 6

6 pressed garlic cloves
Olive oil
6 cups chicken broth
1 cup shell macaroni
1 can garbanzo beans

- Brown garlic cloves in olive oil.
- Add chicken broth.
- Bring to a boil, add macaroni and cook until soft.
- Add garbanzo beans and simmer 5 minutes.

Chablis Cheddar Soup

Serves 4

2 tablespoons butter
3 green onions with tops,
 thinly sliced
½ cup diced celery
1 can condensed cheese soup
½ cup water
½ cup half and half
1 teaspoon instant chicken
 bouillon
⅛ teaspoon ground nutmeg
¼ cup chablis
Paprika and croutons for
 garnish

- Melt butter in saucepan. Stir in onions and celery until tender.
- Stir in soup, mixing until smooth.
- Return to medium heat and add all but chablis. Cook until thick, about 9 minutes.
- Stir in chablis. Sprinkle with paprika. Garnish with croutons.

Fish Chowder

Serves 6-8

½ pound Polish sausage,
 sliced
1 large onion, chopped
2 tablespoons butter
1 cup raw diced potatoes
¾ cup sliced carrots
1 pound skinned and boned
 fish (grouper, trout, turbot)
1 cup water
2 cups milk
1 (17-ounce) can creamed
 corn
1 (13-ounce) can evaporated
 milk
1 teaspoon salt
½ teaspoon white pepper

- In a large soup pot, sauté sausage and onion in butter until onion is tender.
- Add potatoes, carrots, fish and water.
- Cover and simmer 30 minutes or until fish flakes easily and vegetables are tender.
- Add remaining ingredients and heat until serving temperature.

Conch Chowder

Serves 10-12

6-8 conch, cleaned and
 chopped (easy in a food
 processor, especially if
 partially frozen)
3 quarts water
2 tablespoons lime juice or
 vinegar
1-2 tablespoons salt
¼ pound salt pork, diced
1 cup chopped onion
½ cup chopped green pepper
½ cup chopped celery
4 garlic cloves, chopped
1 (20-ounce) can tomatoes
1 (6-ounce) can tomato paste
½ cup chopped parsley
½ teaspoon crushed red
 pepper
½ teaspoon dried thyme
3 pounds potatoes, peeled
 and diced
Salt and pepper to taste

- Combine diced conch, water, lime juice and salt in pot and bring to boil.
- Lower heat and simmer 30 minutes.
- Meanwhile fry salt pork and sauté onion, green pepper, celery and garlic in same pan until soft but not brown.
- Add to conch, along with tomatoes, tomato paste and remaining ingredients.
- Potatoes may be added after chowder has cooked 1 hour. Cook chowder an additional 30 minutes.

Crab Soup

Serves 6-8

1 can tomato soup
1 can green pea soup
1-2 cups crabmeat
1 cup cream
Sherry to taste
¼ teaspoon curry powder
 (optional)
½ teaspoon paprika (optional)

- Mix all ingredients. Heat over medium burner until hot. Do not boil.

Zucchini Soup

Serves 4-6

2 large zucchini
1 green pepper
1 carrot
1 celery stalk
1 medium onion
3 cups chicken stock
1 (8-ounce) carton sour
  cream
1 tablespoon chopped parsley
½ teaspoon dillweed
Salt and pepper to taste

- Cut up vegetables and cook in chicken stock until tender. Strain and retain stock.
- Put vegetables in processor and purée.
- Add purée of vegetables to stock and beat in sour cream.
- Add parsley, dill, salt and pepper. Chill.
- May be served hot or thoroughly chilled. Sprinkle additional dill on each bowl if desired.

Ybor City Gazpacho

Serves 6

1 cup finely chopped peeled
  tomatoes
½ cup finely chopped green
  pepper
½ cup finely chopped celery
½ cup finely chopped cucumber
¼ cup finely chopped onion
2 teaspoons snipped parsley
1 teaspoon snipped chives
1 small garlic clove, minced
1-2 teaspoons tarragon
1 tablespoon wine vinegar or
  lemon juice
2 tablespoons olive oil
1 teaspoon salt
¼ teaspoon pepper
½ teaspoon Worcestershire
  sauce
2 cups tomato juice

- Combine all ingredients in a stainless steel or glass bowl.
- Cover and chill at least 4 hours.
- Serve with chopped pepper, onion, cucumbers, hard-boiled eggs, croutons, as desired.

Lentil Soup with Lamb and Sausage

Serves 4-6

1 (8-ounce) package sweet
  Italian sausage, peeled and
  cut into 1-inch pieces
2 cups lentils
6 cups water
2 large carrots, sliced
1 large onion, chopped
1 large clove garlic, minced
1½ teaspoon salt, or to taste
½ teaspoon oregano
¼ teaspoon pepper, or to
  taste
2 small lamb shanks (½ pound
  each)
1 cup dry white or red wine
1 medium onion, diced

- Brown sausage in skillet. Set aside.
- In Dutch oven combine lentils, water, carrots, onion, garlic, salt, oregano and pepper. Bring to boil.
- Add lamb. Cover and simmer for 1 hour.
- Add wine and sausage.
- Simmer until all is tender and flavors well blended.
- Remove lamb shanks. Cut off meat and discard bones. Return meat to soup. Heat and serve. Sprinkle finely diced onion on top when served.

Neptune Chowder

Serves 4-6

1 pound white fish
½ teaspoon salt
2 potatoes, peeled and diced
1 medium onion, diced
1 tablespoon butter
2-3 cups half and half
Tabasco to taste
White pepper to taste
Parsley to taste

- Cover fish with water. Add salt. Cook until fish flakes, 12-15 minutes.
- Remove fish. When fish has cooled, remove bones and any dark parts.
- Cook potatoes and onion in same water as fish. Cook until tender.
- Return fish to pot. Add half and half and butter.
- Heat slowly. Do not allow to boil.
- Add seasonings to taste.

Mainland Minestrone

Serves 10-12

2 pounds beef soup bones
  with meat
3 quarts water
1 (28-ounce) can tomatoes in
  purée or juice, undrained
2 medium onions, coarsely
  diced
¼ cup coarsely chopped
  parsley
Salt to taste
1½ teaspoons basil leaves,
  crushed
½ teaspoon ground black
  pepper
2 cloves garlic, crushed
2 cups sliced carrots
2 cups sliced celery
4 cups uncooked shell
  macaroni
2 (9-ounce) packages frozen
  Italian green beans
Parmesan cheese, grated

- Place soup bones in large pot. Add water. Bring to boil. Skim surface of liquid, if desired.
- Add tomatoes, onions, parsley, salt, pepper, basil leaves, garlic.
- Bring to boil again. Reduce heat. Cover and simmer 1 hour.
- Add carrots and celery. Cover and simmer ½ hour longer or until meat is fork tender.
- Remove bones from pot. Trim meat and return to pot.
- Return soup to boiling and add macaroni and green beans, stirring until soup returns to boil.
- Lower heat, cover and simmer 20-25 minutes longer or until macaroni is tender. Stir occasionally.
- Serve with Parmesan cheese sprinkled over top.

Onion Soup

Serves 6-8

6-8 large onions, thinly sliced
1 stick butter
½ teaspoon sugar
2 tablespoons flour
Salt and pepper to taste
2 quarts chicken or beef stock
1 cup wine
Toasted French bread
Grated Gruyère or Swiss
  cheese

- Cook onions in butter until soft.
- Add sugar, flour, salt and pepper. Blend well.
- Cook for 2-3 minutes.
- Add stock gradually, stirring well.
- Cook for 30 minutes.
- When cooking is completed, add the wine.
- Pour over toasted French bread. Sprinkle grated cheese on top.

Onion Wine Soup
from First Lady Nancy Reagan

Serves 6-8

¼ cup butter
5 large onions, chopped
5 cups beef broth
½ cup celery leaves
1 large potato, sliced
1 cup dry white wine
1 tablespoon vinegar
2 teaspoons sugar
1 cup light cream
1 tablespoon minced parsley
Salt and pepper

- Melt butter in large saucepan. Add onion and mix well.
- Add beef broth, celery leaves and potato.
- Bring to boiling. Cover and simmer for 30 minutes.
- Purée mixture in a blender. Return to saucepan and blend in wine, vinegar and sugar.
- Bring to boiling and simmer 5 minutes.
- Stir in cream, parsley and salt and pepper to taste.
- Heat thoroughly but do not boil.

Eau Gallie Oyster Bisque
A New Year's Day Tradition

Serves 4

2 cups milk
2 cups half and half
1 cup heavy cream
½ onion, sliced
2 stalks celery with leaves, chopped
2 sprigs parsley
1 bay leaf
¼ teaspoon ground nutmeg
1 quart shucked oysters with juice
3 tablespoons butter
3 tablespoons flour
Salt and cayenne pepper to taste

- Place first 8 ingredients in pot.
- Bring to boil slowly. Reduce heat and simmer 15 minutes. Strain.
- Discard vegetables and return milk mixture to heat.
- Add oysters and simmer about 5 minutes, until edges of oysters curl.
- In separate pan, melt butter. Add flour and stir well.
- Add 1 cup milk mixture to flour mixture. Blend thoroughly.
- Pour slowly into soup, stirring constantly until blended well.
- Season with salt and cayenne.

Camp Stew

Yields 6 quarts

1 baking chicken
1 pound boneless stew beef
1½ pounds pork
2 (16-ounce) cans tomatoes
1 (32-ounce) bottle catsup
2 cups chopped onion
½ cup Worcestershire sauce
2 teaspoons Louisiana hot
  sauce
2 teaspoons salt
5 large baking potatoes
1 (17-ounce) can green peas
  (optional)
1 (16-ounce) can whole kernel
  corn (optional)

- In large pot, cover chicken with water and boil until tender.
- Debone, skin and cut up meat.
- Boil beef and pork until tender.
- Retain stock from hen and beef.
- Place cut up beef, pork, chicken, tomatoes, catsup, onions and seasonings in 6-quart boiler.
- Add stock and let simmer 3 hours.
- When meat begins to shred, add cut up potatoes and cook until done.
- Add peas and corn last.
- As the stew thickens, you will need to stir constantly with wooden spoon.

Hint: Freezes well. When heating, water or V-8 juice may be used to thin.

Romaine Soup

Serves 8

2 packages frozen, chopped
  spinach
1 (4-ounce) can mushrooms
1 stick margarine
1 small onion, finely chopped
3 cloves garlic, finely
  chopped
6 chicken bouillon cubes
2 cups whipping cream
2 cups half and half
White pepper to taste

- Prepare spinach according to directions, omitting any salt. Drain well. Purée in blender.
- Add mushrooms and quickly chop in blender.
- Melt margarine in heavy saucepan and add onion and garlic. Cook for several minutes.
- Add bouillon cubes and mash.
- On low heat, add spinach mixture and creams.
- Heat thoroughly, but slowly. Do not allow cream to boil.
- Add white pepper to taste.

SALADS &
SALAD
DRESSINGS

½ Dozen Blue Crabs, By Mari M. Conneen.

Salads

Salad Dressings

* Denotes Quick and Easy Recipes

Hearts of Palm Salad

Serves 4

1 can hearts of palm
1 large avocado, sliced into
  wedges
½ cup olive oil
Juice of 1 lemon
1 clove minced garlic
Salt and pepper to taste
Blanched almonds
Ripe, pitted olives

- Marinate hearts of palm in dressing made of oil, lemon juice, garlic, salt and pepper for several hours.
- Drain and reserve dressing.
- Arrange avocado wedges and hearts of palm on lettuce. Top with dressing.
- Sprinkle blanched almonds and sliced black olives over salad.

Fresh Asparagus Salad with Radish Fans

Serves 4-6

1½-2 pounds fresh asparagus,
  sliced lengthwise in thin
  strips
4 teaspoons soy sauce
1 teaspoon sugar
2 teaspoons sesame seed oil
24 radishes, cut into
  accordians
1 teaspoon salt
1 tablespoon sugar

- Boil asparagus for 1 minute. Drain and rinse with cold water. Pat dry on paper towels.
- Combine soy sauce, 1 teaspoon sugar and sesame oil. Toss with asparagus. Chill at least 2 hours or overnight.
- Place radishes, salt and 1 tablespoon sugar in a 1-quart glass jar. Shake vigorously.
- Marinate at room temperature for at least 6 hours. Liquid will collect in jar.
- Arrange asparagus in long serving dish and top with radish fans.

Mandarin Avocado Salad

Serves 6

½ cup red wine vinegar
1 cup salad oil
1 small onion, finely chopped
½ teaspoon celery seed
1 teaspoon dry mustard
1 teaspoon salt
½ cup sugar
2 heads Boston lettuce
2 green onions and tops,
    chopped
1 can mandarin oranges,
    drained
1 ripe avocado, sliced

- Mix first 7 ingredients and chill overnight.
- Break lettuce into bite-size pieces.
- Mix lettuce, onions, oranges and avocado.
- Pour oil mixture over lettuce mixture.
- Toss gently and serve.

Easy Caesar Salad

Serves 6-8

Dressing
1 cup salad or olive oil
2-3 cloves garlic
1 tablespoon Worcestershire
    sauce
½ teaspoon salt
¼ teaspoon pepper
4 tablespoons lemon juice
1 egg
Anchovy paste (optional)

- Cut garlic into quarters and add to oil. Let stand several hours.
- Add other dressing ingredients, except egg. Mix well.
- Add raw egg and mix well.
- Anchovy paste may be added to taste, if desired.

2 heads romaine lettuce,
    washed and patted dry
Bleu cheese
Croutons
Parmesan cheese

- Serve over romaine, crumbled bleu cheese, croutons and Parmesan cheese.
- Keep dressing in tightly sealed glass jar for several weeks.

Curb-the-Urge Salad

Serves 6-8

2 (1-pound) cans French-style
  green beans
1 (1-pound) can wax beans
2 (4-ounce) cans mushrooms
1 medium green pepper,
  diced
½ cup wine vinegar
½ teaspoon salt
½ teaspoon garlic salt
Coarsely ground pepper

- Drain beans and mushrooms.
- Combine remaining ingredients.
- Refrigerate several hours or
  overnight.

Indian River Cole Slaw

Serves 12

3 pounds white cabbage,
  shredded or chopped
1 green bell pepper, chopped
2 onions, chopped
½ red bell pepper, chopped
1 carrot, shredded (optional
  for color)
1½ cups sugar (less, if
  desired)
1 cup vegetable oil
1 cup vinegar
1-2 tablespoons celery seed
1 tablespoon salt

- Combine cabbage, pepper and
  onions in a large bowl.
- Pour sugar over mix and let
  stand. (Amount of sugar may be
  decreased according to taste.)
- Mix oil, vinegar, celery seed and
  salt in a saucepan. Bring to a
  boil.
- Pour over cabbage mixture while
  hot.
- Cover and refrigerate.

Hint: Should be made a day in advance to enhance flavors.

Foo Young Toss

Serves 6-8

1 head romaine lettuce, torn
  into bite-size pieces
1 (16-ounce) can bean
  sprouts, drained
1 (5-ounce) can water
  chestnuts, sliced
5 slices bacon, crisply
  cooked, drained and
  crumbled
2 hard-boiled eggs, sliced

Dressing
1 cup salad oil
½ cup sugar
¼ cup catsup
¼ cup vinegar
2 teaspoons grated onion
2 teaspoons Worcestershire
  sauce

- In salad bowl combine romaine, bean sprouts, water chestnuts, bacon and eggs.
- Sprinkle lightly with salt and pepper.
- Combine ingredients for dressing and blend in blender.
- Add to salad. Toss lightly and serve.

Granny Lil's Cranberry Salad

Serves 6-8

2 (3-ounce) packages
  softened cream cheese
¼ cup mayonnaise
¼ cup lemon juice
⅛ teaspoon salt
1 (1-pound) can cranberry
  sauce
1 cup crushed pineapple,
  drained
1 cup chopped pecans
1 cup sliced bananas
1 pint Cool Whip

- Whip together softened cream cheese, mayonnaise, lemon juice, salt and cranberry sauce.
- Fold in pineapple, pecans, bananas and Cool Whip.
- Pour into 9 x 13-inch pan. Cover and freeze. Take from freezer 30 minutes before serving.
- Cut into squares and serve on bed of lettuce.

Guacamole Salad

Serves 10

½ head lettuce
¼ cup chopped green onions
2 diced tomatoes
1 cup grated cheddar cheese
1 cup black olives, chopped
1 cup Fritos

Dressing:
1 avocado
½ cup sour cream
5 tablespoons salad oil
1 tablespoon lemon juice
½ teaspoon salt
¼ teaspoon chili powder
¼ teaspoon Tabasco
Garlic salt

- Toss together all salad ingredients, except Fritos.
- Mash avocado. Blend together all dressing ingredients.
- Add dressing and Fritos to salad at last minute.

Italian Salad

Serves 10-12

6 ounces cubed summer
  sausage
6 ounces cubed ham
6 ounces sliced salami
4 ounces cubed American
  cheese
4 ounces cubed Swiss cheese
4 ounces salad oil
1 cup wine vinegar
4 hard-boiled eggs
4 ounces chopped onions
1 red onion, thinly sliced
4 ounces chopped green
  peppers
Salt
Crushed pepper to taste

- Toss all ingredients and allow to chill overnight.
- Place in glass bowl and decorate with sliced salami and hard-boiled eggs. Vary ingredients by adding other vegetables, cheeses, etc. Good at large buffets or cocktail parties, if meat and cheeses are in cubes or slices. Serve with toothpicks.

Patches Salad

Serves 6-8

1 small head of lettuce, cut in
   bite-sized pieces
1 can chick peas, drained and
   chilled
1 small sweet onion, cut in
   rings
3 hard-boiled eggs, sliced
1 tomato, cut into wedges
6 slices bacon, cooked and
   crumbled
Salt and pepper to taste

Dressing
¼ cup mayonnaise
1½ teaspoons catsup
¼ teaspoon Worcestershire
   sauce
1 teaspoon wine vinegar
1 teaspoon oil

- Toss all ingredients together.
  Top with dressing.
- Stir first 3 dressing ingredients
  together. Add remaining
  ingredients. Stir thoroughly.
- Cover and chill.

Picnic Potato Salad

Serves 6

2 pounds new potatoes
½ cup chopped onion
½ cup chopped celery
2 hard-boiled eggs, chopped
8 slices bacon, cooked,
   drained and crumbled
½ cup mayonnaise
½ cup sour cream
¼ cup tarragon vinegar
Salt and pepper

- Cook potatoes in boiling salted
  water until tender.
- Drain, peel and cut into cubes.
  Cool.
- Toss together potatoes, onion,
  celery, eggs and bacon.
- Mix mayonnaise, sour cream and
  vinegar. Toss with potato
  mixture.
- Season with salt and pepper.
  Chill.

Potpourri Salad

Serves 6

Rare leftover sirloin, cut into
  bite-sized pieces
1 small head lettuce, torn into
  bite-sized pieces
2 ripe tomatoes, cut into
  wedges
1 small onion, sliced
2-3 ripe peaches, peeled and
  sliced

Dressing
¼ cup salad oil
2 tablespoons lemon juice
1 teaspoon seasoned salt
1 tablespoon horseradish
Salt and pepper to taste

- Place salad ingredients in large bowl.
- Mix dressing ingredients together and refrigerate.
- When ready to serve, toss with dressing.

Orange Spinach Salad

Serves 10-12

1 (10-ounce) bag fresh
  spinach, washed and
  drained
1 head iceberg lettuce
2 tablespoons diced onion
2 tablespoons diced green
  pepper
2 large oranges, sectioned
1 cucumber, shredded

Honey Dill Dressing
¾ cup mayonnaise
2 tablespoons honey
1 tablespoon lemon juice
1 tablespoon dill seed
1 teaspoon mustard
1 tablespoon Grand Marnier
1 teaspoon allspice

- Mix together all ingredients for dressing and refrigerate.
- Tear spinach and lettuce into bite-sized pieces.
- Add remaining ingredients and toss.
- To serve toss with honey dill dressing.

Susan's Specialty Salad

Serves 6

2 cups torn iceberg lettuce
2 cups torn curly endive
2 cups torn romaine lettuce
6 tablespoons mayonnaise
1 medium red onion, thinly
  sliced
1½ cups canned garden peas
½ cup grated cheddar cheese
½ cup grated Swiss cheese
6 slices bacon, crisply cooked
  and crumbled
6-10 fresh mushrooms, thinly
  sliced

- Place a third of the salad greens into a bowl. Dot with some mayonnaise.
- Top with a third of the onion slices, sprinkle with sugar (about 1 teaspoon). Dash with pepper and salt.
- Add a third of the peas and cheeses.
- Repeat layers, seasoning each.
- Do not toss until served.
- Cover, chill 2 hours.
- Just before serving, top with bacon and mushrooms. Toss.

Summer Sauerkraut

Serves 6

½ cup vinegar
½ cup sugar
¼ cup salad oil
¼ teaspoon salt
1 (16-ounce) can sauerkraut,
  rinsed and drained
1 cup finely chopped celery
1 small onion, finely chopped
½ medium green pepper,
  finely chopped
1 (2-ounce) jar pimiento,
  chopped
½ teaspoon caraway seed

- Combine and heat vinegar, sugar, oil and salt until sugar dissolves.
- Pour over sauerkraut. Stir in remaining ingredients.
- Cover. Chill several hours or overnight.

Tabuli-Lebanese Salad

Serves 6

1 cup fine bulgar wheat, well washed
2 cups finely chopped parsley
1 cup finely chopped green onions
2 tomatoes, chopped
1 cucumber, chopped
¼ cup lemon juice
½ teaspoon salt
¼ cup olive oil
Lettuce

- Cover wheat with cold water and soak for 1 hour. Drain.
- Mix with parsley, green onions, tomatoes and cucumber.
- Add lemon juice, salt and olive oil.
- Toss and refrigerate 1 hour before serving.
- Serve on a bed of lettuce.

Tack Room Salad

Serves 6-8

1½ cups raw cauliflower, cut in ½-inch pieces
1½ teaspoons salt
8 cups lettuce, cut in 1½-inch chunks
7 cups romaine, cut in 1-inch wide strips, 2-inches long
1½ cups White French Salad Dressing (page 109)
5 tablespoons bleu cheese, crumbled
5 tablespoons bacon, crumbled
16 half wedges of tomato
Watercress

- Combine cauliflower pieces, salt and chilled cut greens. Toss together.
- Add dressing and toss to coat all greens.
- Line a large salad serving bowl with lettuce leaves. Heap tossed greens into bowl.
- Sprinkle bleu cheese and bacon crumbs over the top.
- Garnish with tomato wedges and watercress.

 If salad greens are wet and you need them right away, place in a pillow case and spin dry in washing machine for 30-40 seconds.

Tomato and Cucumber Refresher

Serves 6

3 medium tomatoes, sliced in
wedges
1 cucumber, sliced
1 small onion, chopped
1 tablespoon salt
¼ teaspoon black pepper
¼ cup vinegar
¼ cup sugar
1 cup cold water

- Place sliced tomatoes and cucumber in shallow serving dish.
- Mix together remaining ingredients and pour over the top.
- Cover and chill at least 3 hours.

Tropical Salad

Serves 6-8

½ bunch romaine lettuce
3 medium bananas, sliced
3 oranges, peeled and sliced
1 green pepper, sliced in rings
1 small red onion, thinly
sliced

Dressing
½ cup salad oil
2 tablespoons vinegar
2 tablespoons lemon juice
2 tablespoons sugar
1 teaspoon dry mustard
½ teaspoon salt

- Tear romaine into bite-sized pieces. Combine with next 4 ingredients.
- Combine dressing ingredients. Mix well. Chill.
- Toss together when ready to serve.

Artichoke Pasta Salad

Serves 6

4 ounces shell macaroni,
  cooked and drained
1 (6-ounce) jar marinated
  artichoke hearts and liquid
¼ pound fresh mushrooms,
  sliced
1 cup cherry tomatoes,
  halved
1 cup pitted ripe olives
1 tablespoon chopped parsley
½ teaspoon dry basil leaves
1 teaspoon capers
Salt and pepper to taste

- Toss all ingredients together. Cover and chill at least 4 hours.

Artichoke Rice

Serves 6

1 package chicken-flavored
  rice
2 (6-ounce) jars marinated
  artichoke hearts
4 green onions, chopped
1½ green peppers, chopped
12 stuffed olives, chopped
¾ teaspoon curry powder
5-6 tablespoons mayonnaise

- Cook rice and cool.
- Drain artichokes, saving juice from one jar. Slice artichokes in half.
- Combine reserved artichoke juice with mayonnaise and curry powder.
- Combine all ingredients. Chill and serve.

Buccaneer Salad

Serves 6

3 cups long-grain rice,
    cooked, rinsed and drained
½ cup mayonnaise
2 teaspoons Worcestershire
    sauce
2 teaspoons lemon juice
¼ teaspoon salt
1 cup grated raw carrots
¼ cup thinly sliced scallions

- In large bowl combine rice, mayonnaise, Worcestershire sauce, lemon juice and salt. Mix well.
- Add carrots and scallions. Toss lightly.
- Chill 6-8 hours before serving.

Bombay Rice Salad

Serves 6-8

4 cups white rice, cooked and
    chilled
¾ cup thinly sliced celery
1 cup frozen peas, cooked,
    drained and chilled
½-¾ cup salted peanuts or
    toasted almonds
½ cup mayonnaise
½ cup sour cream
4-6 tablespoons mango
    chutney
2 teaspoons curry powder, or
    to taste

- Place rice, celery, peas and nuts in large bowl.
- In small bowl prepare dressing by mixing mayonnaise and sour cream with curry powder, chutney, salt and pepper.
- Carefully mix the rice mixture with the dressing and chill at least 6-8 hours for the flavors to combine nicely.
- Serve with peanuts or almonds sprinkled over salad.

Marco Polo Salad

Serves 16

2 tablespoons butter
2½ cups raw rice
5 cups boiling water
2 green peppers
1 apple
½ cup pitted olives
¼ cup red radishes
½ cup celery
½ cup pignoli nuts or toasted
  almonds
6 anchovy fillets
½ cup raisins; soak in water
  1 hour, drain
½ cup oil
¼ cup lemon juice
1 teaspoon salt
Pinch of pepper
4 tablespoons mayonnaise
Sliced hard-boiled eggs
Tomato slices
Sliced ripe olives
Parsley

*Variation: For main dish,
  chopped chicken or ham may
  be added.*

*Hint: Best when made a day
  ahead.*

- Heat butter in large skillet to simmering.
- Pour in rice and fry 5 minutes, stirring constantly with wooden spoon.
- When rice is slightly brown, add boiling water.
- When water resumes boiling, remove from heat. Cover tightly, and bake at 400° for exactly 18 minutes. Rice will be perfectly cooked.
- While rice is cooling, finely chop peppers, apple, olives, radishes, celery, nuts, anchovies and raisins.
- Mix cooled rice with above ingredients and season with oil, lemon juice, salt and pepper. Add mayonnaise to bind salad.
- When well mixed, shape into large melon on serving platter.
- Cover with mayonnaise and decorate with egg slices, tomato slices, ripe olive slices and parsley.
- Cover lightly and refrigerate until serving.

Crab Salad
from the Grant Seafood Festival

Serves 4

1 pound crabmeat
3 hard-boiled eggs
1 cup chopped celery
1 medium onion, chopped
¼ cup pickle relish
Mayonnaise to taste
Salt and pepper to taste

- Pick over crabmeat for shells. Toss all ingredients thoroughly with enough mayonnaise to hold together. Chill before serving.

Confetti Salad

Serves 8

4 cups cooked rice, fluffy
4 scallions, sliced
2 bell peppers, 1 green and 1
   red
2 medium tomatoes, peeled,
   seeded and diced
4 radishes, sliced
½ pound Muenster or Swiss
   cheese, cubed
12 green olives, chopped
12 black olives, chopped
¼ cup parsley or mixed fresh
   herbs
½ cup highly seasoned oil
   dressing
Salt and pepper to taste

- Mix all ingredients in an
  attractive, large serving bowl at
  least 1 hour before serving.
- Refrigerate so flavors can blend.
- Serve at room temperature.
- Add extra lemon juice and salt to
  taste at last minute.

Raft-up Salad

Serves 4-6

1 cup shell macaroni
1 pound cooked, cleaned
   shrimp
½ green pepper, chopped
2 stalks celery, chopped
2 teaspoons horseradish
6 tablespoons mayonnaise
Juice of ½ lemon

- Cook macaroni according to
  package directions. Rinse and
  drain.
- Combine with remaining
  ingredients. Chill.

Apricot Cheese Delight

Serves 10-12

2 (3-ounce) packages orange-flavored gelatin
2 cups hot water
1 (17-ounce) can apricots, drained and chopped (reserve juice)
1 (16-ounce) can crushed pineapple, drained (reserve juice)
1 cup apricot juice
1 cup (or more) miniature marshmallows

Topping
½ cup sugar
3 tablespoons flour
1 egg, slightly beaten
2 tablespoons butter
1 cup pineapple juice
1 cup whipping cream (or whipped topping)
¾ cup grated cheddar cheese

- Dissolve gelatin in hot water. Add apricots, pineapple and apricot juice with enough water to make 1 cup.
- Pour into 9 x 13-inch dish. Chill.
- Put marshmallows on top of gelatin after gelatin congeals.
- Combine sugar and flour. Add pineapple juice and stir to dissolve.
- Blend in beaten egg and butter. Cook over low heat, stirring constantly until thick.
- Let cool thoroughly. Fold in whipped cream.
- Spread over congealed salad. Sprinkle with grated cheese.
- Serve on lettuce leaf.

Strawberry Buttermilk Salad

Serves 15-20

1 (6-ounce) package strawberry gelatin
1 (20-ounce) can crushed pineapple, undrained
2 cups buttermilk
1 cup chopped pecans
1 (8-ounce) carton whipped topping

- Heat gelatin and pineapple with juice in a large saucepan on low heat until the gelatin dissolves. Do not boil. Cool.
- Mix in buttermilk, nuts and topping until blended.
- Pour into a 9 x 13-inch oblong dish.
- Refrigerate until firm.

Blueberry Salad

Serves 12-15

2 (3-ounce) packages grape, blackberry or raspberry gelatin
2 cups boiling water
1 (16-ounce) can crushed pineapple, undrained
1 (21-ounce) can blueberry pie filling

Topping
1 (8-ounce) carton sour cream
1 (8-ounce) package cream cheese, softened
½ cup sugar
1 teaspoon vanilla
½ cup chopped nuts (optional)

- Mix together gelatin, boiling water, crushed pineapple and pie filling.
- Put into 9 x 13-inch pan or similar size dish.
- Refrigerate until set.
- Mix together topping ingredients and spread on top of congealed salad.
- Add ½ cup chopped nuts.
- Refrigerate until needed.

Guacamole Mold

Serves 10

1½ tablespoons unflavored gelatin
½ cup cold water
¾ cup boiling water
2 tablespoons lemon juice
1¼ teaspoon salt
1 teaspoon grated onion
2 dashes Tabasco
2½ cups mashed avocado
1 cup sour cream
1 cup mayonnaise
1 (6-cup) mold

- Soften gelatin in cold water, dissolve in boiling water.
- Add next 4 ingredients and cool.
- Combine avocado, sour cream and mayonnaise. Blend in gelatin mixture.
- Pour into one 6-cup mold.
- Chill 6 hours or overnight.

Cucumber Ring

Serves 8-10

First Layer
½ envelope gelatin
1 tablespoon sugar
½ teaspoon salt
¾ cup boiling water
2 tablespoons lemon juice
Thinly sliced cucumbers

Second Layer
1 envelope gelatin
2 tablespoons sugar
¾ teaspoon salt
½ cup boiling water
¾ tablespoon lemon juice
6 pared and seeded
  cucumbers
1 (8-ounce) package cream
  cheese
1 cup mayonnaise
¼ cup minced onion
¼ cup minced parsley

- Mix gelatin, sugar and salt.
- Add boiling water and lemon juice.
- Overlap cucumber slices in bottom of 6½-cup round mold.
- Carefully pour gelatin mixture over cucumbers, trying to keep in overlapping pattern.
- Chill until firm.
- While first layer is chilling, prepare second layer.
- Mix gelatin, sugar and salt. Add water and lemon juice.
- Process cucumber in blender and measure 2 cups.
- Soften cream cheese and add processed cucumbers, mayonnaise, onion and parsley.
- Stir in gelatin mixture and pour over first layer.
- Chill until firm.

Curry Pear Salad

Serves 4

Lettuce
8 canned pear halves
4 scoops cottage cheese
4 tablespoons mayonnaise
1 cup raisins
1 cup Spanish peanuts
Curry powder

- Arrange on individual salad plates in order listed.
- Use more or less of any ingredient to suit your own taste.

Frosted Salad

Serves 12-16

2 (6-ounce) boxes lemon
  gelatin
2 cups boiling water
16 ounces 7-Up
1 (16-ounce) can crushed
  pineapple, drained (reserve
  juice)
½ cup chopped nuts
2 large bananas, sliced
½ cup white sugar
2 tablespoons flour
1 cup pineapple juice
1 egg, slightly beaten
2 tablespoons butter
4 ounces cream cheese
½ pint whipping cream
Yellow food coloring

- Dissolve gelatin in boiling water.
- Add 7-Up and chill in 9 x 13-inch pan until consistency of heavy corn syrup.
- Add drained pineapple, nuts and bananas. Chill until firm.
- Combine sugar, flour, pineapple juice and egg in saucepan.
- Cook over low heat until thick.
- Remove from heat. Add butter.
- Stir in cream cheese and chill.
- Whip cream until stiff. Fold in cream cheese mixture.
- Add yellow food coloring.
- Spread evenly over firm gelatin.
- Sprinkle nuts on top and chill until serving time.
- Cut in squares to serve.

Spinach Salad Mold

Serves 8

2 (10-ounce) packages frozen
  chopped spinach
4 hard-boiled eggs, chopped
¾ cup mayonnaise
1 (10-ounce) can consomme´, hot
2 envelopes unflavored gelatin
1¾ teaspoons salt
3 teaspoons Worcestershire
  sauce
2 tablespoons lemon juice
¼ teaspoon Tabasco sauce
8 lettuce leaves

- Cook spinach according to package directions. Drain thoroughly.
- Combine spinach, eggs and mayonnaise.
- Dissolve gelatin in hot consomme´.
- Fold in spinach mixture. Add salt, Worcestershire, lemon juice and Tabasco.
- Turn into oiled 2-quart mold.
- Chill 3-4 hours.
- Unmold on bed of lettuce.

Strawberry Pretzel Salad

Serves 12

¾ cup margarine
3 tablespoons brown sugar
2½ cups coarsely crushed
   pretzels
1 (6-ounce) package
   strawberry gelatin
2 cups boiling water
3 cups chilled strawberries or
   1 pound package frozen,
   slightly-thawed
   strawberries
1 (8-ounce) package cream
   cheese
1 scant cup sugar
1 (4-ounce) carton frozen
   whipped topping

- Combine margarine, sugar and pretzels. Pat into lightly buttered 9 x 13-inch pan.
- Bake at 350° for 10 minutes.
- Dissolve gelatin in boiling water.
- While still hot, add chilled berries.
- Cool until mixture begins to set.
- Meanwhile, cream the cream cheese with sugar. Fold in whipped topping.
- Spread over cooled crust.
- When gelatin mixture begins to set, pour gelatin mixture over cheese mixture.
- Refrigerate until firm.

Santa's Christmas Salad

Serves 8

1 (16-ounce) can crushed
   pineapple
1 (3-ounce) package lime
   gelatin
1 (8-ounce) package cream
   cheese
½ pint coffee cream or half
   and half

*Variation: Serve with a mara-
schino cherry on top of each
portion. Can also add
peaches, fruit cocktail or
mandarin oranges.*

- Bring pineapple (with juice) to boil over medium high heat.
- Remove from stove and add gelatin.
- Stir until dissolved and set aside to cool.
- Beat cream cheese, adding coffee cream slowly until smooth.
- Blend pineapple and cheese mixture and pour into 7 x 11-inch pan.
- Chill until set.

Thanksgiving Mold

Serves 12

1 (16-ounce) can whole
  cranberry sauce
1 (3-ounce) package lemon
  gelatin
1 (3-ounce) package
  raspberry gelatin
2½ cups boiling water
1 (8-ounce) can crushed
  pineapple, drained
¾ cup diced apple, unpeeled
¾ cup diced celery
½ cup chopped nuts

- Mash cranberry sauce in large bowl.
- Dissolve gelatin in hot water and add to cranberry sauce.
- Cool until consistency of egg whites.
- Fold in pineapple, apple, celery, and nuts.
- Pour into 8-cup mold that has been sprayed with Pam and rinsed with ice water. (This makes mold very glossy.)
- Chill until firm.

Tropicana Salad

Serves 8-12

2 (6-ounce) packages
  strawberry gelatin
2 cups boiling water
2 (3-ounce) packages frozen
  strawberries (thaw with
  juice)
1 (20-ounce) can crushed
  pineapple, drained
3 medium bananas, mashed
1 cup chopped pecans
1 pint sour cream

- Dissolve gelatin in boiling water.
- Fold in strawberries with juice, drained pineapple, bananas and nuts.
- Put ½ in an oblong casserole dish. Refrigerate until firm.
- Pour on the sour cream and spread evenly.
- Pour on remaining mixture and chill until firm.

Vegetable Aspic

Serves 18

4 cups tomato juice
3-4 envelopes plain gelatin
½ teaspoon salt
2 medium cucumbers,
    chopped
½ green pepper, chopped
½ large Spanish onion,
    chopped
2-3 stalks celery, chopped
1 (5-ounce) jar pimiento
    stuffed Spanish olives
Tabasco to taste

- Heat tomato juice until warm enough to dissolve gelatin. Add salt and gelatin. Mix well. Cool.
- Cut olives in half.
- Add all ingredients to cooled gelatin mixture.
- Pour into a greased mold or 9 x 13-inch pan.

Frosty Cherry Salad

Serves 10

1 (21-ounce) can cherry pie
    filling
1 (15-ounce) can sweetened
    condensed milk
1 (20-ounce) can chunk
    pineapple
1 (12-ounce) container frozen
    whipped topping

- Mix pie filling and condensed milk.
- Drain pineapple and slice chunks in half. Add to pie filling mixture.
- Fold in thawed whipped topping. Pour into an 8-inch casserole dish and freeze.
- Before serving, let stand at room temperature 5-10 minutes.
- Cut into squares.
- May be served as dessert.

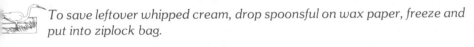 *To save leftover whipped cream, drop spoonsful on wax paper, freeze and put into ziplock bag.*

Tapioca Fruit Salad

Serves 15

½ cup plus 2 tablespoons
   minute tapioca
1 cup sugar
Juice from 1 (16-ounce) can
   pineapple chunks; save
   chunks
3 cups water
1 (6-ounce) can frozen orange
   juice concentrate
1 (16-ounce) can pineapple
   chunks, drained
2 (11-ounce) cans mandarin
   oranges, drained
1-2 cups grapes
2-3 bananas, sliced
Maraschino cherries
   (optional, for color)

- Combine first 4 ingredients. Cook over medium heat until thick and cloudy, stirring constantly.
- Cool about 10 minutes.
- Add orange juice concentrate. Stir until dissolved.
- Add rest of ingredients. Pour into large glass bowl and chill about 4 hours until firm.

Chiles' Chicken Salad Mold

from Governor and Mrs. Lawton Chiles

Yields 1 (3-cup) mold

1 envelope plain gelatin
½ cup cold water
½ teaspoon salt
1 tablespoon sugar
1 tablespoon lemon juice
2-4 tablespoons vinegar
1 cup hot chicken stock
1½ cups bite-sized cooked
   chicken pieces

Sauce
1½ cups plain yogurt
2 tablespoons mayonnaise
1 tablespoon capers
½ cup canned tuna

- Sprinkle gelatin over water. Stir constantly over low heat for 3 minutes until gelatin dissolves. Remove from heat.
- Add salt, sugar, lemon juice, vinegar and chicken stock. Stir until sugar and salt dissolve.
- Refrigerate until slightly thickened.
- Fold in chicken. Pour into greased 3-cup mold and chill until firm.
- When ready to serve, blend sauce ingredients together.
- Remove salad from mold. Top with sauce.

Company Chicken Salad

Serves 4-6

4 cups cubed, cooked
  chicken
1 cup chopped celery
1 medium apple, chopped
1 small package slivered
  almonds, toasted
1 teaspoon salt
1 teaspoon pepper
¼ cup sour cream
¾ cup mayonnaise

- Combine chicken, celery, apple and toasted almonds in large bowl.
- Sprinkle salt and pepper over mixture.
- Add sour cream and mayonnaise and mix thoroughly.
- Chill well before serving.

Cranberry Chicken Mold

Serves 8

2 envelopes gelatin
2 cans whole cranberry sauce
1 (8-ounce) can crushed
  pineapple, drained
½ cup chopped walnuts or
  pecans
1 cup mayonnaise
½ cup evaporated milk
2½-3 cups diced chicken
1 cup diced celery
Salt and pepper to taste

- Soften half of gelatin in ¼ cup cold water.
- Dissolve over hot water.
- Break up cranberry sauce with fork. Add cranberry sauce, pineapple and nuts to gelatin and pour into a 10-cup mold.
- Chill until congealed.
- Dissolve remaining gelatin as before.
- Combine mayonnaise and milk in large bowl.
- Blend in gelatin and remaining ingredients.
- Spoon over cranberry layer. Chill until firm.

Curried Chicken Salad

Serves 4-6

3 pounds chicken breasts,
  cooked, cubed
½ cup celery, thinly sliced
  and cut diagonally
½ cup chopped green pepper
2 teaspoons grated onion
¾-1 cup homemade mayon-
  naise (if commercial
  mayonnaise is used, add 2-
  3 tablespoons light cream)
½-1 teaspoon curry powder
¾ teaspoon salt or to taste
Pepper to taste
¾ cup apple, unpeeled, diced
1 cup white seedless grapes,
  halved

- Remove skin and bones from chicken.
- Combine chicken, celery, green pepper and onion.
- Blend mayonnaise, curry powder, salt and pepper. Add to chicken. If prepared ahead, refrigerate at least 3-4 hours for better flavor.
- Before serving add fruit, correct seasoning and add additional mayonnaise, if required.

Chicken and Fruit Salad

Serves 6

2½-3 cups cooked, diced
  chicken
1 cup sliced celery
2 tablespoons chopped green
  onion
2 tablespoons capers
1 teaspoon salt
2 tablespoons lemon juice
1 (11-ounce) can mandarin
  oranges, drained
1 (9-ounce) can pineapple
  chunks, drained
½ cup slivered almonds, toasted
½ cup mayonnaise
½ teaspoon grated lemon peel

- Combine chicken with celery, green onion and capers.
- Mix in salt and lemon juice. Cover and chill for several hours.
- Just before serving, add oranges. (Reserve a few for garnish), pineapple and almonds.
- Combine mayonnaise and lemon peel. Mix in carefully so as not to break fruit.
- Spoon into a bowl lined with greens. Garnish with reserved oranges.

Mrs. Walter Reich's Crab Louis

Serves 3-4

1 pound lump crabmeat
1 head lettuce
¼ cup finely chopped onion
¼ cup chopped green pepper
2 tablespoons green olives
1 cup mayonnaise
¼ cup chili sauce
1 tablespoon lemon or lime
   juice
1 teaspoon Worcestershire
   sauce
1 teaspoon prepared
   horseradish
1 teaspoon salt
½ teaspoon paprika

- Pick over crab to remove shells.
- Finely chop ½ of lettuce.
- Mix together rest of ingredients.
- Add crab chunks and shredded lettuce. Toss lightly.
- Serve on large plates or soup bowls lined with lettuce leaves.
- Garnish with ripe olives, tomato wedges and quartered hard-boiled eggs.

Seafood Aspic

Serves 8

1 package unflavored gelatin
1 can tomato soup or V-8
   juice
3 ounces cream cheese,
   softened
1 cup cooked shrimp, cleaned
   and broken
1 cup crabmeat, picked and
   broken (may use 2 cups of
   just 1 seafood)
¼ cup diced celery
¼ cup diced onion
¼ cup diced cucumber
¼ cup diced green pepper
1 cup mayonnaise

- Dissolve gelatin in ¼ cup water.
- Warm undiluted soup. Add dissolved gelatin and cream cheese.
- Stir well until mixture is well blended.
- Add seafoods, vegetables and mayonnaise.
- Pour into greased 6-cup mold.
- Refrigerate 24 hours.
- Turn out onto bed of lettuce.

Island Shrimp Salad

Serves 20

2 tablespoons gelatin
½ cup cold water
1 cup chili sauce
2 tablespoons minced onion
½ green pepper, finely chopped
1 teaspoon Worcestershire
  sauce
2 tablespoons India relish
4 cups chopped, cooked shrimp
  (reserve several for garnish)
2 cups mayonnaise

- Soften gelatin in cold water. Dissolve over hot water.
- Combine with remaining ingredients, except mayonnaise. Blend well.
- Add mayonnaise a little at a time. Mix well.
- Pour into individual molds. Place in refrigerator. Turn onto bed of lettuce when ready to serve.

Coastal Summer Salad

Serves 6

7 medium potatoes
1 medium onion
1 (8-ounce) bottle Italian
  salad dressing
1 (7-ounce) can tuna
1 (7¾-ounce) can salmon
1 tablespoon chopped fresh
  dill
Boston lettuce, washed and
  chilled

- Cook potatoes in boiling, salted water until tender. Drain and cool slightly. Peel and slice ¼-inch thick.
- Peel onion, slice and separate into rings.
- In shallow dish, arrange potatoes and onion in alternate layers.
- Pour ¾ cup dressing over all.
- Refrigerate, covered, 3 hours.
- Drain tuna and salmon. Break into chunks and remove bone and skin from salmon.
- Place in small bowl and toss with remaining dressing.
- Refrigerate mixture, covered.
- When ready to serve, arrange potato slices and onion rings in layers alternating with fish mixture. Sprinkle dill on top. Garnish with lettuce.

Avocado Dressing

Yields 3 cups

2 avocados, pitted and
  mashed
2 tablespoons lemon juice
2 tablespoons mayonnaise
½ cup sour cream
½ teaspoon minced onion
  (optional)
2-3 drops Tabasco
¼ cup milk

- Mix thoroughly all ingredients.
- If too thick, add a little milk or
  more mayonnaise.
- Pour over salad greens.

Chart House Bleu Cheese Dressing
from the Chart House, Melbourne

Yields 2½ cups

¾ cup sour cream
½ teaspoon dry mustard
½ teaspoon black pepper
½ teaspoon salt, scant
¼ teaspoon garlic powder
1 teaspoon Worcestershire
  sauce
1¼ cups mayonnaise
4 ounces imported Danish
  bleu cheese

- Blend first 6 ingredients in mixing
  bowl on low speed for 2 minutes.
- Add mayonnaise. Mix ½ minute
  on low speed, then 2 minutes on
  medium speed.
- Crumble cheese with hands into
  small pieces. Add to mixture.
- Blend on low speed no longer
  than 4 minutes.
- Let set in refrigerator at least 24
  hours before serving.

 You may substitute white vinegar, with a small amount of red or rosé wine added, for red wine vinegar.

Brass Door Dressing

Yields 2 cups

1¼ cups mayonnaise
½ cup vegetable oil
¼ cup honey
¼ cup prepared mustard
3 tablespoons fresh lemon juice
2 green onions, finely chopped
1 tablespoon chopped fresh
  parsley
1 teaspoon celery seed
¼ teaspoon dry mustard
¼ teaspoon curry powder

- Combine all ingredients and chill.
- Serve with fresh torn spinach and any combination of chopped eggs, fresh sliced mushrooms, bacon bits and marinated artichokes.

Caesar Salad Dressing

Yield 2½ cups

1 cup mayonnaise
1 cup sour cream
1 medium onion
1-2 cloves garlic
2 tablespoons chopped parsley
½-1 can anchovies
Juice of 1 lemon
¼ cup Parmesan cheese
½ teaspoon curry powder

- Blend all ingredients in food processor or blender.
- Store in refrigerator.
- Toss with romaine or iceberg lettuce and serve.

Sharon's Vinaigrette Dressing

1 cup salad oil
¼ cup cider vinegar
1 teaspoon salt
1 teaspoon garlic salt
1 teaspoon pepper
½ teaspoon dry mustard
Dash cayenne

- Mix all ingredients. Chill.
- Serve over tossed salad. May also be used for pasta or vegetable marinade.

Ramon's Caesar Dressing

from Ramon's, Cocoa Beach

Yields 1½ quarts

6 eggs
1 quart mayonnaise
1 package dried onion soup
  mix
½ teaspoon curry powder
1 teaspoon garlic powder
1¼ cups Parmesan cheese
4 teaspoons anchovy paste

- Beat eggs until frothy.
- Slowly add mayonnaise and remaining ingredients. Mix well.
- Chill.

White French Salad Dressing

Yields 2 cups

3 tablespoons cornstarch
¼ cup cold water
½ cup boiling water
¼ teaspoon paprika
¼ cup hot water
½ cup sugar
2 tablespoons salt
1 teaspoon dry mustard
2¾ cups salad oil
1 cup cider vinegar
½ teaspoon onion juice
1 clove garlic

- Dissolve cornstarch in cold water.
- Add boiling water and cook 3-5 minutes over medium heat until thick, stirring constantly.
- Dissolve paprika in hot water. Add to cornstarch mixture and cook 1 minute longer.
- Add sugar, salt and mustard. Mix well.
- Strain mixture to eliminate lumps.
- Whip hot mixture on medium speed of electric mixer, while gradually adding salad oil alternately with vinegar.
- Add onion juice. Add garlic clove.
- Cover and refrigerate 24 hours to blend flavors. Remove garlic clove after 24 hours.
- Store in refrigerator, covered. Stir well before each use.

Easy Fruit Dressings

Mint Dip

Yields 1 cup

1 cup sour cream
1-2 tablespoons green crème
de menthe

- Mix together.
- Serve with fresh fruit.

Apricot Dip

Yields 1 cup

1 cup sour cream
2-3 tablespoons apricot
preserves or jam
Shaved coconut and chopped
walnuts (optional)

- Mix together.
- Serve with fresh fruit or wheat crackers.

Honey Cream Dip

Yields 2 cups

2 eggs
¼ cup honey
¼ cup lemon juice
1 cup heavy cream, whipped

- Beat eggs until light in top of double boiler.
- Add honey and lemon juice.
- Cook over hot, not boiling water, stirring constantly until thickened. Cool.
- Fold in whipped cream. Chill.

Oriental Dressing
from Piper's Restaurant, North Carolina

Yields 1 pint

1 cup olive oil
½ cup soy sauce
⅛ cup soybean oil
⅛ cup sesame oil
¼ cup red wine vinegar
1 tablespoon black pepper

- Combine all ingredients. This keeps well. Great on spinach salad.

Poppy Seed Dressing for Fruit Salad

Yields 1 cup

¼ cup sugar
1 teaspoon salt
¼ cup white vinegar
1 tablespoon lemon juice
1 teaspoon dry mustard
1 teaspoon onion juice
1 cup salad oil
2 tablespoons poppy seed

- Put all ingredients except oil in deep mixer bowl.
- As you run the mixer on medium speed, slowly add salad oil.

Garlic Salad Dressing

Yields 1 quart

1 cup water
3 cloves garlic, finely chopped
1 tablespoon oregano
1 (2-ounce) can anchovies, chopped
1 ounce Worcestershire
1 tablespoon salt
½ tablespoon pepper
1 pint sour cream
1 pint mayonnaise

- Put water, garlic, oregano, anchovies, Worcestershire, salt and pepper in blender for 3-4 minutes.
- Add sour cream and mayonnaise. Mix for 5 minutes.

Tomato-Herb Salad Dressing

Yields 1½ cups

1 cup tomato vegetable juice
¼ cup red wine vinegar
½ teaspoon sugar
¼ teaspoon ground cumin
¼ teaspoon dried oregano
¼ teaspoon celery salt
1 garlic clove, pressed
⅛ teaspoon fresh ground
   pepper
Dash Worcestershire sauce
2 teaspoons cornstarch
2 tablespoons cold water
2 tablespoons minced chives
1 tablespoon olive oil

- Bring juice, wine vinegar, sugar, cumin, oregano, celery salt, garlic, pepper and Worcestershire sauce to a boil in a small saucepan.
- Stir cornstarch into cold water until dissolved.
- Stir into dressing until thickened. Remove from heat and cool.
- Stir in chives and olive oil.
- Cool and adjust seasoning.
- Best served at room temperature.

Lancer Spinach Salad Dressing

from Nevada Rep. Barbara F. Vucanovich

Yields 2 quarts

¾ teaspoon garlic powder
2 tablespoons sugar
2 tablespoons salt
2 tablespoons dry mustard
1 tablespoon fresh ground
   pepper
½ cup Worcestershire sauce
2 tablespoons A-1 sauce
1 cup Burgundy
1 cup catsup
1 cup cider vinegar
1 cup honey
4 cups salad oil

- Mix all ingredients.
- Pour dressing over spinach salad.

BREADS &
SAUCES

The Fisherman, By Nancy Vice. Collection of The Brevard Art Center and Museum. Photographed by Franko Photo.

Breads

Sauces

* Denotes Quick and Easy Recipes

114

Sunrise Loaf

Yields 1 loaf

1 medium orange
½ cup nuts, coarsely chopped
½ cup dates, finely cut
2 tablespoons butter, melted
½ cup fresh orange juice
1 cup brown sugar
1 egg, slightly beaten
1 teaspoon soda
½ teaspoon salt
2 cups sifted flour
1 teaspoon baking powder

Spread
1 (3-ounce) package cream
  cheese
5 tablespoons orange
  marmalade

- Cut orange into sections and put through a food chopper.
- Add nuts, dates, butter, orange juice, sugar and beaten egg.
- Stir dry ingredients and add to fruit mixture.
- Stir lightly until just mixed.
- Pour into greased 5 x 9-inch loaf pan and bake at 350° for 50-60 minutes.
- Cool thoroughly before slicing.
- Mix together spread ingredients.
- Cut bread into slices and spread with cream cheese mixture.

Apricot Nibble Bread

Yields 1 loaf

6 ounces cream cheese,
  softened
¼ cup sugar
1 tablespoon flour
1 egg
1 teaspoon grated orange
  rind
1 slightly beaten egg
½ cup orange juice
½ cup water
1 (15.7-ounce) package
  apricot-nut quick bread
  mix

- Combine cream cheese, sugar, flour, 1 egg and orange rind. Set aside.
- Combine 1 egg, orange juice and water. Stir in bread mix.
- Turn 2/3 batter into greased and floured 3 x 5 x 9-inch loaf pan.
- Pour cream cheese mixture on top. Spoon on remaining batter.
- Bake at 350° for 1 hour.
- Cool 10 minutes and remove from pan.
- Cool, wrap in foil, and refrigerate.

Coconut Bread

Yields 2 loaves

1¼ cups coconut
1½ cups margarine
1½ cups sugar
6 eggs
4½ cups flour
¾ teaspoon salt
¾ teaspoon baking soda
¾ teaspoon baking powder
1½ cups buttermilk
3 tablespoons coconut
   flavoring (1 small bottle)

- Combine coconut, margarine, sugar and eggs. Mix well.
- Sift flour, salt, soda and baking powder together.
- Add to coconut mixture alternately with buttermilk and flavoring.
- Pour into 2 greased and floured loaf pans. Bake at 325° for 1 hour or until tests done.

Quick Cheese Bread

Yields 1 loaf

3¾ cups flour
5 teaspoons baking powder
½ teaspoon salt
5 tablespoons margarine
2½ cups grated cheddar
   cheese
2 eggs, slightly beaten
1½ cups milk

Variation: Add ½ teaspoon dill weed to dry ingredients.

- Combine dry ingredients.
- Cut in margarine until coarse crumbs form.
- Stir in cheese.
- Add combined eggs and milk, mixing just until moistened.
- Spoon into greased 5 x 9-inch loaf pan.
- Bake at 375° for 1 hour.
- Remove from pan immediately.

 Can you open a coconut? Puncture eyes with ice pick and drain milk. Place coconut in shallow pan and bake at 350° for 45 minutes, until shell begins to crack. Cool enough to handle, then tap firmly with hammer. Shell will almost spring apart. Pry out meat with knife.

Mammy's Corn Bread

Serves 6

1 cup white cornmeal
½ teaspoon baking soda
½ teaspoon salt
1 egg, beaten
1 cup buttermilk
1 tablespoon shortening or
   bacon drippings, melted

- Sift together dry ingredients.
- Mix eggs and buttermilk. Add to dry ingredients.
- Add shortening and pour into a greased shallow pan.
- Bake at 450° for about 18 minutes.

Hot Cross Buns

Yields 4 dozen

8 cups flour
2 cups milk
2 sticks butter
2 packages dry yeast
l lemon rind, grated
1 cup sugar
4 eggs
½ box raisins or currants

Icing
2 cups powdered sugar
¼ teaspoon vanilla
1 small egg
Dash of salt

- Place flour in bowl. Make a well in flour.
- Melt butter in milk. Scald and add to flour in well.
- Add yeast and grated lemon.
- Pull flour over top.
- Sprinkle sugar on top and set aside until yeast bubbles through, about 1 hour.
- Add eggs and raisins.
- Knead and let rise 2 hours.
- Knead again. Drop by tablespoons onto greased cookie sheet.
- Bake at 375° for 15 minutes.
- Combine icing ingredients. Form a cross on bun with icing. May need additional powdered sugar to reach proper thickness.

French Bread

Yields 2 loaves

½ cup milk
1 cup water
1½ teaspoons shortening
1 package dry yeast
¼ cup warm water
1½ tablespoons sugar
4 cups flour
2 teaspoons salt

- Heat milk, water and shortening until lukewarm.
- Sprinkle yeast over ¼ cup warm water and leave 5 minutes.
- Add cooled milk with shortening and ¾ tablespoon sugar.
- Sift flour into warm bowl with salt and remaining sugar. Make a well in center. Pour in yeast mixture.
- Stir thoroughly but do not knead. The dough will be soft.
- Cover with damp cloth. Let rise 2 hours until doubled in bulk.
- Work dough lightly and turn out onto floured board.
- Cut in half and pat into flat rectangles, about 9 x 12 inches.
- Roll up from wide side. Taper dough at ends to form thin loaf.
- Place on greased baking sheet. Cut shallow slits ¼ inch deep across top in several places.
- Cover loaves with damp cloth and let rise 15 to 20 minutes until almost doubled in size.
- Preheat oven to 400°. Place pan of water on bottom shelf of oven. Place bread on top shelf. After 15 minutes, reduce heat to 350°. Bake an additional 30 minutes, until loaves are crisp and brown.
- Cool on wire rack.

Italian Bread

Yields 2 loaves

2 packages active dry yeast
1 tablespoon sugar
1 cup warm water
3½ tablespoons butter
¾ cup hot water
2 teaspoons salt
5½-6 cups flour
Cornmeal
1 egg white, beaten lightly

- Stir yeast, sugar and warm water together in large bowl.
- Let sit until yeast dissolves and starts to bubble.
- Melt butter in hot water. Cool to lukewarm.
- Stir in salt and combine with yeast mixture.
- Stirring vigorously with wooden spoon, add flour, 1 cup at a time, until dough comes away from sides of bowl. (May be sticky.)
- Turn out onto lightly floured board. Knead for 2-4 minutes, keeping hands floured.
- Let rest 5-6 minutes. Divide into 2 parts.
- Roll each part into rectangle 8 x 12 inches. Starting from wide end, roll up tightly, pinching seams as you roll. Baste with butter and sprinkle with cornmeal.
- Place on baking sheet. Let rise 50-60 minutes, until doubled.
- Brush with egg white. Bake at 425° for 40 minutes, until golden and makes hollow sound when tapped. Cool on rack.

 Freshen dried bread by wrapping in damp towel and placing in refrigerator for 24 hours. Remove towel and heat in oven at 300° for 5-10 minutes.

Pumpkin Loaf

Yields 3 loaves

2 beaten eggs
4 cups pumpkin
4 cups sugar
1 cup oil
5 cups flour
4 teaspoons baking soda
1 teaspoon salt
1 teaspoon cinnamon
1 teaspoon cloves
1 cup raisins
1 cup walnuts

- Combine ingredients in order given.
- Pour into greased and wax-paper-lined pans.
- Bake at 350° for 1 hour.

Pumpkin Mincemeat Bread

Yields 2 large loaves

¾ cup vegetable oil
4 eggs, beaten
2 cups mashed pumpkin
1 (18-ounce) jar mincemeat
¼ cup orange marmalade
3½ cups flour
2 teaspoons baking soda
¾ teaspoon cinnamon
½ teaspoon nutmeg
1 teaspoon salt
3 cups sugar
½ cup chopped nuts

- Combine oil, eggs, pumpkin, mincemeat and marmalade in a large bowl.
- Sift dry ingredients together and add to pumpkin mixture. Blend well until moistened.
- Stir in nuts.
- Divide evenly between greased pans, filling about 2/3 full.
- Number of pans will depend upon their size.
- Bake at 350° for 1 hour.

Zucchini Nut Bread

Yields 2 loaves

3 eggs
1 cup cooking oil
2 cups sugar
2 cups unpeeled zucchini,
  grated
3 teaspoons vanilla
3 cups flour
1 teaspoon salt
1 teaspoon soda
3 teaspoons cinnamon
1 cup nuts, chopped

- Mix first 5 ingredients together. Set aside.
- Mix dry ingredients together.
- Add to first mixture and blend.
- Stir in nuts, if desired.
- Pour into 2 greased and floured loaf pans. Bake at 350° for 40-60 minutes.

Variations: Add 1 (8-ounce) can crushed pineapple with syrup to batter, or add ¼ cup cocoa to dry ingredients.

Sausage Bread

Yields 2 loaves

Crust
Pillsbury Hot Roll Mix

Filling
1½-2 pounds sausage
2 eggs
1 pound grated mozzarella
  cheese
5 tablespoons grated
  American cheese
Parsley flakes
1 egg, beaten

- Prepare hot roll mix. Allow to rise according to directions on box.
- Brown sausage and drain.
- Beat eggs in large bowl.
- Add cheese, parsley and drained sausage.
- Roll pastry out in two 8 x 12-inch rectangles. Place half of filling in middle of each rectangle.
- Fold sides and ends of dough toward middle. Pinch seams.
- Place seam-side down on cookie sheet.
- Brush top of loaves with beaten egg.
- Bake at 350° for 30 minutes.

Cheese Braid Coffee Cake

Yields 4 loaves

1 cup sour cream
½ cup sugar
1 teaspoon salt
½ cup melted butter
2 packages yeast
½ cup warm water
2 beaten eggs
4 cups flour

Filling
2 (8-ounce) packages cream
  cheese
¾ cup sugar
1 beaten egg
⅛ teaspoon salt
2 teaspoons vanilla

Glaze
2 cups powdered sugar
3-4 tablespoons milk

- Heat sour cream. Add sugar, salt and butter. Cool.
- Sprinkle yeast over warm water.
- Combine with sour cream mixture in large bowl. Add eggs. Beat.
- Add flour. Mix well.
- Put in air-tight container. Refrigerate overnight.
- Divide dough into 4 parts. Roll each into 8 x 12-inch rectangle.
- For filling, combine cream cheese and sugar. Add other ingredients. Mix well.
- Spread each rectangle with ¼ filling. Roll up, starting with wide side. Put seam down on greased cookie sheets (2 per sheet). Slit top to resemble braiding.
- Cover. Let rise for 1½ hours.
- Bake at 375° for 12-15 minutes.
- Combine glaze ingredients. Spread over warm loaves.

Cobblestone Coffee Cake

Yields 9-12 squares

4 ounces butter, melted
1 cup sugar
4 eggs, added one at a time
1 (8-ounce) can crushed
  pineapple, drained
6 slices white bread, crust
  removed, cubed

- Combine ingredients in order given. Pour into buttered 8 x 8-inch baking dish.
- Bake at 350° for 45 minutes.
- Cut in squares and serve hot.

Golden Raisin Rum Buns

Yields 100

1 cup water
½ cup butter
1 teaspoon sugar
¼ teaspoon salt
1 cup flour
4 eggs
½ cup raisins, soaked in
　water and drained
　(optional)

Icing
1 tablespoon butter
1½ tablespoons heavy cream
1 cup powdered sugar
½ teaspoon lemon extract
½ teaspoon rum
½ teaspoon vanilla

- Combine water, butter, sugar and salt. Bring to boil.
- Add flour all at once and mix with wooden spoon over low heat until mixture leaves side of pan.
- Remove from heat.
- Beat 2 minutes until cool.
- Add eggs, 1 at a time, beating until dough cools slightly.
- Add drained raisins, if desired.
- Drop by teaspoon on cookie sheet.
- Bake at 400° for 30-35 minutes.
- For icing, melt butter. Add cream, sugar and other ingredients.
- Beat until smooth.
- Dip buns in mixture.

Regency Brunch Ring

1 package hot roll mix
1 tablespoon grated lemon
　rind
½ cup sugar
½ cup brown sugar
2 tablespoons cinnamon
¾ cup chopped nuts
½ cup margarine, melted

- Prepare mix as directed.
- Add lemon rind.
- Brush 6-cup Bundt pan with margarine.
- Combine sugars, cinnamon and nuts.
- Make 40 balls from dough. Dip in margarine, then sugar mixture.
- Layer balls in Bundt pan.
- Let rise 20-30 minutes to top of pan.
- Bake on bottom rack at 375° until brown, about 30 minutes.
- Turn out of pan immediately.

MacIntosh Muffins

Yields 3 dozen

1¼ cups oil
2 cups sugar
3 cups flour
3 eggs
2 teaspoons vanilla
1 teaspoon salt
1 teaspoon soda
2 cups chopped MacIntosh
   apples
1 cup chopped pecans or
   walnuts
1 cup coconut

- Mix all ingredients together. Fill greased muffin tins 2/3 full.
- Bake at 350° for 25 minutes.

Oatmeal Muffins

Yields 12 muffins

½ cup plus 2 tablespoons milk
¼ cup vegetable oil
¼ cup molasses
¼ cup brown sugar
1 egg
1 cup whole wheat flour
1 cup quick-cooking oats
1 tablespoon baking powder
¾ teaspoon cinnamon
¼ teaspoon salt
½ cup raisins

- Combine milk, oil, molasses, brown sugar and egg. Mix well.
- Combine remaining ingredients and add to liquid mixture. Mix briefly until dry ingredients are moistened.
- Bake in greased muffin pan at 400° for 15-17 minutes.

 If bread or cake brown too quickly, reduce heat and place a pan of warm water on rack above it.

Rise 'n' Shine

Yields 1 (9-inch) coffee cake

1 cup sugar
3 tablespoons grated orange rind
2 (12-ounce) cans refrigerated buttermilk biscuits
5 tablespoons butter or margarine, melted
1 (3-ounce) package cream cheese, softened
½ cup sifted powdered sugar
2 tablespoons orange juice

- Combine sugar and orange rind.
- Separate biscuits. Dip each in butter and coat with sugar mixture.
- Stand biscuits on side, overlapping edges, in a 9-inch tube pan.
- Bake at 350° for 30 minutes or until golden brown.
- Remove ring from pan. Invert on serving platter.
- Combine cream cheese and powdered sugar, mixing until smooth.
- Add orange juice, stirring well.
- Spoon mixture over top while ring is hot.

Bran Ahead Muffins

Yields 5 dozen

5 cups flour
5 teaspoons baking soda
2 teaspoons salt
2 cups All Bran
2 cups boiling water
2 cups sugar
1 cup margarine, softened
4 eggs
1 quart buttermilk
4 cups Bran Buds
Raisins (optional)

Note: Covered batter will keep 6 weeks in refrigerator.

- Sift together flour, baking soda and salt.
- Pour boiling water over cereal. Set aside.
- Cream sugar and margarine.
- Add eggs. Beat well.
- Blend in buttermilk and Bran Buds.
- Combine all ingredients. Blend well. Fill greased muffin tins 2/3 full.
- Bake at 400° for 25 minutes.

Pineapple Muffins

Yields 18-24 muffins

½ cup margarine, softened
1 cup sugar
2 eggs
1 teaspoon vanilla
2 cups all-purpose flour
2 teaspoons baking powder
½ teaspoon salt
1 (8¼-ounce) can crushed
 pineapple, undrained

- Cream margarine and sugar until light and fluffy. Add eggs, one at a time, beating well after each addition.
- Stir in vanilla.
- Combine flour, baking powder and salt. Add to creamed mixture.
- Stir in pineapple.
- Fill greased or paper-lined muffin pans half full.
- Bake at 375° for 15-20 minutes.

Sweet Potato Muffins

Yields 6 dozen small muffins

½ cup butter
1¼ cups sugar
2 eggs
1¼ cups canned sweet
 potatoes, drained and
 mashed
1½ cups flour
2 teaspoons baking powder
¼ teaspoon salt
¼ teaspoon nutmeg
1 teaspoon cinnamon
1 cup milk
¼ cup chopped pecans
½ cup chopped raisins

- Cream butter and sugar until fluffy. Add eggs. Mix well.
- Blend in sweet potatoes.
- Sift the flour with the baking powder, salt, nutmeg and cinnamon.
- Add alternately with milk. Do not overmix.
- Fold in nuts and raisins. Fill greased muffin tins 2/3 full and bake at 400° for 25 minutes.

 For baking, it's best to use medium to large eggs. Extra large may cause cakes to fall when cooled.

Alice's Croutons

1 clove garlic, mashed
½ cup olive oil
2-3 slices whole wheat bread,
  cubed
Thyme, oregano and basil to
  taste
2 tablespoons butter

- Mash garlic and put in olive oil.
- Refrigerate 1 hour.
- Cut bread into cubes and
  sprinkle with seasonings.
- Put garlic oil and butter in frying
  pan and heat.
- Add seasoned bread cubes.
- Toss until brown and hard.
  Takes 10-15 minutes.

Corn Fritters

Yields 3 dozen

1 (8¾-ounce) can whole
  kernel corn, drained, liquid
  reserved
Milk
1½ cups sifted flour
3 teaspoons baking powder
¾ teaspoon salt
1 egg, beaten
Maple syrup
Powdered sugar

- Add enough milk to liquid from
  corn to measure 1 cup.
- Sift together dry ingredients.
- Combine egg, milk mixture and
  corn.
- Add to dry ingredients. Mix until
  moist.
- Drop batter by heaping
  tablespoons into deep, hot fat.
- Fry until golden, 3-4 minutes.
- Drain on paper towels. Serve
  warm with warmed maple syrup
  or roll in powdered sugar.

Double Good Rolls

Yields 3 dozen large rolls

2 cups milk
½ cup shortening
½ cup sugar
2 packages dry yeast
¾ tablespoon salt
½ teaspoon soda
½ teaspoon baking powder
6 cups flour (approximately)

Note: Dough can be stored before rolls are formed in refrigerator for 7 days.

- Bring milk, shortening and sugar to a boil. Cool to lukewarm.
- Dissolve yeast in a little water. Add to milk mixture.
- In large bowl, add 1 cup flour and 1 cup milk mixture, using all milk and enough flour to make the consistency of cake batter. Mix until smooth after each addition.
- Let rise in large bowl for 2 hours.
- Sift in salt, soda and baking powder. Work in more flour until dough can be handled.
- When rolls are formed, dot with margarine. Let rise for 1½-2 hours.
- Bake at 400° for 15 minutes or until brown on top.

Squash Puffs

Yields about 2 dozen

¾ pound yellow squash, sliced
1 egg, beaten
6 tablespoons flour
5 tablespoons cornmeal
1 teaspoon baking powder
½ teaspoon salt
1 medium onion, grated
Vegetable oil

Variation: For a sweeter puff, sprinkle with powdered sugar. Great with fried fish to replace hush puppies.

- Cover squash with water. Boil 10-15 minutes or until tender.
- Drain. Mash enough squash to measure 1 cup.
- Stir squash and egg together well.
- In separate bowl, combine flour, cornmeal, baking powder and salt. Stir well.
- Add squash mixture and onion. Stir until blended.
- Drop squash mixture by level tablespoons into hot oil.
- Cook until golden brown, turning once. Drain well on paper towels.

Bordelaise Sauce

Yields 2-3 cups

2 tablespoons butter
¾ cup sliced mushrooms
2 tablespoons minced onion
¾ cup dry red wine
1½ cups brown sauce or
   canned beef gravy
2 tablespoons lemon juice
3 tablespoons minced parsley
Salt and cayenne to taste

- Sauté mushrooms in butter.
- Remove and saute onion until transparent.
- Add wine and simmer until reduced to half its volume.
- Stir in remaining ingredients and simmer 30 minutes. Serve over grilled steak or roast beef.

Chicken Barbecue Sauce

Yields sauce for 3 chickens

¼ cup minced onion
3 tablespoons margarine
1 cup catsup
2 teaspoons prepared mustard
¼ cup vinegar
2 tablespoons brown sugar
½ cup water
2 tablespoons
   Worcestershire sauce
⅛ teaspoon salt

- In saucepan, saute' onion in butter until tender.
- Add other ingredients. Simmer 10 minutes, covered.
- Use sauce for basting chickens or pork chops in oven, on grill or in microwave.

 If your brown sugar is hard as a rock and you need it quickly, simply grate the amount called for with a hand grater.

Hot Curry-Mayonnaise Sauce

Yields ½ cup

**2 tablespoons melted butter
or margarine**
**¼ teaspoon finely minced
garlic**
½ teaspoon curry powder
½ cup mayonnaise
1 tablespoon lemon juice

*Hint: This can be mixed in a
small pot and carefully heated
over low heat. Do not allow
to separate.*

- Mix butter, garlic and curry
  powder in a small bowl.
- Add mayonnaise and lemon juice.
- Set in pan of hot water. Let water
  simmer until sauce is heated.
- Serve hot over broccoli or
  Brussels sprouts.

Dijon Mustard

Yields 2 cups

2 cups dry white wine
1 cup chopped onion
2 cloves garlic, minced
1 (4-ounce) can dry mustard
2 tablespoons honey
1 tablespoon vegetable oil
2 teaspoons salt
Few drops Tabasco

- Combine wine, onion and garlic
  in small saucepan. Heat to boiling. Lower heat and simmer 5
  minutes.
- Pour mixture into a bowl. Cool.
- Strain wine mixture into dry
  mustard in small saucepan. Beat
  constantly with wire whip until
  very smooth.
- Blend honey, oil, salt and
  Tabasco into mustard mixture.
- Heat slowly, stirring constantly,
  until mixture thickens. Cool.
- Pour into a container (not metal).
  Cover and chill at least 2 days.
  May be kept in refrigerator for
  long periods.

Sauce Dresden

from Chef Norbert

1 cup sour cream
½ teaspoon chopped fresh
　chives
½ teaspoon fresh, grated
　horseradish
Pinch each salt and pepper

- Mix thoroughly all ingredients
  and keep cool.
- Serve over fresh fish.

Blender Hollandaise

Yields 1¼ cups

3 egg yolks
2 tablespoons lemon juice
1 sprig parsley
1 slice onion
½ teaspoon salt
⅛ teaspoon pepper
⅛ teaspoon cayenne
½ cup butter, melted
½ cup boiling water

- Place all ingredients except
  boiling water into blender. Blend
  5 seconds.
- Add boiling water slowly, in
  steady droplets, continuing to
  blend.
- When all water is added, turn off
  blender and pour into double
  boiler.
- Cook, stirring to custard
  consistency 15-20 minutes. Do
  not allow to boil or sauce will
  curdle.

 If Hollandaise Sauce separates, remove it from heat immediately. Add ice cube and reheat.

Hollandaise Sauce
(Base for Béarnaise Sauce)

Per Serving

1 egg yolk
1 ounce butter, melted and
  cooled to room
  temperature
¼ teaspoon Worcestershire
  sauce
½ teaspoon lemon juice
4 drops Tabasco
Salt to taste

*Variation: For Béarnaise, add a
  pinch of tarragon leaves,
  pinch of dried parsley and a
  dash of tarragon vinegar to
  the Hollandaise and blend
  thoroughly.*

- Place egg yolks in stainless steel bowl and add ½ teaspoon water per egg yolk.
- Place bowl over pot of boiling water.
- Whisk until mixture doubles in volume and thickens. Remove from heat.
- Gradually add melted cooled butter per serving while you continue to whip.
- Add Worcestershire sauce, lemon juice and Tabasco sauce. Salt to taste. Blend thoroughly.

Horseradish Mayonnaise Sauce

Serves 6

2 egg yolks
1 tablespoon Dijon mustard
½ teaspoon salt
2 shakes cayenne pepper
¾ cup vegetable oil
¾ cup olive oil
¼ cup tarragon vinegar
Horseradish to taste

- Put egg yolks and seasonings in mixing bowl.
- Add very small amount of oil and vinegar alternately, beating vigorously until mixture thickens.
- Refrigerate when completed.

Versatile Hot Sauce

Yields 3-4 cups

1 (28-ounce) can crushed
  tomatoes with tomato purée
1 tablespoon vinegar
1 teaspoon garlic juice or ½
  teaspoon garlic powder
1 teaspoon dried mustard
1 chopped jalapeño pepper,
  fresh or canned
1 teaspoon crushed chili
  peppers
1 teaspoon cumin
⅛ teaspoon oregano
⅛ teaspoon onion flakes or
  powder
⅛ teaspoon dried parsley
⅛ teaspoon cayenne pepper
Salt and pepper to taste

- Combine all ingredients. Peppers, chili, jalapeno and cayenne determine the "hotness" and should be used accordingly.
- Keep in container in refrigerator and use with tacos, nachos or other spicy dishes.

Lemon Sauce

Yields 1¾ cups

1 cup sugar
2 tablespoons cornstarch
¼ teaspoon salt
1½ cups water
2 egg yolks, beaten
3 tablespoons lemon juice
1½ teaspoons grated lemon
  rind
4 teaspoons butter

- Blend sugar, cornstarch and salt.
- Gradually add to water in top of double boiler. Heat over rapidly boiling water, beating constantly.
- Cook until mixture is thickened and starch taste disappears.
- Beat a small amount of hot liquid into beaten egg yolks.
- Return to mixture in top of double boiler, beating constantly. Cook 2-3 minutes longer.
- Remove from heat. Add lemon juice, grated rind and butter. Blend well. Serve warm.

Steak Marinade

½ cup soy sauce
4 tablespoons vinegar
6 tablespoons brown sugar
1 teaspoon ginger
1-1½ cups oil
2 scallions

- Mix together and pour over London broil or other 1-1½ inch thick steak.
- Marinate overnight.

Marinara Sauce

Yields 3 cups

4 tablespoons olive oil
2 medium onions, chopped
2 cloves garlic, finely minced
2 (16-ounce) cans Italian peeled tomatoes, drained
¼ cup dry red wine
½ teaspoon oregano
Salt and pepper to taste

- Heat oil. Cook onion and garlic until onions are soft.
- Add remaining ingredients.
- Cook on high heat 3-4 minutes. Reduce heat. Simmer 15-20 minutes.

Variation: For boiled shrimp, add crumbled feta cheese.

Remoulade Sauce

Yields 1 quart

4 hard-boiled egg yolks, sliced
4 cloves garlic, finely chopped
3 tablespoons dark mustard
3 cups mayonnaise
3 tablespoons horseradish
2 tablespoons Worcestershire sauce
Dash Tabasco
4 tablespoons vinegar
4 tablespoons finely chopped parsley
Salt and pepper to taste

- Mix with blender and store in refrigerator.
- Let stand a day or two before using.
- Serve with fried shrimp, clams or any type seafood and fish.

Inlet Shrimp Sauce

Yields 1 quart

1 clove garlic
1 medium onion
1 cup mayonnaise
½ cup vegetable oil
¼ cup catsup
¼ cup chili sauce
1 teaspoon yellow mustard
1 tablespoon Worcestershire
  sauce
½ teaspoon black pepper
2 tablespoons water
Dash Tabasco

- Press garlic and onion through garlic press.
- Combine all ingredients in blender and blend until smooth.
- Chill overnight for best taste.
- Serve with cold boiled shrimp.

Sweet and Sour Sauce

Yields 4 cups

1 cup sugar
1 cup white vinegar
¼ cup water
1 teaspoon salt
1-2 cloves garlic, minced
¾ cup catsup
½ teaspoon ginger
1½ tablespoons cornstarch
1½ tablespoons soy sauce

- Mix first 7 ingredients.
- Pour over meat and let simmer 1 hour.
- Add cornstarch and soy sauce. Let simmer 5 minutes longer.

Fresh Tomato Sauce

Yields 3-4 cups

5 very ripe medium or large
   tomatoes, peeled and
   coarsely chopped
½ cup finely chopped fresh
   basil
2 cloves garlic, peeled
½ cup olive oil or olive oil and
   butter
1 teaspoon salt
¼ teaspoon fresh ground
   black pepper

- Chop tomatoes and basil
  together on a wooden board
  until very finely mixed.
- Place in a skillet.
- Add garlic, salt, pepper, oil and
  butter. Cook no more than 10
  minutes on medium heat.

Vegetable Sauce

Yields 1 cup

1 small onion, grated
1 stick butter
1 cup mayonnaise
1 tablespoon dry horseradish
1 tablespoon prepared
   mustard
1 teaspoon salt
Black or cayenne pepper to
   taste

- Allow butter and onion to soften
  together. (Do not melt.)
- Add other ingredients. Mix well
  and refrigerate.
- Spoon over cooked vegetables
  before serving.

 Lengthen the life of olive oil by adding a cube of sugar to the bottle.

Curry Powder

Yields 1 cup

½ cup ground coriander
¼ cup ground cumin
1½ teaspoons black pepper
1½ teaspoons turmeric
1½ teaspoons mustard seed
1½ teaspoons chili powder
1½ teaspoons ground Star of
   Anise

• Blend well. Store in refrigerator.
  Keeps indefinitely.

*Star of Anise may be found in
  oriental shops.*

Seasoned Salt

Yields 1/3 cup

6 tablespoons salt
½ teaspoon thyme leaves
½ teaspoon marjoram
¼ teaspoon garlic powder
2½ teaspoons paprika
½ teaspoon curry powder
1 teaspoon dry mustard
¼ teaspoon onion powder
⅛ teaspoon dill seed, optional
½ teaspoon celery salt

• Combine all ingredients in small
  jar. Cover and shake until well
  blended.

 1 teaspoon fresh herbs is equivalent to ¼ teaspoon dried herbs.

Squash Pickles

5 pounds medium yellow
   squash, cut in rounds
4 large green peppers,
   sliced and seeded
2-3 hot peppers
5 medium white onions,
   sliced
½ cup salt
4 cups vinegar
4 cups sugar
2 teaspoons celery seed
2 teaspoons mustard seed
1½ teaspoons turmeric

- Place prepared vegetables in a large bowl or dish pan.
- Sprinkle salt over vegetables.
- Set in refrigerator overnight or soak in ice water for three hours.
- Drain and rinse well.
- Mix vinegar, sugar and spices in 6-quart boiler and bring to boil.
- Add vegetables and bring to second boil, heating thoroughly.
- Pack in sterilized pint jars. Pour liquid over and seal.
- Let age approximately 2 weeks.

EGGS, CHEESE, PASTA & RICE

*Gulls In Flight, Long Point Park, South Melbourne Beach.
Photographed by Trent Chase.*

Eggs, Cheese, Pasta and Rice

* Denotes Quick and Easy Recipes

Eggstraordinary

Serves 6

3 tablespoons butter
3 tablespoons flour
½ teaspoon horseradish
¼ teaspoon dill weed
¼ teaspoon basil
½ teaspoon white pepper
1 teaspoon salt
2 cups milk, scalded
10 hard-boiled eggs
12 slices garlic toast or
toasted English muffins

Variation: Omit horseradish, dill weed and basil for milder, tasty breakfast dish.

- Melt butter in top of double boiler. Stir in flour.
- Add seasonings. Stir in milk and cook until smooth.
- Separate hard-boiled eggs. Chop egg whites and add to sauce. Spoon sauce over toast.
- Crumble egg yolks and sprinkle over all.
- Garnish with cherry tomatoes. Perfect for brunch!

Cheese Rarebit

Serves 4

4 tablespoons butter
¼ cup flour
½ teaspoon dry mustard
1 teaspoon salt
¼ teaspoon paprika
1 cup milk
1 cup cream or evaporated
milk
1 drop Tabasco
1 tablespoon Worcestershire
sauce
½ pound shaved sharp
cheese
Almonds, bacon, or onion
rings for garnish

- Cook butter and flour in double boiler.
- Add mustard, salt and paprika.
- Gradually add milk and cream.
- Add Tabasco, Worcestershire sauce and cheese.
- When melted, mixed and heated, serve hot on toast, toasted English muffins or waffles. Top with slivered almonds, chopped bacon or onion rings.

Chili Relleños

Serves 6-8

2 (10-ounce) cans green
  chilies
1 pound sharp cheese
1 pound Monterey Jack
  cheese
5 eggs, separated
1 can evaporated milk
2 teaspoons flour
Salt and pepper
2 (8-ounce) cans tomato
  sauce

- Split chilies; remove seeds.
- Cover bottom of casserole dish with ½ of the chilies and ½ of each cheese.
- Repeat for second layer.
- Beat egg whites until stiff. Set aside.
- Beat egg yolks. Mix evaporated milk, flour, salt and pepper. Add to egg yolks.
- Fold in beaten egg whites.
- Pour over casserole.
- Bake at 325° 45 minutes. Remove from oven.
- Pour tomato sauce over casserole and return to oven.
- Bake again for 30 minutes.

Fritatta

Serves 8

¾ cup chopped green pepper
1½ cups sliced mushrooms
1½ cups chopped zucchini
¾ cup chopped onion
1 large garlic clove, minced
3 tablespoons oil
6 eggs, beaten
¼ cup light cream
1 pound cream cheese, diced
1½ cups grated cheddar
  cheese
2 cups cubed bread
1 teaspoon salt
¼ teaspoon pepper

- Saute' green pepper, mushrooms, zucchini, onion and garlic in oil until zucchini is crisp-tender. Cool slightly.
- Beat eggs with cream.
- Add cream cheese, cheddar cheese, bread, salt, pepper and sauteed vegetables. Mix well.
- Pour into greased 10-inch springform pan.
- Bake at 350° 1 hour or until set in center.
- Cool 10 minutes before cutting. May serve cold.

Saucy Cheese Enchiladas

Serves 6

12 corn tortillas
½ cup oil
2 cups grated Monterey Jack
  cheese
¾ cup chopped onion
¼ cup margarine
¼ cup all-purpose flour
2 cups chicken broth
1 cup sour cream
1 (4-ounce) can green chilies,
  chopped

Spicy Sauce
1 medium tomato, finely
  chopped
½ cup onion, finely chopped
½ teaspoon salt
1 (4-ounce) can green chilies,
  chopped
¼ cup tomato juice

- Warm each tortilla in oil. Drain.
- Place 2 tablespoons grated cheese and 1 tablespoon onion on each tortilla.
- Roll up. Place seam down in greased 9 x 13-inch pan.
- Melt margarine. Blend in flour and add broth. Cook until thick.
- Add sour cream and chilies.
- Pour cream sauce over enchiladas.
- Bake at 425° 20 minutes.
- Drizzle spicy sauce over enchiladas.

Green Chilies and Rice

Serves 8

2 (4-ounce) cans green
  chilies, chopped
¾ pound grated Monterey
  Jack cheese
½ pound grated cheddar
  cheese
2 cups sour cream
2½ cups cooked rice
Sliced ripe olives to taste

- Mix chilies with cheeses, olives and sour cream.
- Stir in rice and olives.
- Bake at 350° 30-45 minutes in 2½-quart casserole.

Huntsman's Souffle'

Serves 10

Souffle'
10 slices bread
1 stick margarine
2 cups grated Cheddar
  cheese
4 eggs
2 cups milk
1 teaspoon Worcestershire
  sauce
½ teaspoon dry mustard

Chicken Sauce
½ cup butter
½ cup flour
1 teaspoon salt
1 cup cream
3 cups milk
2 cups chicken broth
2 cups diced chicken
½ cup blanched almonds
¼ cup chopped pimiento
½ cup sauteed mushrooms
1 cup sliced water chestnuts
½ cup sherry (optional)

- Remove crust from bread. Spread with margarine. Cut in fourths.
- Place 1 layer in bottom of greased 9 x 13-inch casserole.
- Sprinkle with cheese.
- Repeat until all used.
- Beat eggs, milk and seasonings together.
- Pour over bread.
- Cover with foil and refrigerate at least 12 hours.
- Bake at 350° for 45 minutes.
- Prepare sauce by mixing butter, flour, salt, cream, milk and broth.
- Add all other ingredients. Serve thoroughly heated sauce over souffle'.

Pepper and Cheese Custard

Serves 8

2 green peppers, diced
3-4 hot peppers, finely diced
2 cups large curd cottage
  cheese
1 pound cheddar, Swiss,
  Muenster, or any combination of cheeses, grated
10 eggs
1 cup milk

- Mix peppers, cottage cheese and cheeses together.
- Arrange mixture in a greased 9 x 13-inch baking dish or a 2-quart casserole.
- In a bowl, beat eggs and milk thoroughly. Pour egg mixture over cheese mixture.
- Bake at 350° 35-40 minutes or until golden on top. Cool slightly.

Baked Ham and Cheese Surprise

Serves 8

16 slices bread, crusts
  removed
8 slices luncheon ham
8 slices cheddar cheese
3 cups milk
6 eggs, well beaten
½ teaspoon salt
½ teaspoon dry mustard
¼ pound bacon, fried and
  crumbled
½ pound butter, melted
1 cup crushed potato chips

- Butter 9 x 13-inch baking dish. Place 8 slices of bread in bottom.
- Put ham and cheese on bread. Cover with 8 slices of bread.
- Mix milk, eggs, salt and mustard.
- Pour over sandwiches and refrigerate covered overnight. (Sandwiches will be swimming in milk.)
- Before baking, pour bacon, butter and chips on top.
- Bake uncovered 1 hour at 350°.

Cheesy Onion Pie

Serves 6

1 cup Ritz cracker crumbs
  (20 crackers)
¼ cup butter
2 cups onions, thinly sliced
2 tablespoons butter
2 eggs
¾ cup milk
¾ teaspoon salt
Pepper
¼ cup medium cheddar
  cheese, grated
Paprika

- Combine cracker crumbs and melted butter.
- Press into bottom and sides of 8-inch pie plate.
- Saute' onions in 2 tablespoons butter until transparent, but not brown. Spoon into pie shell.
- Mix slightly beaten eggs, milk, salt and pepper. Pour over onions.
- Sprinkle top with shredded cheese and paprika.
- Bake at 350° for 30 minutes or until a knife inserted in center comes out clean.

Omelet Mexicali

Serves 4-6

¾ cup chopped avocado
¼ cup sour cream
1 can green chilies, chopped
and drained
2 tablespoons chopped green
onions
1 teaspoon lemon juice
¼ teaspoon salt
Dash Tabasco
2 tablespoons margarine
2 corn tortillas, torn into 6-8
pieces each
6 eggs, beaten
1 cup grated Monterey Jack
cheese

- In small bowl, combine
avocado, sour cream, chilies,
onion, lemon juice, salt and
Tabasco. Set aside.
- In 10-inch oven-safe skillet,
melt margarine. Add tortillas,
cooking until soft.
- Pour in eggs and cook 3-5
minutes, lifting edges to allow
uncooked eggs to flow under.
- Remove from heat and
sprinkle with cheese.
- Put under broiler just until
cheese melts.
- Spread with avocado mixture
and return to broiler until
bubbly.
- Cut into wedges to serve.

Fettucine alla Bernard

Serves 6

1 (16-ounce) package
fettucine noodles
½ cup olive oil
2 sticks butter, melted
1 (12-ounce) can grated
Parmesan cheese
1 pint heavy cream

- Boil noodles in water with
olive oil for 20 minutes,
stirring frequently.
- Drain noodles, spray with hot
water and return to same pan.
- Place on low heat, adding 1/3
at a time, butter, cheese and
cream, stirring constantly for
10-15 minutes or until very
hot.

Stuffed Eggs au Gratin

Serves 3-4

6 hard-boiled eggs
¼ cup butter, melted
½ teaspoon Worcestershire
  sauce
¼ teaspoon prepared
  mustard
3 green onions, minced
1 tablespoon minced parsley
¼ cup minced ham
Salt and pepper to taste
1 package Knorr Hollandaise
  sauce mix, prepared

- Cut eggs in half.
- In bowl, mash yolks. Add all ingredients, except Hollandaise sauce.
- Stuff egg whites with mixture.
- Arrange in pie plate and top with Hollandaise sauce.
- Bake at 350° just until heated through.

Crab Quiche

Serves 6

½ lb. crabmeat, washed and
  drained
9-inch unbaked pie shell
1 (4-ounce) can mushrooms
1½ cups grated Swiss cheese
¾ cup sour cream
¼ cup mayonnaise
½ teaspoon salt
1 tablespoon flour
¼ cup light cream
2 eggs, slightly beaten
Tabasco sauce

- Sprinkle crabmeat on bottom of pie shell.
- Saute' mushrooms and put on top of crabmeat.
- Sprinkle cheese over mushrooms.
- Combine remaining ingredients and mix well.
- Pour into pie shell.
- Bake at 350° 50-55 minutes.
- Let stand 15 minutes before serving.

Scalloped Eggs

Serves 12

¼ cup butter
3 tablespoons flour
1 cup half and half
1 cup milk
1 pound sharp cheddar
  cheese, grated
¼ cup chopped celery
¾ teaspoon Lawry's Pinch of
  Herbs Seasoning
⅛ teaspoon garlic salt
1 pound bacon, fried and
  crumbled
18 hard-boiled eggs, sliced
Pepperidge Farm herb
  stuffing mix
4-6 tablespoons melted butter

- Melt butter. Add flour with whisk.
- Add half and half and milk. Bring slowly to boil. Boil 2-3 minutes.
- Add cheese, celery and seasonings.
- Stir until cheese melts.
- In 13 x 9-inch glass dish, alternate layers of sauce, bacon and eggs.
- Top with ⅓ package Pepperidge Farm stuffing tossed with 4-6 tablespoons melted butter.
- Bake at 350° 20-25 minutes.

Arroz Cubano

Serves 8-10

1 cup uncooked white rice
1 cup chopped onion
½ cup melted butter or
  margarine
½ cup seedless raisins
1 (4-ounce) can sliced
  mushrooms, drained
2 (10½-ounce) cans
  consomme'
½ cup chopped peanuts
¾ cup chopped celery

- Lightly brown rice and onion in butter.
- Add raisins, mushrooms, consomme', peanuts and celery to rice mixture. Mix well.
- Pour into a 2-quart casserole.
- Bake uncovered at 250° 50-60 minutes or until rice is done.

 Pierce the end of an egg with a pin. It will not break when boiled.

Swiss Scrambled Eggs

Serves 4

2 tablespoons butter or
   margarine
8 eggs
¼ cup half and half or light
   cream
½ teaspoon salt
Cayenne pepper
¾ cup shredded Swiss cheese
Parsley and toast points, for
   garnish

- Melt butter in 8-inch skillet.
- In medium bowl, beat eggs lightly with half and half, salt and dash cayenne.
- Fold in ½ cup of the cheese.
- Pour mixture into hot skillet. Cook over medium heat 2 minutes, stirring gently but constantly until eggs are moist and slightly underdone.
- Sprinkle remaining ¼ cup cheese over eggs and cook until eggs are set. (They will stay soft.)
- Garnish with parsley, toast points and a very light sprinkle of cayenne.

Bernie's Fluffy Omelette

Serves 2

⅛ stick butter
3 eggs
½ cup ham, diced
2 slices American cheese

To serve: Slide ½ of the omelette from pan to plate and use the side of the pan to fold other ½ over top. This omelette, when served folded, should be approximately 3 inches thick and very fluffy. Many substitutes for the ham: sausage, mushrooms, vegetables, and seafood.

- Melt butter in egg pan over medium-high heat.
- Beat eggs with wire whisk. Stir in ham. Pour into pan.
- As omelette starts to cook, use handle of wooden spoon to pull omelette back towards center of pan, tilting pan away from you. Continue this until omelette is no longer runny.
- Lay cheese on omelette.
- Cover pan immediately and remove from burner. Let stand about 1 minute and serve immediately.

Oeufs au Crouton

Serves 6

8 slices fried bacon, crumbled
1 medium onion, diced
2 cups croutons
1 cup shredded cheddar
  cheese
4 eggs, beaten
2 cups milk
½ teaspoon salt
½ teaspoon prepared
  mustard
⅛ teaspoon onion powder
Dash pepper

*Variation: Add mushrooms,
  ham, or sausage pieces.*

- Saute' onion in bacon fat.
- Butter a 10 x 16-inch glass
  baking dish.
- Spread croutons in dish and
  sprinkle with cheese.
- Mix eggs, milk, salt, mustard,
  onion powder and pepper
  with a fork.
- Pour over croutons and
  cheese.
- Sprinkle onion and bacon
  pieces on top.
- Bake at 325° for 60 minutes
  until set.

Noodle Casserole

Serves 8

1 (8-ounce) package Kluski
  noodles
2 cups ricotta cheese
2 cups sour cream
1 cup chopped onion
1 tablespoon Worcestershire
  sauce
½ cup melted butter
1-2 cloves garlic, finely
  minced
Tabasco to taste
Salt and pepper to taste
Parmesan cheese

- Cook noodles in boiling, salted
  water for 10 minutes. Rinse in
  cold water.
- Combine remaining ingredients
  except for Parmesan cheese. Stir
  into noodles.
- Pour into buttered 2-quart
  casserole.
- Sprinkle with Parmesan
  cheese.
- Bake at 350° 40 minutes.

Spaghetti and Spinach Casserole

Serves 4

4 ounces spaghetti, cooked
  and drained
1 (10-ounce) box frozen
  chopped spinach, cooked
  and drained well
1 egg, beaten
½ cup sour cream
¼ cup milk
4 tablespoons Parmesan
  cheese
1 tablespoon minced dry
  onion
1 garlic clove, minced
½ teaspoon salt
Dash pepper
2 cups grated Monterey Jack
  cheese
Parmesan cheese

- Combine egg, sour cream, milk, Parmesan cheese, onion, garlic, salt and pepper.
- Add Monterey Jack cheese and mix well.
- Add cooked, drained spaghetti and spinach. Mix well again.
- Put into a 10 x 6 x 2-inch baking dish.
- Sprinkle top with additional Parmesan cheese.
- Bake covered at 350° 15 minutes. Uncover, bake 15-20 minutes more or until heated through.

Southern Ham and Cheese Pie

Serves 6

1 cup shredded Swiss cheese
1 cup chopped cooked ham
½ cup chopped onion
1 (13-ounce) can evaporated
  milk
3 eggs
1 cup hot, cooked, quick grits
1 tablespoon chopped parsley
Salt to taste
¼ teaspoon dry mustard
⅛ teaspoon cayenne
9-inch unbaked pie shell

- Sprinkle cheese, ham and onion over bottom of pie shell.
- Combine and beat remaining ingredients. Pour into pie shell.
- Bake at 375° 45 minutes or until knife inserted into center comes out clean.
- Let stand 10 minutes before serving.

Spaghetti Cheese Pie

Serves 6

1 (8-ounce) package spaghetti
½ pound sliced bacon
½ cup chopped onions
¼ pound sliced fresh
mushrooms
3 eggs
1 cup milk
¼ teaspoon pepper
1 teaspoon Worcestershire
sauce
2 cups shredded cheddar
cheese
¼ cup buttered fresh bread
crumbs
2 tablespoons chopped
parsley for garnish

- Cook and drain spaghetti as label directs.
- In large skillet, saute' bacon. Remove bacon. Reserve 1 tablespoon drippings.
- Add onions and mushrooms. Brown lightly.
- Break bacon into 1-inch pieces.
- Arrange cooked spaghetti in 10-inch pie plate. Place mushroom mixture and bacon on top.
- In medium bowl, beat eggs slightly. Beat in milk, pepper and Worcestershire sauce. Stir in cheese.
- Pour over spaghetti. Top with bread crumbs.
- Bake 25 minutes at 350°. Let stand 5 minutes before serving. Sprinkle with parsley.

Kugel

Serves 10

1 (16-ounce) package wide
egg noodles
8 eggs
1 (16-ounce) container sour
cream
2 cups sugar
¼ pound margarine

- Cook noodles. Drain and return to pan.
- Add eggs, sour cream and sugar. Mix well.
- Melt margarine in 9 x 13-inch pan and add noodle mixture.
- Bake at 350° 45-50 minutes or until brown.

Spaghetti with Butter Crab Sauce

Serves 4-6

½ cup butter
1 small onion, minced
½ cup beer
Dash nutmeg
½ teaspoon ground black
  pepper
Dash cayenne pepper
6½ ounces crabmeat, flaked
  and drained
¼ cup coarsely chopped
  parsley
1 pound linguine or spaghetti,
  cooked and drained

- Melt butter in skillet.
- Add onion and beer. Cook on
  low heat until onion is soft
  and golden.
- Add nutmeg, pepper, cayenne
  and crabmeat.
- Stir to blend and heat gently
  until crab is very hot.
- Stir in parsley and salt to
  taste. Cook one minute
  longer.
- Pour sauce over hot spaghetti
  and toss.
- Serve immediately.

Italian Sausage Quiche

Serves 4-6

1 pound Italian sausage, bulk
  type
1 pound fresh mushrooms,
  sliced
2 cups shredded Gruyere or
  Swiss cheese
4 eggs, beaten
1 cup whipping cream
¼ teaspoon salt
Pastry for 10-inch pie

- Line quiche dish with pastry;
  trim around edges, prick bottom and sides. Bake at 425° 6-
  8 minutes. Cool.
- Cook sausage until browned.
  Drain, but reserve drippings.
- Saute' mushrooms in drippings for 5 minutes or until
  tender. Drain.
- Combine sausage, mush-
  rooms, cheese, eggs, cream
  and salt. Mix well.
- Pour into pastry and bake 45
  minutes at 350° or until set.

Cracker-style Grits

Serves 8-10

1 cup grits, uncooked
4 cups water
1 teaspoon salt
1 stick butter
1 roll garlic cheese
8 ounces sharp cheddar
   cheese, grated
2 tablespoons
   Worcestershire sauce
Paprika

- Cook grits in salted water until done.
- Add remaining ingredients. Stir until butter and cheese have melted.
- Pour into greased 2-quart casserole and sprinkle top with paprika.
- Bake at 350° for 20 minutes.

Asparagus Tourtière

Serves 6

3 tablespoons margarine
1 tablespoon cornstarch
¾ teaspoon salt
⅛ teaspoon pepper
1 cup milk
¼ cup mayonnaise
2 cups diced cooked ham
2 (10-ounce) packages frozen
   cut asparagus, cooked
1 tablespoon lemon juice
9-inch pastry, baked
¼ cup grated Parmesan
   cheese

- Melt margarine over medium heat.
- Stir in next 3 ingredients. Remove from heat.
- Gradually stir in milk until smooth.
- Cook over medium heat, stirring constantly, until boiling for 1 minute.
- Stir small amount of hot mixture into mayonnaise, then stir into hot milk mixture.
- Add ham, asparagus and lemon juice.
- Cook until heated.
- Pour into pastry shell. Sprinkle with cheese.
- Broil 2 minutes or until lightly browned.

Cauliflower Pie with Potato Crust

Serves 4-5

Crust
2 cups packed, grated raw
  potato (peeled if desired)
½ teaspoon salt
1 egg, beaten
¼ cup grated onion

Filling
1 cup chopped onions
1 medium clove garlic,
  crushed
3 tablespoons butter
Dash thyme
½ teaspoon basil
½ teaspoon salt
1 small cauliflower, broken
  into small florets
1½-2 cups grated cheddar
  cheese
2 eggs and ¼ cup milk,
  beaten together
Paprika

- Put freshly grated potato in colander over bowl.
- Add salt and leave for 10 minutes.
- Squeeze out remaining excess moisture.
- Mix potato with egg and onion.
- Pat mixture into well-oiled 9-inch pie plate, building up sides of crust with lightly floured fingers.
- Bake at 400° 30 minutes. Brush with oil and continue baking 15 minutes until golden brown.
- Sauté onions and garlic in butter for 5 minutes.
- Add thyme, basil, garlic and cauliflower. Cook for 10 minutes, stirring occasionally.
- Spread ½ of cheese into baked crust.
- Pour cauliflower mixture over cheese. Add remaining cheese.
- Pour egg and milk mixture over pie. Sprinkle with paprika.
- Bake at 375° 35-40 minutes or until set.

 To stop rice, macaroni or potatoes from boiling over while cooking, grease the top of the boiler about 1-inch deep all the way around.

Fromage Florentine

Serves 6

½ cup fine bread crumbs
¼ cup freshly grated
   Parmesan cheese
2 tablespoons melted butter
1 pound ricotta cheese
2 tablespoons sour cream
2 tablespoons flour
2 eggs
1 (10-ounce) package frozen
   chopped spinach, cooked
   and drained
¼ cup finely diced ham
¼ teaspoon Lawry's seasoned
   pepper
1 tablespoon bread crumbs
1 cup sour cream

- Mix bread crumbs with 2 table-spoons Parmesan cheese.
- Blend in melted butter
- Press into bottom and sides of a 9-inch pie plate.
- Place ricotta, 3 tablespoons Parmesan cheese, sour cream, flour and eggs in large bowl. Beat until smooth.
- Add salt to taste.
- Mix ½ of cheese mixture with spinach and spread evenly in prepared pie shell.
- Add ham to remaining cheese mixture and spread evenly over spinach layer.
- Sprinkle top with seasoned pepper and bread crumbs.
- Bake at 350° 40 minutes. Pass sour cream separately as sauce.

Wild Rice Pilaf

Serves 6-8

1 cup wild rice
1 cup chicken broth
4 tablespoons butter
1¾ cups water
1 teaspoon salt
Pepper to taste
1 cup sliced, fresh
   mushrooms
¼ cup chopped parsley
Parmesan cheese (optional)

- Heat rice, broth and butter until butter is melted.
- Add water, salt, pepper and mushrooms.
- Pour into a 1-quart baking dish and cover. Bake at 350° 1 hour.
- Do not stir until ready to serve.
- When liquid is absorbed, add parsley. Mix gently and serve.
- May top with Parmesan cheese.

MEATS

Boy On The Beach, By Nancy Vice. Photographed by Franko Photo.

Meats

Key West Piccadillo

½ cup olive oil
2 onions, diced
3 cloves garlic, diced
½ can tomatoes, chopped
1 sweet pepper, diced
1 pound fried ground beef
½ cup raisins
¼ cup green olives

- Put first 6 ingredients in heavy skillet and simmer.
- Half hour before serving add raisins and green olives.
- Serve over hot rice.

Hint: Better when made days ahead.

Baked Stuffed Flank Steak

Serves 6

Rice Stuffing
¼ cup butter
½ cup chopped onions
1 clove garlic, crushed
1½ cups cooked rice
½ cup chopped parsley
½ cup grated Parmesan cheese
½ teaspoon salt
¼ teaspoon pepper

Flank Steak
2 pounds flank steak
1 clove garlic, crushed
2 tablespoons soy sauce
½ teaspoon pepper
2 tablespoons butter
½ cup condensed beef broth
½ cup water
1 teaspoon ginger

- In butter saute' onion and garlic until onion is golden.
- Remove from heat. Stir in rice, parsley, cheese, salt and pepper.
- Wipe steak with damp cloth.
- Score both sides lightly into diamonds. Rub steak with garlic.
- Brush both sides with soy sauce and pepper.
- Spread steak with 1 tablespoon butter.
- Place stuffing on steak. Roll from end to end and fasten with skewers or twine.
- Spread remainder of butter on steak. Place in roasting pan.
- Dilute beef broth with water.
- Pour over roll. Sprinkle with ginger.
- Roast at 350° 45-60 minutes, basting occasionally.
- Pour juices into a bowl to serve with meat.
- Remove skewers or twine and slice.

Beef Tyrolean

Serves 6-8

1 (3-pound) London broil
Salt
Pepper
Mashed garlic
2 tablespoons margarine
1 large onion, chopped
1 carrot, chopped
½ cup chopped celery
2 (6-ounce) packages Swiss
   cheese
Toothpicks and string

- Have butcher slash filet lengthwise on 1 side, stopping about 1 inch or more before cutting through filet, forming pocket.
- Sprinkle meat on all sides with salt and pepper. Rub with garlic.
- Heat margarine. Saute' onion, carrot and celery until soft and lightly brown.
- Put mixture on cut surface of filet.
- Finely dice 6 ounces of cheese and sprinkle over vegetables.
- Fold over meat and fasten opening with toothpick and string.
- Place in shallow pan. Cook at 400° for 40 minutes.
- Remove from oven. Remove string and toothpicks.
- Place remaining slices of cheese over roast. Place in oven and heat another 5 minutes.

London Broil Deseret

Serves 4-8

2-3 pounds London Broil
1 (5-ounce) bottle soy sauce
5 teaspoons red wine vinegar
5 dashes Worcestershire
   sauce
Sprinkle of minced garlic
Pepper to taste

- Mix ingredients and marinate meat 24 hours.
- Cook on low heat (gas grill) or indirect heat (charcoal grill) for 35 minutes (medium rare) to an hour (well done). If cooked in oven, place under broiler for 10-15 minutes.

Sesame Steak

Serves 8

½ cup salad oil
¼ cup sesame seeds
4 medium onions, thickly
   sliced
½ cup soy sauce
½ cup lemon juice
1 tablespoon sugar
¼ teaspoon cracked pepper
2 garlic cloves, crushed
2½-3 pounds boneless top
   sirloin, cut 1½ inch thick

- 5 hours before serving prepare marinade.
- Cook sesame seeds in hot oil over medium-high heat, stirring frequently, until golden. In 9 x 13-inch baking dish, mix sesame seed oil mixture with remaining ingredients, except steak.
- Trim excess fat from steak. Place steak in marinade, turning to coat both sides.
- Cover and refrigerate at least 4 hours, turning steak occasionally.
- Before serving, preheat broiler. Place steak and onions on rack in broiling pan. Broil 20-25 minutes for rare.
- Brush often with marinade. Turn steak once.
- Stir onions to prevent burning.

Steak and Kidney Pie

Serves 6

1½ pounds stewing beef,
   diced
6 ounces kidney, sliced
½ pound mushrooms, sliced
1 cup chopped onion
¼ cup parsley
½ bay leaf, crumbled
1 teaspoon salt
1 cup butter
3 cups sifted self-rising flour
1 cup milk

- Put first 7 ingredients into baking dish with 2 cups of water.
- Cut butter into flour until it resembles coarse meal. Add milk. Mix lightly to form soft dough.
- Turn out on floured board and roll ⅛ inch thick.
- Place on top of baking dish.
- Cut slits in dough to let steam escape.
- Bake at 325° for 1¾ hours.

Steak Sicilione

Serves 4-5

2½ pounds top round steak

Sauce
1 cup Burgundy wine
1 tablespoon Worcestershire
  sauce
1 small onion, minced
¼ teaspoon pepper
1 teaspoon salt
2 tablespoons parsley
1 tablespoon sugar
¼ teaspoon oregano
2 tablespoons horseradish
2 tablespoons prepared
  mustard
2 tablespoons olive oil or
  butter

- Heat sauce until hot. Cool.
- Put on top of round steak and marinate 2-3 hours in refrigerator.
- Cook on grill for 15 minutes, 7-8 minutes on each side.
- Before serving, cut steak in thin slices across the grain.

Teriyaki Steak

Serves 4

2 pounds flank steak, scored
  in diamond pattern
¼ cup soy sauce
3 tablespoons honey
2 tablespoons vinegar
1½ teaspoons garlic powder
1½ teaspoons ginger

- In blender container, combine all ingredients except flank steak.
- Blend on high speed for 1 minute.
- Pour marinade over meat and refrigerate for at least 24 hours, turning frequently.
- Cook on charcoal grill to desired doneness.
- Heat marinade to pass with meat.
- Slice meat into thin slices to serve.

Beef Parmesan

Serves 6-8

1½ pounds round steak, ⅜
   inch thick
1 egg, beaten
½ cup Parmesan cheese
½ cup bread crumbs
½ cup oil
1 onion, minced
1 teaspoon salt
¼ teaspoon pepper
½ teaspoon sugar
½ teaspoon margarine
1 (6-ounce) can tomato paste
   or 2 cans tomato sauce
2 cups hot water
¼ pound mozzarella cheese
   (optional)
Oregano or basil, to taste
   (optional)

- Trim meat and cut into pieces.
- Dip pieces in egg. Roll in cheese and bread crumbs.
- Heat oil in skillet. Brown meat.
- Add onion and cook until tender over low heat.
- Stir in next 5 ingredients.
- Gradually add hot water.
- Boil 5 minutes. Add scrapings and any left-over cheese and bread crumbs.
- Top with mozzarella cheese.
- Bake at 350° for 1½ hours until tender. Serve over noodles.

Spicy Pepper Steak

Serves 6

4 tablespoons oil
1 teaspoon salt
1 teaspoon ginger
½ teaspoon pepper
1-2 pounds round steak,
   thinly sliced
4-6 tablespoons soy sauce
½ teaspoon sugar
2 green peppers, slice in strips
1 large onion, thinly sliced
Sliced, fresh mushrooms
   (optional)
1 tablespoon cornstarch
1 cup water

- Heat, medium-high, in 10-12-inch skillet: oil, salt, ginger and pepper.
- Brown sliced round steak.
- Add soy sauce and sugar. Cover and simmer meat 5-10 minutes.
- Remove meat. Add green peppers, onion and mushrooms to juice in pan.
- Cover and cook briskly.
- Put meat back in pan.
- Mix cornstarch with water and add to mixture in skillet. Cook over medium heat until mixture thickens slightly, about 5 minutes.

Stir-fry Beef with Broccoli

Serves 2-3

1 pound flank or other steak,
   cut into ¼ inch slices about
   2 inches long
¼ cup soy sauce
1 tablespoon cornstarch
1 tablespoon dry sherry
1 teaspoon sugar
½ bunch broccoli
5 tablespoons vegetable oil
½ teaspoon salt
1 slice ginger root or ¼ cup
   sliced onion

- Mix first 5 ingredients. Set aside.
- Cut broccoli in 2 inch long florets.
- Peel stalk and slice in 2 inch lengths less that ½ inch thick.
- Put 2 tablespoons oil in hot skillet or wok over high heat.
- Stir-fry salt and broccoli, turning constantly until broccoli is dark green (not over 2 minutes).
- Remove from skillet.
- Put remaining oil in skillet. Add ginger root (or onion) and beef mixture.
- Stir-fry for about 2 minutes.
- Add broccoli and mix well.
- Serve at once with rice.

Beef Ragout

Serves 6

2½ pounds beef chuck, cut
   into 1-inch cubes
2 tablespoons bacon drippings,
   butter or margarine
1 teaspoon salt
½ teaspoon pepper
1 teaspoon ground marjoram
2 cloves garlic, minced
1 medium onion, chopped
2 tablespoons chopped parsley
1 cup thinly sliced carrots
½ cup chopped celery
¾ cup red wine
2 cans undiluted tomato soup
2 bay leaves

- Place ½ of meat at a time in Dutch oven. Brown well in drippings.
- Return all meat to pan. Sprinkle with salt, pepper and marjoram.
- Add garlic, onion, parsley, carrots and celery.
- Cook uncovered over medium heat, stirring frequently until liquid is reduced to less than 2 tablespoons (about 15-20 minutes).
- Stir in wine, soup and bay leaf.
- Cover and simmer for about 1 hour, stirring occasionally.
- Serve with buttered noodles.

Sukiyaki

Serves 4-6

4 tablespoons margarine
1½ pounds round steak, cut
   in strips across the grain
¼ cup beef bouillon
¼ cup soy sauce
2 tablespoons sugar
2 bunches green onions, cut
   in 2-inch pieces
1 Spanish onion, thinly sliced
½ pound fresh mushrooms,
   sliced
1 pound fresh spinach, washed
1 (7-ounce) can bamboo
   shoots, drained
1 (8-ounce) can water chestnuts, sliced and drained

- Melt margarine in skillet over medium-high heat.
- Saute' beef quickly until browned.
- Add bouillon, soy sauce and sugar.
- Cover and cook over low heat for 30 minutes.
- Add vegetables in order listed and cook covered for 10 minutes.
- Serve over rice.

Lemon Beef Marinade

Serves 6-8

1 large freezer zip-lock bag
1 teaspoon salt
1 teaspoon pepper
2 teaspoons oregano
3 cloves garlic
½ cup fresh lemon juice
½ cup olive oil
1 tablespoon grated lemon
   rind
3 pound roast

Hint: Let roast stand about 15 minutes after cooking for easier carving.

- Place roast in bag. Combine remaining ingredients and pour over roast. Close bag tightly; turn bag several times to distribute marinade. Refrigerate 24 hours, turning occasionally.
- About 2 hours before serving, remove roast from bag. Save marinade. Place roast fat side up on a rack in a shallow open pan.
- Roast at 325° for 1½-1¾ hours or until 160° internally for medium doneness. Baste with marinade during last 30 minutes.

165

Rancher's Rave

Serves 8

3 pounds lean chuck roast or
   fresh pork roast
1 large onion, chopped
1 cup chopped celery
2 tablespoons vinegar
2 tablespoons brown sugar
4 tablespoons lemon juice
½ cup catsup
½ cup chili sauce
3 tablespoons
   Worcestershire sauce
1 teaspoon chili powder
1½ cups water

- Place raw meat in roaster. Combine remaining ingredients and pour over meat.
- Cover and cook at 350° for 3 hours or until meat is very tender and will shred with 2 forks.
- Remove meat from roaster and discard fat and bone.
- Shred with forks while still hot.
- Return meat to sauce. Serve in hamburger buns.

Beef 'n' Beer

Serves 4-6

¼ cup oil
6 small onions, sliced
1 clove garlic, chopped
2 pounds stew beef
5 tablespoons flour
1 teaspoon salt
½ teaspoon pepper
1 (12 ounce) can beer or
   1¼ cups red wine
1 bay leaf
2 tablespoons dried parsley
¼ teaspoon thyme

- Cook onions and garlic until tender in oil. Set aside.
- Dredge meat in flour, salt and pepper. Brown meat in oil.
- Put all ingredients in 2-quart casserole. (If flour is left over after dredging meat, add to casserole.)
- Cover and cook at 350° for 2½ hours until very tender. May also be cooked in crockpot 10 hours on low.

Boeuf Bourguignonne

Serves 6

½ pound bacon, cut into
    ½-inch pieces
3 pounds beef round, cut
    into ½-inch cubes
1 large carrot, peeled and
    sliced
1 large onion, sliced
1 (10-ounce) can clear beef
    broth
2 tablespoons tomato paste
2 cloves garlic, minced
1 teaspoon whole thyme
1 whole bay leaf
½ pound pearl onions, peeled
1 pound fresh mushrooms,
    sliced and sautéed
¾ cup red wine
3 tablespoons cornstarch

- Cook and drain bacon.
- Add beef and brown.
- Brown carrot and onion.
- In a large pot, place bacon, beef,
  carrot, onion, broth, tomato
  paste, garlic, thyme, bay leaf and
  pearl onions.
- Season with 1½ teaspoons salt
  and ¼ teaspoon pepper.
- Simmer for 8-10 hours.
- Before serving, add sautéed
  mushrooms and wine.
- Cornstarch should also be added
  slowly to obtain desired
  thickness.
- Serve over white rice.

Prime Rib

Serves 6

¼ cup flour
6 tablespoons butter
1 tablespoon dry mustard
1 teaspoon paprika
¼ teaspoon pepper
6 pound standing rib roast

- In heavy skillet over moderate
  heat pour and stir flour until
  lightly browned. Set aside.
- Cream butter. Add dry mustard,
  paprika, pepper and browned
  flour.
- Blend all into a paste.
- Place roast, standing on bones,
  into a roasting pan. Spread paste
  over roast.
- Bake at 325° to desired
  doneness.

Beef McCarthy

Serves 4-6

3 pounds stew beef or chuck
    roast, cut in 1-inch cubes
Flour
Salt
Pepper
1 (28-ounce) can tomatoes
½ cup catsup
1 teaspoon chili powder
1 teaspoon oregano
2 tablespoons brown sugar
6 large carrots, pared and cut
    into quarters
6 large potatoes, pared and
    cut into quarters
4 large onions, peeled and cut
    into quarters

- Flour and season beef and brown in lightly greased skillet. Remove from heat.
- In medium saucepan, combine tomatoes, catsup, chili powder, oregano, brown sugar, salt and pepper to taste. Boil 5 minutes.
- Combine meat and vegetables in large casserole. Pour sauce over all.
- Cover and bake at 250° for 4 hours.

Beef Stroganoff

Serves 6

1 medium onion, finely
    chopped
1 teaspoon finely chopped
    garlic
1 (4-ounce) can sliced
    mushrooms, drained
    (reserve liquid)
8 tablespoons butter or
    margarine
2 pounds round steak,
    trimmed and cut into
    ½-inch cubes
1 (6-ounce) can tomato paste
1 pint sour cream, divided

- Sauté onion, garlic and mushrooms in 4 tablespoons butter until onions are soft. Set aside.
- Sauté meat with 4 tablespoons butter until brown.
- Put mushroom liquid and onion mixture in small roaster. Add tomato paste and ½ pint sour cream. Mix until smooth.
- Add meat.
- Cover and refrigerate overnight. Bake, covered, 250° for 3½ hours.
- Just before serving, add remaining sour cream and heat slowly.

Greenbrier Beef Stroganoff

Serves 4

1 pound lean beef filet
1 tablespoon paprika
3 tablespoons olive oil
4 ounces sliced mushrooms
1 cup dry sherry
½ cup beef stock or canned
  condensed beef broth
1 cup dairy sour cream
1 teaspoon lemon juice
Salt to taste
Fine noodles, cooked

*Hint: To slice meat very thin, cut
when still partially frozen.*

- Cut beef into ¼-inch thick strips. Add paprika.
- Heat olive oil and saute' beef strips very quickly for 2-4 minutes.
- Remove meat from pan.
- Add mushrooms to pan and saute' 2-4 minutes. Remove from pan.
- Add dry sherry to pan. Reduce to ½ its volume by boiling.
- Add beef stock and let boil briskly, uncovered, for 5 minutes.
- Add sour cream, lemon juice and salt to taste.
- Add meat and mushrooms. Bring just to boiling. Do not let boil when sour cream is in the sauce.
- Spoon over fine noodles, which are well-drained and hot.
- Garnish with chopped chives.

Spicy Roast

2-3 pounds chuck roast
2 cloves garlic
1 envelope onion soup mix
2 teaspoons sweet basil
1-2 teaspoons crushed red
  pepper
1 teaspoon oregano

- Stuff garlic cloves into roast.
- Place roast in roasting pan.
- Mix onion soup, basil, red pepper and oregano. Top roast with the mixture.
- Cover with water.
- Bake at 350° for 4-5 hours, turning often.

Planter's Palette

Serves 4

1½ pounds beef shoulder, cut
   into 1-inch cubes
3 tablespoons flour
Salt and pepper to taste
Cooking oil for browning meat
1 (16-ounce) can tomatoes,
   drained, reserve liquid
Small amount beef bouillon, if
   needed for liquid
1½ cups finely chopped celery
1 cup finely chopped carrots
2 green peppers, finely chopped
3 tablespoons instant minced
   onions or sautéed fresh
   onions
1 teaspoon crumbled dried basil
1 teaspoon crumbled dried
   tarragon leaves

- Trim excess fat from meat. Sprinkle well with flour, salt and pepper, reserving excess flour.
- Brown well on all sides in oil.
- Remove meat to 2-quart casserole with cover.
- Mix reserved flour with fat and meat bits in pan, until dissolved. Gradually add liquid from tomatoes.
- Cook over low heat. Whisk constantly until thick. Add water or bouillon to make 1 cup sauce.
- Pour sauce over browned meat in casserole. Top with tomatoes.
- Cover dish and bake in preheated oven at 325° for 1 hour.
- Remove from oven. Add vegetables, onions, basil and tarragon.
- Cover and bake 1 hour longer.
- Flavor improves if prepared in advance.

Oven Bar-B-Q Ribs

Serves 6-8

1-1½ pounds beef or pork
   ribs
1 lemon
1 medium onion
1½ cups catsup
1 (8-ounce) can tomato sauce
2 dashes Tabasco
¼ cup Worcestershire sauce
Water
Salt to taste
Brown sugar to taste, about 3
   tablespoons

- Place ribs on foil in shallow pan, meaty side up.
- Cut lemon and onion in large slices over ribs.
- Place in 450° oven for 30 minutes.
- Combine remaining ingredients and bring to boil. Add water if too thick.
- Pour part of sauce over ribs and bake at 350° for 50-60 minutes, basting with additional sauce every 15-20 minutes.
- May be cooked on grill.

Ground Beef-Rice Surprise

Serves 4-6

1 pound ground beef
¾ cup chopped onion
1 tablespoon vegetable oil
1½ teaspoons salt
Dash pepper
½ small bay leaf
⅛ teaspoon garlic powder,
   thyme and oregano
1 can cream of mushroom soup
1 (12-ounce) can tomatoes
1 cup uncooked instant rice
2-3 slices American cheese
Sliced stuffed olives

- Brown meat in oil. Add onion. Cook until tender.
- Stir in seasonings, soup, tomatoes and rice.
- Reduce heat and simmer 5 minutes.
- Spoon into 1½-quart baking dish.
- Criss-cross cheese over top and top with olives.
- Broil until cheese melts.

Straw Hats

Serves 8

1 cup chopped onion
½ cup chopped celery
½ cup chopped green pepper
2 pounds ground beef
2-3 tablespoons chili powder,
   or to taste
2 teaspoon salt
¼ teaspoon pepper
2 (6-ounce) cans tomato
   sauce
½ cup catsup
2 cups water
2 tablespoons Worcestershire
   sauce
2 dashes red pepper sauce
1 (12-ounce) package corn
   chips
2 cups shredded American
   cheese

- Brown ground beef and drain.
- Saute' onions, celery and green pepper.
- Add ground beef and remaining ingredients, except corn chips and cheese.
- Simmer 30 minutes, stirring occasionally.
- Serve meat sauce over corn chips and top with cheese.

171

Gulf Coast Casserole

Serves 12

4 pounds ground round or
  chuck
2 large onions, chopped
2 garlic cloves, minced
¼ cup chili powder (or to
  taste)
6 cups tomato sauce
1 teaspoon sugar
1½ tablespoons salt
2 cups sliced black olives
2 (4-ounce) cans diced green
  chilies
24 corn tortillas
Cooking oil
4 cups small curd cottage
  cheese
2 eggs
1 pound thinly sliced
  Monterey Jack cheese
2 cups grated cheddar cheese
1 cup chopped green onion
1 cup sour cream
Avocado

- Brown meat in batches in a large heavy frying pan or Dutch oven.
- Saute' onion and garlic with last batch of meat.
- Return all meat to pan.
- Sprinkle chili powder over meat and mix well.
- Add tomato sauce, sugar, salt, half the olives and green chilies.
- Simmer over low heat 15 minutes.
- While sauce cooks, fry tortillas in hot oil, 1 at a time. Do not allow to brown. Drain on paper towels and cut into quarters.
- Beat cottage cheese and eggs together and set aside.
- Spread 1/3 meat-tomato sauce mixture in bottom of 6-quart casserole. Cover with ½ pound sliced cheese, half cottage cheese-eggs mixture and half of the cooked tortillas.
- Repeat, finishing with a final layer of meat.
- Top with grated cheddar cheese and bake, uncovered at 350° for 30 minutes or until casserole is thoroughly heated and cheese is melted.
- Top with chopped green onions, sour cream, black olives and sliced avocado.

Aunt Susan's Meat Loaf

Serves 6

2 eggs
2 pounds ground chuck
2 cups finely crumbled day-
old bread crumbs
¾ cup minced onion
¼ cup seeded chopped green
pepper
1 tablespoon salt
6 teaspoons bottled
horseradish (drained)
1 teaspoon dry mustard
¼ cup milk
¼ cup catsup
½ cup catsup

- Beat eggs in bowl with 2-tined fork.
- Add ground chuck. Toss together lightly with fork (over-mixing makes meat tough).
- Toss bread crumbs, onion and green pepper with the meat.
- With fork lightly combine salt, horseradish, dry mustard, milk and ¼ cup catsup. Add to meat.
- Shape into 3 mounds in 3 flat (well-greased) baking dishes.
- Spread ½ cup catsup on mounds.
- Bake at 400° for 40 minutes.
- May be shaped into loaves; do not put into loaf pans.

Mozzarella Burgers

Serves 4

1 pound ground beef
½ teaspoon garlic salt
1 cup shredded mozzarella
cheese
1 (8-ounce) can tomato sauce
1 (2½-ounce) jar mushroom
caps, drained
½ teaspoon oregano
1 cup onion rings, sauteed
4 hamburger buns, split and
toasted

- Combine meat and garlic salt. Shape into 8 thin patties.
- Top each of 4 patties with ¼ cup cheese and put second patty on top. Seal edges firmly.
- Broil on both sides to desired doneness.
- Heat together tomato sauce, mushrooms and oregano. Simmer 10 minutes.
- For each burger spread bottom half of bun with sauce. Top with onion, beef patty and additional sauce.
- Top with top half of bun.

Poor Boy Filets

Serves 5

1 pound lean ground beef
5 slices bacon
Lemon pepper
¼ cup grated Parmesan
cheese
12 ounce can mushroom bits,
drained
3 tablespoons finely chopped
stuffed olives
2 tablespoons finely chopped
onion
2 tablespoons finely chopped
green pepper

- In a skillet, partially cook bacon. Drain on towel.
- On waxed paper, pat beef into a 12 x 7½ x ¼-inch rectangle.
- Sprinkle lightly with salt and lemon pepper.
- Top with Parmesan cheese.
- Combine mushrooms, olives, onion and green pepper.
- Sprinkle evenly over meat.
- Roll up jelly-roll style, starting from the short end.
- Cut into 1½-inch slices.
- Wrap edge of each slice with bacon. Secure with wooden picks.
- Grill over medium coals 8 minutes on each side.

Scottish Mince

Serves 3-4

1 pound ground lean beef
1 onion, chopped
½ teaspoon salt
2 rounded tablespoons flour
Boiling water
Several dashes
Worcestershire sauce
Sherry or vermouth to taste
Pepper to taste
Mushrooms (optional)

- Put ground beef, onion and salt in heavy skillet.
- Brown beef, breaking it into fine pieces.
- Pour off excess fat and sprinkle with flour.
- Add sufficient water or wine to prevent beef from burning and to make a sauce.
- Add mushrooms.
- Allow to stew gently 30 minutes or so, adding liquid if necessary.
- Adjust seasonings if desired.

Spinach-stuffed Shells

Serves 6

1 pound ground beef
1 tablespoon cooking oil
1 small onion, chopped
1 (15-ounce) can peeled
  tomatoes
1 (4-ounce) can tomato paste
¼ teaspoon oregano
¼ teaspoon garlic
¼ teaspoon basil
Parsley to taste
1 crushed bay leaf
1 teaspoon sugar
1 box jumbo pasta shells
2 packages frozen creamed
  spinach
1 pound ricotta cheese
8 ounces grated mozzarella
  cheese
Salt and pepper to taste
Parmesan cheese

- Brown ground beef over medium heat. Drain off fat.
- In medium saucepan, saute' onion in hot oil.
- Add tomatoes, tomato paste and water, if necessary.
- Add spices, sugar and ground beef. Stir well.
- Bring to boil. Simmer, covered, for 1 hour. Uncover during last 10 minutes.
- Cook shells according to package directions. Drain.
- Cook spinach according to package directions. Let cool.
- In medium mixing bowl, mix spinach, ricotta, mozzarella, salt and pepper.
- Stuff each shell with 2-3 heaping teaspoons of spinach mixture.
- Place 4 shells in each of 6 individual casserole dishes. Cover with sauce and sprinkle generously with Parmesan cheese.
- Bake at 350° for 25-30 minutes.

 Add a tablespoon of olive oil to cooking water. Noodles will not boil over or stick together — and the flavor will be more interesting!

175

Swedish Meatballs

Serves 6-8

Meatballs
2 pounds ground round
1 cup cornflake crumbs
5 tablespoons dried parsley
  flakes
½ teaspoon garlic powder
¼ cup catsup
2 eggs
2 tablespoons soy sauce
¼ teaspoon pepper
2 tablespoons instant minced
  onion

Sauce
2 cups sour cream
2 tablespoons Worcestershire
2 cans mushroom soup

- Blend meatball ingredients well. Form into meatballs the size of walnuts for entreé, smaller for appetizers.
- Arrange in shallow 10 x 15-inch pan. Bake uncovered at 350° for 30 minutes or until nicely browned.
- Drain all grease.
- Mix sauce ingredients and heat until smooth, adding milk to thin if necessary.
- Pour over meatballs and bake about 30 minutes.
- Serve over fancy noodles or with toothpicks for an appetizer.

Corned Beef and Cabbage Cajun Style

Serves 8

12 ounces sauterne
4 shakes Worcestershire
  sauce
3 shakes hot sauce to taste
1 clove garlic, finely chopped
1 tablespoon salt
6 pounds brisket of corned
  beef
2 large onions, peeled (whole)
2 large heads cabbage, cut
  into wedges

- Fill ¾ of a 12-quart pot with water.
- Add sauterne, Worcestershire, hot sauce, garlic and salt.
- Bring to a boil. Add corned beef and onions.
- Reduce heat to simmer. Cook until meat is tender, 2-3 hours.
- Remove beef after tender to cool (will not slice well when hot).
- Place cabbage in boiling juice from beef.
- Cook until tender and serve with corned beef.

Stuffed Cabbage

Serves 16-20

1 (4-pound) head cabbage
1½ pounds ground pork butt
½ pound ground beef
½ cup raw long-grain rice
2 eggs
1 teaspoon salt
¼ teaspoon pepper
1 medium onion, chopped
½ cup catsup

Sauce
1 (16-ounce) can tomatoes
2 cans tomato soup
1½ tablespoons cider vinegar
2 tablespoons brown sugar
Bay leaf

- Remove core from cabbage. Place cabbage in deep pot of hot water and bring to boil.
- Rotate cabbage with slotted spoon and gently remove outer layers as they soften.
- When cool, thinly trim thick rib of each leaf. Prepare 16-20 leaves.
- Combine pork, beef, rice, eggs, salt, pepper, onion and catsup. Mix well.
- Divide the mixture, placing small amount on center of each leaf.
- Fold sides of leaf over meat and roll jelly-roll fashion.
- Cover bottom of 4-quart Dutch oven with remaining cabbage. Layer rolls in pan.
- Cut up canned tomatoes, retaining liquid. Add soup and ½ cup water. Stir to dissolve.
- Add cider vinegar and brown sugar.
- Pour over cabbage rolls.
- Add layer of cabbage leaves, if any remaining.
- Add bay leaf. Cover. Bake at 325° for 1½ hours.

 While cooking vegetables that give off unpleasant odors, simmer a small pan of vinegar on top of stove.

Kazuko Fried Rice

Serves 4

4 pork chops, chopped into
  small pieces
1 tablespoon butter or
  margarine
3 stalks celery, chopped
½ cup chopped onion
1 (6-ounce) can mushrooms,
  drained
½ cup finely chopped carrots
3 tablespoons soy sauce
1 teaspoon sugar
2-3 cups cooked rice
Salt and pepper to taste

- Brown chopped pork chops in butter.
- Stir in celery, onion, mushrooms and carrots. Fry with meat for 3-4 minutes.
- Add soy sauce and sugar.
- Add rice.
- Salt and pepper to taste.

Panhandle Pork Chops

Serves 8

8 rib pork chops, 1½ inches
  thick
3 cups fresh bread crumbs,
  without crusts
1 cup ground ham
⅛ teaspoon pepper
¼ teaspoon nutmeg
1 egg, beaten
1¼ cups beef broth
1 teaspoon salt
¼ teaspoon sage
¼ teaspoon ground thyme
Salad oil
8 canned pineapple slices

- Cut deep pocket in each chop.
- Combine bread crumbs, ham, pepper, nutmeg and ½ cup broth mixed with beaten egg.
- Rub chops inside and out with combined salt, sage and thyme.
- Stuff chops with bread mixture.
- Brush chops on both sides with oil and place in foil-lined pan.
- Bake uncovered at 450° for 30 minutes.
- Remove from oven. Reduce heat to 400°. Drain all fat from pan.
- Mix ½ cup water with remaining broth. Pour over chops. Cover and bake 50-60 minutes or until very tender.
- Serve garnished with pineapple slices.

Pork Chops Italiano

6 lean chops, 1½-inch thick
1½ teaspoons rubbed sage
1 teaspoon rosemary
1½ teaspoons chopped garlic
Salt and pepper to taste
2 tablespoons butter or
  margarine
2 tablespoons olive or
  vegetable oil
Dry vermouth

- Rub chops with herbs, garlic, salt
  and pepper.
- Place in skillet and brown in
  butter and oil.
- After browned, remove from
  pan. Pour off drippings.
- Add vermouth.
- Return chops to skillet. Cover
  and reduce to simmer. Cook
  until tender for 45-60 minutes.

Quarterback Pork Chops

Serves 6

6 pork chops
Oil or bacon drippings for
  browning
2 large onions, sliced
4 medium potatoes, sliced
1 can cheddar cheese soup
2 cans mushroom soup
Salt and pepper to taste

- Brown chops in hot oil. Place in a
  9 x 13-inch baking dish.
- Alternate layers of onion,
  potatoes, cheese and mushroom
  soup. Bake at 325° for 1½ hours.

*A favorite meal of Bob Griese —
and a big hit with Miami dolphin
teammates and their families
during the early '70's.*

 *Brown flour makes gravy more attractive. Brown flour in 325° oven for
30 minutes until golden, stirring occasionally. Keeps well when stored
in an airtight container.*

Speak Easy Pork Chops

Serves 4

4 pork chops, cut 1-inch thick
Salt and pepper to taste
¼ cup gin
¼ cup orange juice

- Rub chops with salt and pepper.
- Brown in heavy pan over high heat. Reduce heat. Add gin and orange juice.
- Cover tightly. Simmer until chops are tender. If more liquid is needed, add orange juice or gin.

Indonesian Pork

Serves 6-8

1 (4-5 pound) pork roast
Salt and pepper
1 cup hot water
¼ cup molasses
¼ cup prepared mustard
¼ cup vinegar
¼ cup orange marmalade
¼ teaspoon ground ginger

- Place metal rack or trivet in bottom of slow cooking pot.
- Sprinkle pork roast with salt and pepper. Put on trivet in pot.
- Pour hot water around pork. Cover and cook on low for 8-10 hours or until done.
- Remove meat from pot.
- Place on broiler pan or oven-proof platter.
- Combine molasses, mustard, vinegar, marmalade and ginger. Brush over cooked pork.
- Brown in 400° oven for 30 minutes, brushing several times with sauce.

Stuffed Crown Roast of Pork Flambe'

Serves 8

1 crown pork roast (about 5 pounds)
Vegetable oil
Salt and pepper
¼ cup butter or margarine
3 green onions and tops, sliced
4 large fresh mushrooms, sliced
2 tart apples, diced
3 cups packaged stuffing mix
½ cup applesauce
3 tablespoons apple brandy
1 (10-ounce) jar apricot preserves
½ cup apple brandy
Preserved kumquats

- Brush meat with vegetable oil. Rub salt and pepper into meat.
- Place meat on triple thickness of aluminum foil same diameter as roast. Place in roasting pan.
- Cover bone tips with foil.
- Insert meat thermometer in thickest part of meat so tip does not touch bone or rest in fat.
- Heat butter in large skillet until it bubbles. Cook and stir onions in butter until tender.
- Add mushrooms. Cook and stir until mushrooms are just tender.
- Add apples; cook and stir 1 minute.
- Stir in stuffing mix, applesauce, and 3 tablespoons brandy (add more applesauce if stuffing seems dry). Pack in prepared roast, mounding high.
- Cover stuffing with foil cap.
- Roast 2½ hours at 325°.
- Remove foil from stuffing.
- Heat apricot preserves and ¼ cup brandy in small saucepan.
- Brush preserves mixture (reserving ¼ cup) on meat every 10 minutes.
- Roast until 170°, about ½ hour.
- Remove from oven. Let stand 15 minutes.
- Cut ends off kumquats. Scoop out centers with melon baller.
- Garnish bone tips with kumquats.
- Heat reserved ¼ preserves mixture. Float remaining ¼ cup brandy on top.
- Ignite and pour over roast.

Stuffed Loin of Pork

Serves 6

4 pound boneless pork loin
12 pitted prunes
2 teaspoons salt
1 teaspoon ginger
½ teaspoon pepper

Sauce
1 apple
1 yellow onion
4 prunes
2 cups water
2 tablespoons soy sauce
1 tablespoon flour

- Make a hole straight through meat with handle of wooden spoon.
- Cover pitted prunes with boiling water and soak for 30 minutes.
- Drain and stuff prunes in hole of roast, evenly distributed.
- Roast should be tied with kitchen string, making loops and knotting along the horizontal surface of the rolled meat.
- Mix seasonings and rub on meat.
- Cut apple, onion and prunes in pieces.
- Put a meat thermometer in roast and place in roasting pan with fruits and onion.
- Add water and soy sauce. Roast at 325° approximately 45 minutes per pound, or until thermometer registers 185 degrees.
- Baste frequently.
- Set meat aside. Drain liquid from pan and beat in flour. Let boil for 5 minutes.

 For roasts having little fat, place 2 or 3 slices of bacon over the top while cooking ... makes good drippings for gravy and keeps meat from sticking.

Sweet and Sour Pork

Serves 6-8

3 pounds pork, cut in 1-inch
   cubes, seasoned
¾ cup brown sugar
3 tablespoons cornstarch
2 teaspoons dry mustard
2 green peppers, chopped
2 onions, chopped
¾ cup vinegar
1 cup pineapple chunks,
   undrained
½ cup catsup
½ cup water
2 tablespoons soy sauce
Salt and pepper to taste

- Brown seasoned pork.
- Place in casserole.
- Combine other ingredients. Pour over pork.
- Bake at 350° for 1½ hours.
- Add pepper and onion last 10 minutes of cooking, if you prefer them crisp.

Variation: May use chicken cubes instead of pork.

Sausage Ponce de Leon

Serves 8-10

1 cup uncooked rice
2 cups chopped carrots
1 large onion, chopped
1 cup chopped celery
1 cup chopped green pepper
1 (14½-ounce) can chicken
   broth
¼ cup water
1 pound bulk pork sausage

- Spread rice evenly in a lightly greased 3-quart casserole.
- Spoon vegetables over rice.
- Pour chicken broth and water over vegetables.
- Cook sausage until browned. Drain well.
- Spoon sausage over vegetables.
- Cover and bake at 350° for 30 minutes.
- Remove from oven and stir well.
- Cover and bake an additional 30 minutes.
- Garnish with mushrooms and parsley, if desired.

Pizza Strata

from Senator and Mrs. Paul Laxalt

Serves 6-8

8 slices white bread
1 pound hot Italian sausage
½ cup chopped onion
4 ounces sliced mozzarella
  cheese
1 (8-ounce) can pizza sauce
3 beaten eggs
1¾ cups milk
1 tablespoon snipped parsley
½ teaspoon dried oregano,
  crushed
¼ cup grated Parmesan
  cheese

- Remove crusts from 4 slices of bread. Reserve crusts.
- Use remaining 4 slices of bread and crusts to cover the bottom of a greased 8 x 8 x 2-inch baking dish.
- In skillet cook sausage and onion until sausage is brown, about 10 minutes. Drain thoroughly.
- Spread meat-onion mixture over bread in baking dish.
- Cover meat with sliced mozzarella cheese. Spread pizza sauce over cheese.
- Cut the remaining 4 slices of trimmed bread on the diagonal. Place in 2 rows atop sauce. (Bases should overlap points of preceding triangles.)
- Combine eggs, milk, parsley and oregano. Pour over bread.
- Cover tightly and chill overnight.
- Bake, covered, at 325° for 30 minutes.
- Uncover. Bake 30 minutes longer.
- Sprinkle with Parmesan cheese.
- Continue baking until firm, about 10 minutes longer.
- Let stand 5-10 minutes before cutting and serving.
- Cut the strata into squares.

Sausage Strata

Serves 8

6-8 slices white bread, crusts
  removed, cubed
1 pound lean bulk sausage,
  cooked and drained
½ cup Swiss cheese,
  shredded
½ cup sharp cheddar cheese,
  grated
½ cup mushrooms, fresh or
  canned
1 teaspoon prepared mustard
1½ cups milk
¾ cup light cream
5 eggs beaten slightly
1 teaspoon Worcestershire
Salt and pepper to taste

- Arrange bread in greased 9 x 13-inch baking dish.
- Layer sausage, cheese and mushrooms over bread in that order.
- Combine mustard with some of milk.
- Combine with remaining milk, cream, eggs and seasonings. Pour over mushrooms.
- Refrigerate overnight.
- Bake at 350° 35-45 minutes.
- Cool 5 minutes before serving.

Savory Sausage Roll

Serves 6-8

2 pounds sausage
1 cup grated apple
1 cup bread crumbs
1 small onion, grated
½ cup sharp cheddar cheese,
  grated
1 teaspoon curry powder
  (optional)
1 teaspoon sugar
½ teaspoon salt
¼ teaspoon black pepper

- Place sausage on a sheet of waxed paper and spread out to ½-inch thickness.
- Mix other ingredients together and spread on the sausage meat.
- Roll up, as for a sponge roll, using the waxed paper to help.
- Wrap the roll completely in a sheet of aluminum foil and place in a lightly greased large baking dish.
- Bake at 350° for 1 hour. Turn occasionally.

Company Ham

Serves 3-4

1 cup cooked ham in julienne
  strips
¼ cup chopped onion
2 tablespoons butter
2 teaspoons flour
1 cup sour cream
1 (6-ounce) can sliced
  mushrooms, drained

- In skillet or blazer pan of chafing dish, sauté ham and onion in butter until onion is tender but not brown.
- Sprinkle with flour.
- Gradually stir in sour cream.
- Add mushrooms.
- Cook and stir over low heat just until mixture thickens.
- If using chafing dish, keep warm over hot water.
- Serve over fluffy rice.

Ham Loaf with Mustard Sauce

Serves 6-8

1½ pounds cured ham,
  ground
1½ pounds pork shoulder,
  ground
1 egg
1 cup bread crumbs
¾ cup milk
½ teaspoons paprika
½ can condensed tomato
  soup

Mustard Sauce
½ can condensed tomato
  soup
½ cup vinegar
½ cup margarine
½ cup mustard
½ cup sugar
3 beaten egg yolks

- Ask butcher to grind cured ham and pork shoulder together.
- Mix all ingredients. Shape into a loaf.
- Bake in greased 8 x 12-inch pan at 350° for 1 hour or until done.
- If grease collects, draw off with baster.
- Combine sauce ingredients and cook in double boiler until somewhat thick.
- Serve with ham loaf.

Norbert's Veal Oscar

Serves 1

5 ounces thinly sliced veal
  scalloppini
Salt and pepper
Flour
1 teaspoon melted butter
1½ ounces brandy
½ ounce au jus stock or beef
  broth
5 green asparagus spears,
  cooked until crisp tender
3 ounces crabmeat
1 teaspoon lemon juice
1 teaspoon melted butter
Béarnaise sauce, to taste

- Season veal to taste with salt and pepper. Flour both sides.
- Sauté veal in melted butter.
- Remove to heated serving plate.
- Deglaze sauté pan with brandy (pour 1½ ounce brandy into warm pan and ignite ... wait for flames to die).
- Add ½ ounce au jus stock or beef broth. Mix and pour over veal.
- Top with hot asparagus.
- Sauté crabmeat in lemon juice and butter. Strain and place crabmeat over asparagus. Top with Béarnaise sauce.

Veal Cutlets alla Bolognese

Serves 6

6 veal cutlets
1 egg, beaten
1 cup bread crumbs
½ cup grated Parmesan
  cheese
½ teaspoon salt
Freshly ground black pepper
½ cup shortening
6 slices boiled ham
1 cup milk
1 cup canned tomato sauce

- Beat egg with 2 tablespoons water.
- Dip cutlets into egg mixture and then into bread crumbs which have been combined with 2 tablespoons cheese, salt and pepper.
- Saute' in boiling hot shortening for 10 minutes.
- Top cutlets with ham and sprinkle with remaining cheese.
- Combine milk and tomato sauce. Add to cutlets in skillet.
- Cover and simmer for 25 minutes.

Veal in White Sauce

Serves 4

3 tablespoons flour
1 teaspoon salt
⅛ teaspoon pepper
1-1½ pounds veal
¼ cup olive oil
1 clove garlic
3 thin slices lemon
¾ cup sliced onions
4 ounces canned or fresh
    mushrooms, sliced
¾ cup white table wine or
    sherry
1 cup water

- Dip veal into combined flour, salt and pepper.
- Saute' garlic and brown veal in hot oil in heavy skillet on medium heat. Remove garlic.
- Reduce heat. Add lemon slices, onion and mushrooms.
- Combine wine and water. Add ½ of this mixture.
- Cover and simmer gently for 25-30 minutes.
- Add remaining wine and water as needed.
- Serve over wide egg noodles or rice.

Veal Scalloppini

Serves 4

1 pound veal cut in thin strips
½ cup flour
½ teaspoon salt
Pepper to taste
1 clove garlic, minced
¼ cup olive oil
1¾ cups tomatoes, sieved
¼ teaspoon parsley
¼ teaspoon oregano
½ cup Burgundy
1 green pepper, cut bite size
½ pound fresh mushrooms,
    sliced
3 tablespoons butter
Noodles, cooked

- Coat veal strips in flour, salt and pepper
- Brown veal and garlic in olive oil.
- Prepare tomatoes in blender, adding salt and pepper to taste, oregano and parsley.
- Slowly add to the browned veal.
- Cover and simmer 25 minutes.
- Add ½ cup Burgundy.
- Cook green pepper and mushrooms in butter.
- Add to veal. Simmer a few more minutes.
- Serve over noodles.

Luscious Lamb Chops

Serves 6

6 shoulder or sirloin lamb
  chops
1 (10½-ounce) can
  consomme'
½ cup chopped celery
½ cup chopped green onions
  with tops
½ teaspoon dried thyme
1 (3-ounce) can mushrooms
3 tablespoons all-purpose
  flour
1 tablespooon dried parsley
  flakes

- In large skillet brown lamb chops in hot shortening.
- Sprinkle with salt and pepper. Drain off fat.
- Add consomme', celery, green onions and thyme.
- Cover and simmer for 40-45 minutes, until meat is tender.
- Stack chops to the side of pan.
- Drain can of mushrooms, reserving liquid.
- Stir and blend mushroom liquid slowly into flour. Gradually stir flour mixture into consomme' in skillet.
- Cook and stir until bubbly and thickened.
- Add mushrooms and parsley flakes. Heat through.

 Freeze leftover gravy in ice cube trays and transfer to a plastic bag when frozen. Simply warm to serve.

St. Maarten Rack of Lamb

Serves 8-10

1 fresh rack of lamb (about 10
  pounds)
Fresh garlic
Salt
Pepper
Morton's Nature's seasoning
4 mint leaves

Sauce
1 stick butter
2 cloves garlic
Fresh parsley
Fresh shallots
4 tablespoons olive oil
1 teaspoon pepper
½-¾ cup Progresso Italian bread
  crumbs
⅛ teaspoon mint extract

- Trim rack of lamb. Slice cuts in fat and place slices of fresh garlic throughout.
- Salt and pepper rack. Apply liberal amounts of Nature's Seasoning.
- Wipe entire rack with mint leaves.
- Place in large roasting pan and bake at 450° for 1 hour.
- Reduce oven to 375° for second hour.
- Remove from oven and spread sauce over entire rack.
- Return to 375° oven for 30 minutes or until sauce hardens into a crust.
- Slice into chops and serve with excess sauce basted lightly over chops.
- To make sauce: combine all ingredients in saucepan. Cook over medium heat until well blended.

 To remove excess grease from soups and gravies, drop in several ice cubes. The grease will cling to the cubes and can be easily removed.

POULTRY

STS 37, "The Night Before Launch", Photographed by Roland Miller.

Poultry

* Denotes Quick and Easy Recipes

Cornish Hens à l' Orange

Serves 6

6 Cornish hens, cleaned and
   split
Butter, melted

Sauce
1 cup orange marmalade
¼ cup brown sugar
3 tablespoons wine vinegar
2 teaspoons Worcestershire
   sauce
½ teaspoon curry powder
½ teaspoon ground ginger
1 tablespoon M.S.G.
Dash cayenne
Salt and pepper

- Preheat oven to 350°.
- Wash and dry hens. Brush with melted butter.
- Place game hen halves, skin side down on foil-lined broiler pan.
- Combine marmalade, brown sugar, vinegar, Worcestershire sauce, curry powder, ginger, M.S.G., cayenne, salt and pepper in saucepan.
- Heat over medium heat to boiling point. Simmer 2 minutes, stirring constantly.
- Brush surface of game hens with sauce.
- Bake for 30 minutes at 350°. Turn. Bake 30 minutes longer, brushing often with sauce.

Almond Chicken

Serves 6

3 large whole chicken
   breasts, skinned, boned
   and halved
¼ cup butter
4 tablespoons sherry
¼ pound fresh mushrooms,
   chopped
½ garlic clove, crushed
1 (2½-ounce) package sliced
   almonds
1 teaspoon cornstarch
¾ cup chicken stock (may
   use bouillon cube)
¾ cup white wine
Salt and pepper to taste

- Brown chicken breasts in butter in skillet. Remove to platter.
- Pour sherry over chicken.
- To skillet, add mushrooms, garlic and almonds. Sauté several minutes.
- Add cornstarch to bouillon. Stir. Pour into frying pan.
- Add chicken, wine, salt and pepper.
- Cover and simmer 30 minutes.

Aloha Chicken

Serves 6

3 pounds chicken pieces
3 cups pineapple chunks
1 cup pineapple juice
1 cup soy sauce
2 tablespoons freshly grated
  ginger root or 1¼
  teaspoons ground ginger
2 teaspoons liquid garlic
Shortening

- Prepare marinade from ingredients listed. Pour over chicken. Marinate at least 4 hours in refrigerator, turning pieces once or twice.
- Drain chicken and set aside remaining marinade.
- Brown chicken in shortening. Add reserved marinade and simmer for 10 minutes.
- Transfer to casserole. Bake uncovered at 325° for 1 hour, basting twice. May top with toasted almonds before serving.

Chicken Boursin

Serves 6

6 boneless chicken breasts,
  skinned
Seasoned flour
Salt and pepper to taste
7 ounces herbed Boursin
  cheese
6 slices Proscuitto ham
1 tablespoon oil
3 tablespoons butter
½ pound mushrooms, sliced
4 green onions, chopped
2 tablespoons brandy
½ cup white wine
1 cup chicken stock
¼ cup parsley, chopped

- Coat chicken breasts with flour seasoned with salt and pepper.
- Spread ½ tablespoon cheese on each breast. Cover with slice of ham.
- Roll and secure with toothpicks.
- Brown in oil and butter.
- Add mushrooms and onions. Saute'.
- Add brandy and ignite.
- Add wine, chicken stock and parsley.
- Cover and simmer 30-40 minutes. Remove toothpicks before serving.

Chicken Breasts Florentine

Serves 8

Flour
Salt and freshly ground black
    pepper to taste
4 whole chicken breasts,
    boned, skinned and halved
1 egg
1 tablespoon water
¼ cup grated Parmesan
    cheese
½ cup dry bread crumbs
¾ cup butter
2 pounds spinach, cooked
    and drained (may
    substitute 2 packages
    frozen)
1 pound mushrooms, sliced
Chopped parsley

- Dredge breasts in flour seasoned with salt and pepper.
- Dip breasts in egg lightly beaten with water. Coat with mixture of Parmesan cheese and bread crumbs.
- Refrigerate for at least 1 hour.
- In a large skillet, heat ½ cup butter. Add chicken and brown on both sides.
- Lower heat. Cover and cook until tender, about 25 minutes.
- Coarsely chop spinach. Season with lemon juice.
- Pile spinach on platter. Arrange chicken breasts on top. Keep hot.
- To skillet add 2 tablespoons butter and mushrooms. Saute' until mushrooms are tender.
- Spoon over chicken.
- Brown remaining butter in same pan and pour through a fine sieve over the dish.
- Sprinkle with chopped parsley and serve.

 For golden brown fried chicken every time, put a few drops of yellow food coloring in shortening after it has heated.

Champagne Chicken

Serves 4

3 ounces butter
1 tender frying chicken
2 ounces brandy (or to taste)
1 tablespoon chopped parsley
1 box peeled and chopped
  shallots
½ cup champagne (or to
  taste)
¾ cup heavy whipping cream
Dash salt and pepper

- Heat butter in large skillet. Add cut up chicken. Let cook slowly until golden brown.
- Heat brandy in a boiler. Light with a long-stem match and pour over chicken.
- Shake the skillet until the flames die out.
- Add parsley, shallots and champagne.
- Cover skillet. Let contents cook slowly until chicken is tender, 35 minutes.
- Remove chicken only to a hot platter.
- To the remaining liquids add whipping cream.
- Correct seasoning and cook to thicken. Pour these ingredients over the chicken and serve.

Chicken Dijon

Serves 4

4 chicken breasts, split,
  skinned and boned
3 tablespoons butter
2 tablespoons flour
1 cup chicken broth
½ cup light or heavy cream
2 tablespoons Dijon mustard

- In a large skillet, cook chicken in butter until tender, about 20 minutes.
- Remove chicken. Stir flour into skillet drippings.
- Add chicken broth and cream.
- Cook and stir until mixture thickens and bubbles.
- Stir in mustard.
- Add chicken, cover and heat 10 minutes.

Chicken in a Blanket

Serves 4

4 deboned chicken breasts
1 package cream cheese
4 strips bacon
1 can mushroom soup
1 cup water or white wine

- Place ¼ of cream cheese in the middle of each chicken breast.
- Wrap uncooked bacon strips around chicken. Place in pan.
- Pour mushroom soup and water or wine over chicken.
- Cook at 350° for 40 minutes.

Chicken in Spaghetti Sauce

Serves 4-6

8 pieces chicken
1 large onion, thinly sliced
1½ cups prepared spaghetti sauce, meatless
½ cup Burgundy or red wine
1 (4-ounce) can sliced mushrooms, not drained
1 clove minced garlic
¾ teaspoon basil
½ teaspoon oregano

- Arrange chicken pieces in baking dish. Top with sliced onion.
- Combine remaining ingredients. Pour over chicken.
- Bake at 350° for 45 minutes or until chicken is done.

Chicken Indigo

Serves 6

6 chicken pieces
1½ cups poultry stuffing mix
2 tablespoons grated Romano cheese
½ clove garlic, crushed
Dijon mustard, optional
½ stick butter, melted

- Crumble stuffing mix in blender. Stir in cheese.
- Add garlic and Dijon mustard to butter.
- Dip chicken in butter, then in crumbs.
- Bake at 350° for 1 hour.

Ella's Old St. Augustine Chicken Perloo

Serves 4-6

¼ cup shortening
1 pound onions, chopped
1 (20-ounce) can tomatoes
1 teaspoon salt
1 teaspoon sugar
¼ teaspoon thyme
¼ teaspoon cayenne
1 large fryer, cut into 8 pieces
2 cups chicken broth
1 cup rice, uncooked
Datil vinegar or datil relish

- In large, heavy pot melt shortening. When hot, but not smoking, add onions. Simmer over low heat for 10 minutes.
- Add mashed tomatoes, salt, sugar, thyme and cayenne.
- Simmer until thick. Stir constantly. Add chicken. Simmer 20 minutes.
- Add broth and rice. Cover and simmer 1 hour on low. Stir once.
- Let stand for 10-20 minutes to allow flavors to blend.
- Use datil vinegar or datil relish as an accompaniment.

Chicken Saronno

Serves 6

6 boneless and skinless
  chicken breast halves
Dash salt, pepper, garlic
  powder and curry powder
½ cup flour
¼ cup butter
½ pound mushrooms, thickly
  sliced
¼ cup Amaretto di Saronno
Grated rind and juice of 1
  lemon
1½ cups chicken broth
1 tablespoon cornstarch
6 patty shells, cooked

- Cut chicken into 1-inch strips.
- Sprinkle with salt, pepper, garlic powder and curry powder. Roll strips in flour.
- Heat butter in large skillet. Brown chicken on both sides.
- Add mushrooms, Amaretto, grated lemon and juice. Simmer 5 minutes.
- Mix chicken broth and cornstarch.
- Stir into mixture. Cook over low heat until mixture bubbles and thickens.
- Spoon mixture into patty shells.

Chicken Queen Elizabeth

Serves 6

**6 chicken breast halves,
  boned, skinned and
  pounded thin**
Seasoned salt
Freshly ground pepper
**6 teaspoons finely chopped
  fresh parsley**
6 thin slices Swiss cheese
6 thin slices ham
¼ cup melted butter
1 cup fresh bread crumbs
3 cups cooked rice
Apricot halves

Sauce
**1½ cups canned whole
  tomatoes, partially drained**
¾ cup whipping cream
1 tablespoon dry white wine
1 teaspoon salt
1 teaspoon sugar
Pinch garlic powder
**Pinch freshly ground white
  pepper**

- Season chicken breasts with salt and pepper.
- Top each with 1 teaspoon parsley, 1 slice cheese and 1 slice ham. Roll tightly.
- Brush with some of butter and sprinkle with half of crumbs.
- Arrange compactly, crumbed side down, in 6-inch square baking dish.
- Pour remaining butter over top. Sprinkle with remaining crumbs.
- Cover and bake at 325° for 45 minutes.
- Remove cover and continue baking until top is golden brown, about 30 minutes.
- Set aside and keep warm while preparing sauce.
- Combine all ingredients in medium saucepan over medium-high heat and bring to boil.
- Reduce heat and simmer sauce for 3-5 minutes.
- Spoon hot rice onto serving platter. Arrange chicken over top.
- Cover with sauce and garnish with apricot halves.

 Keep parsley fresh and crisp by storing in wide-mouth jar with tight lid.

Coq au Vin

Serves 4-6

1 large onion, sliced
1 carrot, sliced
1 clove garlic, minced
1 tablespoon oil
3 tablespoons margarine
2½-3 pounds chicken, cut up
2 tablespoons flour
½ teaspoon salt
¼ teaspoon pepper
1 tablespoon parsley
1 bay leaf
Pinch thyme
1 cup water
1 cup white wine
1 (4-ounce) can mushrooms,
   drained

- Simmer onion, carrot and garlic in oil and margarine. Remove and add chicken.
- Sprinkle chicken with flour and seasonings. Return vegetables.
- Add water and wine.
- Cook 1 hour and remove chicken from bones.
- Thicken sauce if necessary and return chicken.
- Add mushrooms.
- Heat thoroughly. Serve over rice or noodles.

Cutlets Italiano

Serves 4-6

2-3 chicken breasts, halved,
   skinned and boned
2 tablespoons flour
1 egg
1 tablespoon water
½ cup Italian bread crumbs,
   seasoned with ½ cup
   Parmesan, salt and pepper
3 tablespoons oil
1 (15½-ounce) jar marinara
   sauce (or 15-ounce can
   tomato sauce, 1 clove
   garlic, 1 tablespoon sugar
   and ½ teaspoon oregano)
6-8 ounces mozzarella cheese

- Freeze chicken 30 minutes or until firm. Slice in thin cutlets.
- Dredge chicken in flour.
- Dip cutlets in egg mixed with water, then in crumb mixture.
- Heat oil in skillet and saute' cutlets until golden.
- Put layer of sauce in 9 x 13-inch pan. Add cutlets and remaining sauce.
- Bake at 350° for 15-20 minutes or until hot and bubbly.
- Put slice of mozzarella on each cutlet. Sprinkle with oregano and Parmesan, if desired.
- Bake uncovered 3-5 minutes, until cheese is melted.

Lemon Chicken

Serves 3-4

2 large whole chicken
  breasts, halved, skinned
  and boned
Garlic powder
½ cup lemon juice
¼ cup soy sauce
3 tablespoons margarine

- Cut chicken on diagonal into 8-12 pieces.
- Sprinkle chicken liberally with garlic powder.
- Marinate chicken in lemon juice and soy sauce at least 2 hours in refrigerator.
- Drain marinade and saute' chicken in margarine over medium heat about 7 minutes.

Marty's Party Chicken

Serves 8

1 large jar dried beef
12 boneless chicken breasts
12 slices bacon
16 ounces sour cream
2 cans cream of mushroom
  soup
Salt and pepper to taste

- Line bottom of casserole dish with dried beef.
- Wrap each chicken breast with slice of bacon and place on top of dried beef.
- Mix sour cream with soup. Pour over chicken.
- Bake uncovered for 2½ hours at 275°.

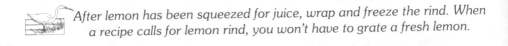

After lemon has been squeezed for juice, wrap and freeze the rind. When a recipe calls for lemon rind, you won't have to grate a fresh lemon.

Pullet en Papillote

Serves 4

1 (3-pound) broiler-fryer
1 lemon, halved
1 onion, halved or quartered
2 tablespoons butter or
   margarine, melted
Seasoned salt to taste
4-5 potatoes, peeled and
   halved
4 carrots, peeled and halved
   crosswise
1 cooking bag

- Stuff cavity of chicken with lemon and onion.
- Rub outside of chicken with melted butter. Sprinkle all of chicken liberally with seasoned salt.
- Put chicken in cooking bag. Place vegetables around chicken. Secure bag and puncture 3 or 4 times. Place bag with contents in large pan.
- Roast at 400° for 1 hour and 15 minutes. Let set for 15 minutes.
- Carve. Place chicken on platter. Surround with vegetables. Garnish with parsley and lemon twists.

Summer Chicken Saute'

Serves 4-6

6-8 deboned chicken breasts
2 tablespoons vegetable oil
1 onion, cut in eighths
1 clove garlic, mashed
2 tomatoes, peeled and
   quartered
1 medium eggplant, cubed
2 tablespoons finely chopped
   parsley
1 teaspoon chopped thyme
1 bay leaf

- Salt and pepper chicken. Brown in oil.
- Add onion and garlic. Cook 5 minutes, stirring occasionally.
- Add remaining ingredients. Salt and pepper to taste.
- Cover tightly and cook over medium heat in Dutch oven until chicken is tender, 30-40 minutes.
- If sauce is not thick enough, raise temperature for last 10 minutes.

The Slim Gourmet's Chicken Cordon Bleu

Serves 6

1 pound (6 small) deboned
   chicken breasts
¼ pound cooked, pressed
   ham, thinly sliced
¼ pound Swiss cheese, thinly
   sliced
2 teaspoons parsley flakes
Salt and pepper to taste
Garlic powder (optional)
½ cup bread crumbs
1 teaspoon salad oil
Fresh parsley and sliced
   tomatoes for garnish

- Slice chicken into 12 equal
  pieces.
- Divide ham and cheese into 6
  equal portions and slice into ½-
  inch strips.
- Sprinkle chicken with parsley,
  salt, pepper and garlic powder, if
  desired.
- Arrange ham and cheese into 6
  packets, alternating strips.
- Top a chicken piece with 1 packet, then cover with another chicken piece. Fasten with toothpicks. (Chicken is on outside
  and completely covers each
  layered packet of ham and
  cheese strips.)
- Mix bread crumbs with oil and
  pour onto a flat plate. Coat each
  chicken packet lightly on all
  sides.
- Place chicken packet on a non-
  stick baking tray in preheated
  350° oven. Bake, without
  turning, approximately 30-40
  minutes.
- Remove toothpicks before
  serving.
- Garnish with fresh parsley and
  sliced tomatoes.

Oven-fried Chicken

Serves 4

1 frying chicken
½ cup Parmesan cheese
½ cup wheat germ
½ teaspoon salt
⅛ teaspoon pepper
¼ teaspoon onion powder
¼ teaspoon garlic powder
¼ teaspoon rosemary
Buttermilk

- Wipe chicken with damp cloth and dry.
- Mix cheese, wheat germ and seasonings.
- Dip each piece chicken in buttermilk. Roll in dry mixture.
- Place on lightly greased baking sheet and bake at 325° for at least 1 hour.

Aunt Jo's Chicken-Broccoli Casserole

Serves 8-10

Sauce
2 cans cream of chicken soup
1 soup can milk
1 (8-ounce) carton sour cream
1½ teaspoons Worcestershire sauce
1½ teaspoons parsley flakes
1 pound grated sharp cheese (reserve some for top)

2 cups Pepperidge Farm stuffing mix
2 packages chopped, frozen broccoli, cooked and drained
2 teaspoons lemon juice
6 chicken breasts, cooked and cut into chunks
1 can French-fried onions
1½ teaspoons minced, dehydrated onion

- Mix sauce ingredients in bowl and spread 4-5 tablespoons in bottom of greased 9 x 13-inch dish.
- Spread layer of dressing mix (not entire package), then a layer of broccoli.
- Sprinkle broccoli with lemon juice.
- Add layer of chicken, dehydrated onions and French-fried onions.
- Pour sauce over top. Cover with foil.
- Bake at 350° for 30 minutes.
- Cover top with grated cheese.
- Heat 15 minutes longer or until bubbly.

Chicken Divan

Serves 6-8

4 large chicken breasts,
  halved
2 packages frozen broccoli
2 cans condensed cream of
  chicken soup
1 cup mayonnaise
½ cup grated cheddar cheese
1 tablespoon lemon juice
1 teaspoon curry powder
  (optional)

Optional Topping
1 cup bread crumbs
1 tablespoon butter

- Simmer chicken until tender.
  Cool. Remove skin and bones.
  Cut into long pieces.
- Cook broccoli in same water
  chicken was cooked in. Cool.
- Place chicken in bottom of 9 x
  13-inch dish.
- Place broccoli over chicken.
- Mix soup, mayonnaise, cheese,
  lemon juice and curry. Pour over
  chicken and broccoli.
- Sprinkle crumbs over casserole.
  Dot with butter, if desired.
- Bake at 350° for 1 hour.

Adele's Chicken Spaghetti

Serves 18-20

1 large hen or fryers to equal
  6 pounds
1 green pepper, chopped
2 large onions, chopped
1½ sticks margarine
24 ounces spaghetti noodles
3 cups Velveeta cheese, cubed
1 (14-ounce) can English peas
1 (10-ounce) can Rotelle
  tomatoes (or add ½
  teaspoon red pepper flakes
  to regular tomatoes)

*Hint: May serve immediately or put
  in casseroles and heat later. If
  heating later, heat at 350° for 30
  to 45 minutes until heated
  thoroughly.*

- Cover chicken with water in
  large kettle and cook until done.
  Cool and debone.
- Sauté pepper and onions in
  margarine until tender.
- Cook spaghetti in chicken broth
  (add chicken bouillon, if
  necessary).
- Drain broth when done.
- Add cubed cheese to spaghetti.
- When cheese is melted, add
  remaining ingredients.

Chicken and Noodles

Serves 8

1 (10-ounce) package egg
  noodles, cooked and drained
1 teaspoon butter
3 (10-ounce) packages frozen,
  chopped broccoli
2 teaspoons lime juice
3-4 cups cooked, sliced
  chicken (about 2 fryers)

Sauce
2 cans cream of chicken soup
1 cup mayonnaise
1 teaspoon Worcestershire
  sauce
½ teaspoon curry powder
½ cup grated sharp cheddar
  cheese

Topping
¼ cup bread crumbs
Grated cheese to taste

- Butter large 3-quart oblong
  casserole.
- Place thick layer of noodles on
  bottom. Dot with butter.
- Place layer of thawed broccoli.
  Sprinkle with lime juice.
- Make layer of chicken.
- Mix sauce ingredients and pour
  over all.
- Top with bread crumbs and
  grated cheese.
- Bake at 350° for 1 hour.

Brunch Party Chicken

Serves 4

2 cups chicken, cooked and
  chopped
1 cup chopped celery
½ cup slivered almonds
2 tablespoons
  Worcestershire sauce
½ teaspoon onion juice
1 can cream of chicken soup
2 hard-boiled eggs, chopped
1 cup crushed potato chips

- Mix all ingredients, except potato
  chips.
- Place in buttered baking dish.
  Top with potato chips and bake
  at 350° for 45-50 minutes.

Chicken à la King

Serves 8

¼ cup chopped green pepper
1 cup thinly sliced mushrooms
2 tablespoons butter
2 tablespoons flour
¾ teaspoon salt
2 cups light cream
3 cups cooked chicken, cut
  into pieces
3 egg yolks
½ teaspoon paprika
¼ cup soft butter
1 teaspoon onion juice
1 tablespoon lemon juice
2 tablespoons sherry
¼ cup diced pimiento

*Hint: Serve with rice, on toast,
or in a pastry shell.*

- Cook green pepper and mushrooms in 2 tablespoons butter until tender but not brown.
- Push vegetables to 1 side of pan. Blend flour and salt into butter.
- Gradually stir in cream. Cook and stir until sauce thickens.
- Add chicken and heat thoroughly, stirring occasionally.
- In small bowl, blend egg yolks, paprika and ¼ cup soft butter. Set aside.
- To chicken, add onion juice, lemon juice and sherry. When bubbling, add egg yolk mixture all at once. Stir until blended.
- Remove immediately from heat and add pimiento.

Chicken Divine

Serves 4

2 cups cooked rice
2 cups diced chicken breasts,
  cooked
2 cups diced celery
½ cup slivered almonds
2 tablespoons minced onion
2 tablespoons lemon juice
½ tablespoon salt
1 cup mayonnaise
1 (8-ounce) can water chestnuts, sliced
1 cup crushed potato chips
½ cup sharp cheddar cheese,
  grated

- Mix first 9 ingredients in casserole.
- Top with potato chips and cheese.
- Bake at 450° for 15-20 minutes.

Chicken Huntington

Serves 12

8 slices of bread (no crust)
7 chicken breasts, cooked,
boned and shredded
½ pound fresh mushrooms
1 stick butter
1 small can water chestnuts,
sliced
½ cup mayonnaise
8 slices American cheese
4 eggs
2 cups milk
1 teaspoon salt
1 can cream of mushroom
soup
1 can cream of celery soup
1 (2-ounce) jar pimientos
2 cups buttered bread crumbs

- Line bottom of 9 x 13-inch baking dish with bread and layer rest of ingredients: chicken, mushrooms sauteed in butter, sliced water chestnuts, mayonnaise (spread on top), and cheese.
- Beat together eggs, milk, salt and pour over top.
- Mix together soups and pour over top.
- Spread pimientos on top.
- Cover with foil and refrigerate overnight.
- Bake uncovered for 1 hour at 325°.
- Add bread crumbs on top and bake another 15 minutes.

Chicken 'n' Chokes

Serves 10

8-10 chicken breasts (or 2
whole chickens)
3 packages frozen artichoke
hearts, cooked and halved
1 pound fresh mushrooms,
sliced
3 tablespoons butter
3 cans cream of mushroom
soup
2 tablespoons
Worcestershire sauce
¼ cup white wine
¼ cup Parmesan cheese
Paprika

- Cook and dice chicken.
- Butter large shallow baking dish.
- Layer artichokes and chicken.
- Saute' mushrooms in butter for 6 minutes. Add to casserole dish.
- In separate bowl mix soup, Worcestershire and wine. Pour over casserole.
- Top with Parmesan cheese and paprika.
- Bake at 375° for 30-40 minutes until bubbly.

Chicken Pot Pie

Serves 8

4 chicken breasts
2 (29-ounce) cans chunky
  mixed vegetables
1 small onion, finely chopped
1 (10½-ounce) can cream of
  chicken soup
1 (10½-ounce) can cream of
  celery soup
2 cups chicken broth
½ (20-ounce) bag frozen peas

Topping
2 cups Bisquick
1½ sticks butter, softened
1½ cups milk

- Boil chicken. Bone, skin and reserve broth. Shred chicken in 9 x 13-inch baking dish.
- Drain canned vegetables and add to chicken.
- Sprinkle onion and frozen peas on top.
- Mix soups with about 2 cups broth (more or less depending on desired consistency). Pour over chicken and vegetable mixture. Mix well.
- For topping, mix Bisquick with soft butter; add milk and beat well. Mixture will be runny. Pour over chicken mixture.
- Bake in preheated oven at 375° for 40-45 minutes or until golden brown. Do not cover.

Chicken Sopa

Serves 6-8

1 large chicken
6 corn tortillas
1 (10-ounce) can green
  chilies, chopped
2 cans cream of chicken soup
1 pint sour cream
⅛ teaspoon garlic powder
⅛ teaspoon onion powder
Salt to taste
1 cup grated cheddar cheese

- Boil and debone chicken.
- In 9 x 13-inch greased pan, place tortillas in bottom and along sides.
- Layer with chicken and green chilies.
- Mix soup, sour cream, garlic powder, salt and onion powder.
- Pour on top of chicken. Sprinkle with cheese.
- Bake at 325° until bubbly.

Chicken with Sugar Pea Pods

Serves 4

2 whole chicken breasts,
  boned, skinned and cut
  against grain into ⅛-inch
  slices
1 egg white
1 teaspoon cornstarch
1 tablespoon sherry
2 teaspoons salt
6 tablespoons oil
8 ounces sugar pea pods
½ teaspoon M.S.G.
¼ cup water

- Marinate chicken in egg white, cornstarch, sherry and 1 teaspoon salt for 1 hour.
- Heat 2 tablespoons oil in pan or wok until hot.
- Stir fry pea pods and 1 teaspoon salt for 2 minutes. Remove from pan. Set aside.
- Heat 4 tablespoons oil until hot.
- Stir fry chicken 3 minutes or until chicken turns white.
- Add cooked pea pods, M.S.G. and water. Cook 2 minutes longer.

Chinese Chicken

Serves 6

2 tablespoons oil
4-6 chicken breasts, cubed
1 cup sliced green onions
½ cup chopped celery
1 (8-ounce) can sliced water
  chestnuts
1 package frozen pea pods
Rice

Sauce
2 tablespoons cornstarch
1 tablespoon sugar
10 tablespoons soy sauce
1 cup water

- Heat oil in wok or frying pan.
- Sauté chicken until done. Set aside.
- Sauté onions, celery, water chestnuts and pea pods.
- Add chicken. Cook for 5 minutes.
- Combine cornstarch and sugar.
- Add soy sauce and water. Blend well.
- Pour over chicken mixture. Stir constantly until thick. Serve over cooked rice.

Down Home Chicken and Dumplin's

Serves 6-8

1 (3-4 pound) hen or cut-up
   fryer
3 quarts water
1 large chopped onion
½ cup chopped celery
2 carrots, finely chopped
   (optional for color)
4 teaspoons salt

Dumplings
2 cups flour
1 teaspoon salt
2½ teaspoons baking powder
¼ teaspoon pepper
4 teaspoons shortening
¾ cup cold milk

- Cover chicken with water. Add onion, celery, salt and carrots, if desired.
- Cook 2-3 hours until tender.
- Remove chicken from stock. Let cool. Remove from bones.
- Sift together flour, salt, baking powder and pepper.
- Cut in shortening with fork.
- Add milk all at once and mix until stiff batter is formed.
- Drop dumplings from spoon into boiling stock and cook covered about 15 minutes.
- Add chicken and heat through.

Marco's Pollo y Fettucine

Serves 4

½ cup oil
3 chicken breasts, diced
3 cups broccoli florets
1 clove minced garlic
⅛ teaspoon ginger
½ cup chicken broth
¼ cup soy sauce
1 (16-ounce) package
   fettucine
3 tablespoons butter
½ cup grated Parmesan
   cheese
½ cup toasted almonds

- Heat oil in wok or large skillet.
- Stir fry chicken. Remove excess oil.
- Add broccoli, garlic and ginger.
- Stir fry until broccoli is tender.
- Add chicken broth and soy sauce. Simmer.
- Cook fettucine in boiling water according to package directions. Drain. Add butter.
- Toss all ingredients in large serving bowl.
- Add Parmesan and toss again.
- Garnish with toasted almonds.

Saucy Chicken Crunch

Serves 4

2 tablespoons vegetable oil
1 large green pepper, cut into
  ¼ inch strips
4 chicken breast halves,
  skinned, boned, cut into ½
  inch strips
2 tablespoons soy sauce
1 tablespoon cornstarch
½ cup cold chicken broth
2 tablespoons dry white wine
½ cup cashews

- Heat oil in wok or skillet. Add pepper. Stir-fry 2 minutes. Push aside.
- Stir-fry chicken 3-4 minutes, until done.
- Return pepper to chicken in wok.
- Combine and stir in soy sauce, cornstarch, chicken broth and wine.
- Heat, stir gently until sauce is thickened and clear. Add cashews.
- Serve at once with rice.

Super Chicken

Serves 6

1 (6-ounce) package long
  grain and wild rice mix
¼ cup butter
¼ cup chopped onion
5-6 tablespoons flour
1 cup half and half
1 cup chicken broth
1 teaspoon salt
Dash pepper
2 cups sliced cooked chicken
1 teaspoon chopped fresh
  parsley

- Prepare rice according to package directions.
- Melt butter in saucepan. Add onion and cook until transparent.
- Blend in flour and cook 1 minute.
- Gradually add half and half and broth. Cook, stirring constantly, until thickened.
- Stir in salt and pepper.
- Add rice, chicken and parsley.
- Spoon mixture into a lightly greased 2-quart casserole.
- Bake at 425° for 30 minutes or until bubbly.

Swiss Chicken

Serves 6

4 cups diced, cooked chicken
2 cups sliced celery
2 cups toasted bread cubes
1 cup mayonnaise
½ cup milk
¼ cup diced onion
1 teaspoon salt
½ teaspoon pepper
6-8 ounces Swiss cheese, cut
   in julienne strips
½ cup walnut or pecan pieces

- Combine all ingredients, except nuts.
- Turn into 2-quart casserole and sprinkle with nuts.
- Bake 350° for 30 minutes or until hot.

Town and Country Casserole

Serves 8

1 pound zucchini squash,
   sliced
1 medium onion, sliced
2-3 cups cooked, shredded
   chicken
1 can cream of chicken soup
8 ounces sour cream
½ cup mayonnaise
¼ pound margarine
1 (8-ounce) package herb
   stuffing mix

- Combine squash and onion in saucepan.
- Add water and boil 5 minutes. Drain.
- Combine all ingredients except margarine and stuffing mix.
- In lightly greased 9 x 13-inch dish, put half of the stuffing mix which has been mixed with the margarine.
- Top with chicken mixture. Top with remaining stuffing mix.
- Bake at 350° for 40 minutes.

Turkey Noodle Encore

Serves 6

8 ounces medium or wide egg
   noodles
2 cups diced cooked turkey
12 spears broccoli, cooked
   and drained
8 ounces grated American
   cheese
2 (10¾-ounce) cans cream of
   chicken soup
1 can water
1 (3-ounce) can fried onions

- Cook noodles as directed on package. Drain.
- Place noodles in buttered 9 x 13 pan. Cover with turkey and broccoli. Top with half the cheese.
- Blend soup and water. Pour over cheese.
- Sprinkle with remaining cheese.
- Bake at 350° for 25 minutes.
- Top with fried onions. Bake 5 minutes more.

Ella's Doves in Wine Sauce

Serves 4

4 tablespoons butter
4 tablespoons flour
2 cups cream
Salt and pepper to taste
8 doves, cleaned
8 slices bacon
2 cups white wine, warmed

- In heavy saucepan, melt butter. Stir in flour. Blend well over low heat.
- Stir in cream, blending with wire whisk.
- Bring slowly to boil. Cook 2 minutes, stirring constantly.
- Season with salt and pepper.
- Wrap each dove with a slice of bacon.
- Cover doves with sauce in deep, heavy pan.
- Bake at 350° for 1 hour.
- Pour 1 cup wine over doves, stirring well. Continue baking until done, about 30 minutes longer.
- Pour remaining wine over doves and serve.

Duckling with Bing Cherry Sauce

from Chef Norbert

Serves 4

1 (4-5 pound) Long Island
   duckling

Bing Cherry Sauce
½ cup drained, dark, sweet
   cherries
1 cup sweet cherry juice
½ teaspoon cornstarch
2 ounces Burgundy
½ ounce Kirschwasser

- Roast duckling tied and seasoned with salt, pepper and paprika oil for 35 minutes at 500°.
- Drain fat, turning duck on side and roast for 25 minutes more at 400°.
- Split duck and bone.
- Bring cherry juice to a boil. Mix cornstarch with 3 teaspoons of juice in small separate bowl.
- Return this mixture to remainder of boiling juice, stirring. Add cherries and Burgundy. Simmer for 10 minutes.
- Remove sauce from heat and add Kirschwasser. Stir. Spread hot sauce generously over boned duckling and serve.

Pheasant in Sherry

Serves 4

2 pheasants, split and cleaned
½ cup butter
½ cup chopped green onions
2 (4-ounce) cans mushrooms
¼ cup sherry
1 tablespoon lemon juice
Salt and pepper to taste
1 cup chicken stock or 2
   chicken bouillon cubes in 1
   cup hot water

- Brown pheasant in butter in large skillet for 10 minutes. Remove.
- Saute' onions in skillet until tender.
- Return pheasant and add rest of ingredients.
- Cover and cook on low for 1 hour. Serve with wild rice.

Quail Simplified

Serves 4

8 quail, dressed and rinsed
1 stick butter
1 tablespoon Worcestershire
  sauce
Salt and pepper to taste
1 cup water

- Brown quail in butter in skillet.
- Add Worcestershire sauce, salt pepper and water. Cover and cook on top of range for 1-1½ hours. Very moist and tender.

Quail Southern Style

Serves 2

2 tablespoons oil
2 quail
2 tablespoons flour
1 teaspoon salt
½ teaspoon pepper
¾ cup light cream

- Heat oil in covered skillet.
- Split quail. Dust with flour, salt and pepper. Brown in oil.
- Pour in cream. Cover and cook over low heat 25 minutes.
- Thicken gravy as desired.

Stir-fry Venison

Serves 6

Oil
2 large onions, sliced
2 cups sliced celery
1 pound venison steaks
2 cups sliced mushrooms
6 ounces bean sprouts
1 small can sliced water
  chestnuts
2 tablespoons cornstarch
1 tablespoon sugar
½ cup soy sauce
1 cup water

- In large fry pan or wok, heat oil. Quickly stir fry onions and celery for 2 minutes.
- Cut venison into julienne strips. Add to skillet with mushrooms, bean sprouts and water chestnuts. Cook, stirring quickly, 2 minutes.
- Pour mixture of cornstarch, sugar, soy sauce and water over meat and vegetables.
- Cover and simmer 2 minutes. Serve over rice.

SEAFOOD

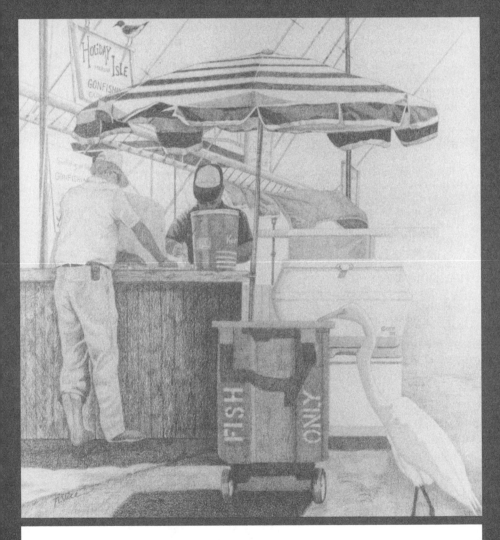

Fish Only, By Nancy Vice. Photographed by Franko Photo.

Seafood

* Denotes Quick and Easy Recipes

Florida Cracked Conch

Serves 4-6

2 pounds conch
2 eggs
½ cup milk
Italian bread crumbs
Salt and pepper, to taste
Olive oil

- Clean and thinly slice conch. Tenderize with mallet into paper-thin slices.
- Mix eggs and milk. Dip conch into mixture.
- Season bread crumbs with salt and pepper.
- Roll conch in bread crumbs.
- Fry in olive oil until golden.

Deviled Clams
from the Grant Seafood Festival

Serves 20

8 cups ground clams
4 cups bread crumbs
1 cup chopped celery
1 cup chopped green pepper
2 cups chopped onions
2 tablespoons mustard
½ cup melted butter
3 eggs
1 teaspoon black pepper
½ teaspoon seafood
   seasoning
¼ teaspoon thyme
1 cup milk

- Mix all ingredients together.
- Bake in individual baking dishes at 350° for 20-30 minutes.

 To remove onion, garlic or fish odor, rub hands briskly with celery seed and lemon juice.

Clams Casino

Serves 12

5 (8-ounce) cans clams,
   minced and drained
½ pound bacon
1 large onion, chopped
1½ green peppers, chopped
1 teaspoon minced garlic
1 ounce olive oil
Parsley, to taste
1 teaspoon oregano
Salt
Pepper
¾ cups bread crumbs
4 tablespoons Parmesan
   cheese plus desired
   amount for sprinkling
Onion salt, to taste
Clam shells to stuff (24-36)
Paprika

- Cook bacon, drain and set aside.
- Sauté onion and green pepper in bacon fat.
- Add garlic, olive oil, parsley, oregano, salt and pepper.
- Place drained minced clams in a bowl.
- Add above mixture plus bread crumbs, Parmesan cheese and onion salt.
- Fill shells. Sprinkle with additional Parmesan cheese and paprika. Crumble bacon on top.
- Bake 10 minutes at 325°.
- Broil until bubbly, approximately 1 minute.

Note: If using real shells, soak them in cold water for 10 minutes before stuffing.

Crab Puff

Serves 4-6

4 eggs
6 slices white bread, trimmed
   and cubed
1½ cups milk
1 cup grated cheddar cheese
½ cup mayonnaise
1-1½ cups flaked crabmeat
½ teaspoon salt
½ teaspoon dry mustard
1 tablespoon grated onion
¼ teaspoon pepper

- Beat eggs with wire whisk. Add bread, milk, cheese, mayonnaise, crabmeat and seasonings.
- Pour into a well-greased 2½-quart casserole. Cover and refrigerate several hours or overnight.
- Bake at 325° for 1 hour or until center is set.

Jim's Paella

Serves 6

18 mussels or clams, soaked
in brine 2 hours (½ cup salt
and 1 quart water)
1 pound shelled and deveined
shrimp
2 tablespoons fresh lemon juice
2 tablespoons olive oil
¼ teaspoon oregano, divided
3 large sweet Spanish or
Italian sausages
6 chicken legs or thighs
1 small green pepper, chopped
1 large onion, chopped
1¾ cups smoked ham, diced
2¼ cups chicken broth
¾ cup white wine
½ teaspoon paprika
2 packages Vigo brand food
flavoring and coloring
¼ teaspoon each coriander,
thyme, dry mustard and
dry ginger
1 bay leaf, crushed
4 medium garlic cloves, crushed
1¼ cups rice (uncooked)
2 tablespoons butter
½ cup drained canned chick
peas or garbanzo beans
½ cup green peas, canned,
fresh or frozen
3 ripe tomatoes, peeled,
seeded and chopped
1 (2-ounce) jar pimientos, 1
tablespoon chopped and
rest cut in strips for
garnish
4 thin lemon slices
Fresh parsley sprigs for
garnish

- Marinate shrimp in lemon juice, oil and ½ of oregano. Set aside.
- Brown sausages in large skillet.
- Remove sausages. Cut in ½-inch slices and drain on paper towel.
- Brown chicken in drippings (add more oil if necessary). Remove and drain. In same skillet add green pepper, onion and ham to drippings and sauté until onion is tender.
- Add sausage, chicken, broth, wine, remaining oregano, paprika, 1 package Vigo, coriander, thyme, mustard, ginger, bay leaf and garlic. Simmer uncovered 25 minutes. Skim fat.
- Drain mussels. Scrub to remove sand. Set aside.
- In separate pan sauté rice in butter until golden brown and grains are separated.
- Add rice to skillet mixture and simmer uncovered 5 minutes.
- Add shrimp, chick peas, green peas, tomatoes, chopped pimientos and 1 package Vigo to skillet. Stir until well mixed.
- Cover and simmer 5 minutes.
- Arrange mussels on top. Cover tightly and steam about 25-30 minutes or until rice is fluffy and mussels are fully opened.
- Discard any unopened mussels.
- Mound paella on large platter and garnish with lemon slices, pimiento strips and parsley.

Crab Supreme

Serves 8-10

¾ cup butter or margarine
¾ cup flour
2 pints sour cream
2 tablespoons instant onion
2 tablespoons snipped
   parsley
½ teaspoon nutmeg
2 pounds crabmeat, cleaned
4 (4-ounce) cans button
   mushrooms, drained
6 tablespoons dry sherry or
   white wine

- Melt butter. Add flour and stir until smooth.
- Lower heat and stir in remaining ingredients, except sherry.
- Cover and cook 20-25 minutes. Stir often.
- Stir in sherry right before serving.
- Serve on rice or noodles.

Crabmeat Cavalier

Serves 6

2 pounds crabmeat
2 cups thinly sliced celery
½ cup chopped almonds or
   peanuts
½ teaspoon salt
2 teaspoons grated onion
1 cup mayonnaise
2 tablespoons lemon juice
½ cup grated cheddar cheese
1 cup crushed potato chips

- Combine ingredients, except cheese and chips.
- Pile lightly in individual baking dishes or seashells (May also use 2-quart casserole.)
- Sprinkle with cheese and potato chips.
- Bake 10-15 minutes at 450°.
- Bake 30 minutes at 400°.

Variation: May substitute 2 cups cooked, diced chicken for crabmeat.

Crabmeat Harold

Serves 4

White sauce
4 tablespoons butter
2 tablespoons flour
⅛ teaspoon garlic powder
1 cup half and half

1 pound lump crabmeat
2 tablespoons chopped
   pimiento
1 cup sliced sautéed
   mushrooms
1 tablespoon chopped parsley
¼ cup grated Romano cheese
½ cup grated sharp cheddar
   cheese
¼ cup dry white wine
Dash white pepper
Paprika

- Melt butter over low heat in a 1-quart saucepan.
- Add flour and garlic powder
- Cook until smooth (3-4 minutes).
- Slowly stir in half and half. Simmer and stir sauce with wire whisk until thickened and smooth.
- Combine with other ingredients.
- Place in buttered casserole or individual ramekins and top with additional grated cheddar cheese and paprika.
- Bake at 375° until bubbly.

Crabmeat en Brochette
from The Pump Room, Chicago

Serves 6

3 pounds fresh crabmeat
3 cups soft bread crumbs
½ cup dry sherry
1 tablespoon dry mustard
1 tablespoon chopped chives
Bacon slices, cut in half

- Combine crabmeat, bread crumbs, sherry, mustard and chives. Mix well.
- Shape into walnut-sized balls.
- Wrap each ball in a half slice of bacon and fasten bacon with toothpick.
- Thread on skewers and broil under medium heat for 15 minutes or until well browned. Turn frequently.

Deviled Crab

from the Grant Seafood Festival

Serves 4

½ stick butter
2 tablespoons flour
¾ cup evaporated milk
1 egg
½ cup chopped onion
Salt and pepper to taste
Worcestershire sauce to
  taste
Cayenne pepper to taste
Seafood seasoning to taste
1 pound crabmeat
Bread crumbs

- Melt butter in heavy pan.
- Stir in flour and milk until mixture is thick and leaves side of pan.
- Remove from heat and stir in egg, onion and seasonings to taste.
- Add crabmeat.
- Sprinkle with bread crumbs and bake at 350° for 20-25 minutes until lightly browned.
- May bake in individual baking dishes or 1 large casserole.

Deviled Crab Casserole

Serves 6

1 pound crabmeat
3 medium onions, chopped
2-3 cups chopped celery
½ bell pepper, chopped
1 stick butter
2-3 tablespoons mayonnaise
2 teaspoons dry mustard
1 teaspoon Worcestershire
  sauce
1 drop Tabasco
2 ounces sherry, or more to
  taste
2 sleeves saltines, crushed

- Saute' onions, celery and bell pepper with butter.
- Add crab, salt and pepper.
- Cook 10-15 minutes. Remove from heat.
- Add mayonnaise, mustard, Worcestershire, Tabasco, crushed saltines and sherry.
- Place mixture in buttered casserole dish.
- Dot with butter and paprika.
- Bake at 350-375° for 20-25 minutes.

Variation: For individual crab shells, dot with butter and papri- ka. Bake 10-15 minutes at 400°.

Seafood Gumbo

Serves 8-10

6-8 tablespoons flour
¼ cup bacon drippings
1 cup chopped onion
1 cup chopped celery
¼ cup chopped green pepper
2 quarts boiling water
2 (28-ounce) cans tomatoes
10 chopped okra pods
5 bay leaves
5 whole allspice
Salt and pepper
1 pound crabmeat
1½ pounds peeled and
    cleaned shrimp

- In 4-quart Dutch oven, brown flour and bacon drippings until dark brown roux forms. Stir constantly.
- Add vegetables and stir.
- Slowly add boiling water, tomatoes, okra, bay leaves, allspice, salt and pepper to taste.
- Simmer ½-1 hour.
- Before serving add crabmeat and shrimp (oysters, too, if desired).
- Serve over hot rice in large bowls.

Uncle Fred's Crab and Broccoli Casserole

Serves 3-4

1 package frozen broccoli
    spears, cooked and drained
1 cup grated sharp cheddar
    cheese
¼ cup butter
2 tablespoons minced onion
2 tablespoons flour
⅛ teaspoon curry powder
    (optional)
½ teaspoon salt
1 cup milk
1 tablespoon lemon juice
½ pound crabmeat, cleaned
2 tablespoons melted butter
½ cup bread crumbs

- Place broccoli in greased 1-quart casserole. Sprinkle with cheese.
- Melt butter in saucepan. Saute' onion until golden but not brown.
- Stir in flour, curry powder and salt.
- Gradually stir in milk over low heat. Stir constantly, until thickened.
- Stir in lemon juice and crabmeat.
- Pour mixture over broccoli.
- Mix melted butter with bread crumbs and sprinkle on top.
- Cover with foil and bake at 350° for 20 minutes.
- Remove foil and bake 10 minutes until bubbly.

Baked Flounder

Serves 4-6

2-3 pounds fresh flounder
1 cup mayonnaise
¼ cup Parmesan cheese
1 teaspoon lemon juice
1 teaspoon grated onion
½ teaspoon salt
Dash pepper sauce or Tabasco

- Mix all ingredients and spread over flounder.
- Bake at 350° for 25-30 minutes in a greased 9 x 13-inch pan.

Broiled Flounder with Cucumber-Parsley Butter

Serves 4-6

2 medium cucumbers, peeled, seeded and shredded
½ cup butter, softened
1 tablespoon fresh, minced parsley
½ teaspoon salt
2 tablespoons lemon juice
2½ pounds flounder or sole fillets
¼ teaspoon white pepper
¼ teaspoon cayenne pepper

- Mix cucumber with all but 2 tablespoons butter and set aside.
- Mix remaining butter with parsley and 1 tablespoon lemon juice. Set aside.
- Oil a shallow oven-to-table broiling pan. Place fish in 1 layer and sprinkle with 1 tablespoon lemon juice, salt and pepper.
- With a small spatula, spread the cucumber butter evenly over the fillets.
- Broil 3 inches from heat source for 5-8 minutes, depending on thickness of fish.
- Baste once. Do not overcook.

Bob's Fish 'n' Onions

Serves 2

1 medium onion, sliced
¼ pound fresh mushrooms,
  sliced
3 tablespoons butter
1 pound fish fillets
Salt and pepper to taste

- Saute' onions and mushrooms in butter over medium heat until onions become limp.
- Add fish, breaking apart as it cooks. Stir frequently until done.
- Salt and pepper to taste.
- Add additional butter while cooking, if necessary.

Fish 'n' Chips

Serves 4-6

1 cup crushed potato chips
¼ cup grated Parmesan
  cheese
¼ teaspoon thyme
2 pounds fish fillets
¼ cup milk
¼ cup butter, melted

- Combine first 3 ingredients.
- Dip fish in milk. Roll in crumbs.
- Place in well-buttered 8 x 10-inch baking dish. Sprinkle with any remaining crumbs.
- Drizzle with butter.
- Bake at 500° for 12-15 minutes.

 For best results in storing seafood, layer seafood with ice in flat containers. Density, as in quart containers, causes spoilage.

Fish with a Twist

Serves 4-6

1¼-1½ pounds white, flaky fish fillets (cobia, grouper, snapper, trout)
2 cups flour
¼ teaspoon garlic powder
½ teaspoon salt
½ teaspoon pepper
1½ sticks butter
1 teaspoon Worcestershire sauce
½ cup toasted finely chopped pecans

- Wash fish and cut into 2 x 4-inch strips.
- Drain and sprinkle lightly with salt, pepper and garlic powder.
- Shake fillets in flour seasoned with garlic powder, salt and pepper.
- Put ½ stick butter in large frying pan and ½ stick butter in glass casserole. Put casserole in 500° oven to melt butter.
- Heat butter in frying pan on medium-high heat.
- When hot, add fillets and cook 5 minutes on 1 side.
- Remove to glass dish and cook on other side in oven for 5-7 minutes.
- When done, remove to serving plates and spread with paste made of ½ stick butter, Worcestershire sauce and pecans.

Florida Pompano à la Maison
From Chef Norbert

1 fresh Florida pompano fillet per person
1 teaspoon lemon juice
1 teaspoon Worcestershire sauce
Pinch each salt and pepper
1 cup sifted flour
½ cup butter

- Mix lemon juice, Worcestershire, salt and pepper.
- Dip fillets in mixture and gently coat with flour.
- Saute' in foaming, melted butter until golden brown. Serve immediately on warm plate topped with sauce Dresden (See index).

Grilled Fish

Serves 7

4 pounds fish (grouper,
  dolphin, flounder)
Mayonnaise
3 tablespoons lemon juice
4 large green peppers
4 large tomatoes
2 large Spanish onions
Key West or other seafood
  seasoning to taste

- Spread fish out on aluminum foil.
- Brush both sides with
  mayonnaise and lemon juice.
- Cover fish with slices of tomatoes, green peppers and onions.
- Season lightly with Key West
  seasoning.
- Seal up foil and cook on hot grill
  for 25 minutes.

Pensacola Red Snapper

Serves 4

4 (8-10 ounce) red snapper
  fillets
1 teaspoon salt
Pepper to taste
¼ cup lemon juice
2 tablespoons olive oil
1½ teaspoons chopped garlic
1 teaspoon oregano
2 tomatoes, sliced
1 tablespoon parsley
1 (3-ounce) can Romano
  cheese

- Wash and dry fillets.
- Season both sides with salt and
  pepper.
- Combine lemon juice, olive oil,
  garlic and ½ teaspoon oregano in
  shallow baking dish.
- Stir mixture until well blended.
- Add fillets, turning to coat both
  sides.
- Place tomato slices over fillets
  and sprinkle remaining oregano
  and Romano cheese on top.
- Bake for 10-12 minutes at 400° or
  until flaky.
- Sprinkle with parsley and serve.

Red Snapper Sanibel

Serves 4

¼ cup olive or vegetable oil
1 large onion, chopped
1-2 cloves garlic, minced
1 (24-ounce) can peeled
 tomatoes
2 jalapeño peppers, seeded
 and chopped (may use
 dried hot red peppers)
10-12 stuffed green olives,
 chopped
6-8 ripe olives, chopped
Flour seasoned with salt and
 pepper
1½ pounds red snapper fillets
 (may use any white fish)
4 tablespoons butter

- Heat oil in large skillet. Add onion and garlic. Saute' until soft.
- Purée tomatoes and juice in blender.
- Add tomatoes, peppers and olives to onion mixture. Bring to boil. Reduce heat and simmer 20 minutes.
- Coat fish fillets in seasoned flour. Shake off any excess.
- Melt butter in large skillet. Add fish and fry 4-6 minutes on each side or until browned.
- Transfer to warmed serving dish.
- Pour sauce over fish and serve at once.

Snapper à la Surf
from Bernard's Surf, Cocoa Beach

Serves 4

4 (4-ounce) snapper fillets
10 ounces scallops
10 ounces raw, peeled shrimp
10 ounces crabmeat
8 teaspoons Parmesan
 cheese
2 tablespoons garlic powder
2 cups white sauce
2 ounces chopped, fresh
 parsley
Butter for cooking

- Lightly broil snapper. Set aside.
- Chop scallops and shrimp. Sauté in butter.
- Add crabmeat, cheese and garlic powder.
- Heat wine sauce and add parsley.
- Place snapper fillets in serving dish. Sprinkle ¼ of seafood mixture over each fillet.
- Top each fillet with ½ cup white sauce.
- Bake at 400° for 5-10 minutes, until well heated.

Snapper Bonne Femme

Serves 4

2 pounds red snapper
4 tablespoons butter
3 shallots, chopped
2 tablespoons parsley
12 mushrooms sliced
1 teaspoon salt
¼ teaspoon pepper
1 cup vermouth
½ cup heavy cream

- Place the snapper in a deep skillet with 2 tablespoons butter, shallots, parsley, sliced mushrooms, salt, pepper and vermouth.
- Bring to a boil and cook gently until fish flakes with a fork.
- Remove snapper.
- Reduce liquid to about 1/3 of its original quantity and gradually stir in ¼ cup cream and 2 tablespoons butter.
- Add salt and pepper to taste.
- Return snapper to skillet.
- Whip remaining cream with a dash of salt and pepper.
- Spoon on top of snapper and place under broiler until puffy and lightly browned.

Sunshine Snapper

Serves 6

2 pounds snapper fillets
3 tablespoons butter, melted
2 tablespoons Key lime juice or lemon juice
2 teaspoons grated orange or lemon peel
Salt and pepper to taste
1 tablespoon fresh parsley, chopped

- Cut fish into 6 portions.
- Place with skin down in a single layer in a greased, ovenproof pan.
- Combine all remaining ingredients and pour over fish.
- Bake at 350°, uncovered, for 20-25 minutes.
- Garnish with orange or lemon peel and chopped parsley.

Savory Baked Grouper

Serves 4

4 (8-10 ounce) grouper filets
2 teaspoons lemon juice
Dash pepper
6 slices bacon, fried and
   crumbled, reserving fat
1 medium onion, thinly sliced
½ cup soft bread crumbs
2 tablespoons chopped
   parsley

- Grease a shallow baking dish and place fillets in a single layer.
- Sprinkle with lemon juice and pepper.
- Cook onion rings in bacon fat until tender. Arrange over fish.
- Combine bacon, bread crumbs and parsley.
- Sprinkle over fillets and onions.
- Bake for 25-30 minutes at 350° or until fillets flake easily when tested with a fork.

Top of the World Fish Fillets

Serves 3

2 pounds Wahoo fillets
2 lemons, juiced
6 teaspoons Worcestershire
   sauce
1 stick melted butter
1½ cups crushed Ritz
   crackers
1½ cups wheat bread crumbs
Salt and pepper to taste

- Mix lemon juice and Worcestershire for marinade.
- Dip fillets in marinade.
- Dip in melted butter.
- Dip in mixed bread and cracker crumbs.
- Place in oblong baking dish.
- Bake at 400° for 15 minutes.
- Lower temperature to 300° for 10 minutes.

 To prevent bacon from curling while frying, dip strips in cold water first.

Trout Almondine

Serves 4

1 (2-pound) fillet of trout
1 stick butter
4 tablespoons sliced almonds
Juice of ½ lemon
1 teaspoon chopped parsley

- Saute' trout in ½ stick butter until golden brown and cooked through. Set aside.
- Brown almonds in ½ stick butter. Add lemon juice.
- Pour over trout. Sprinkle with parsley.

Lobster Champignon
from Bernard's Surf, Cocoa Beach

Serves 4

4 (5-ounce) lobster tails
10 ounces mushrooms
4 teaspoons Parmesan cheese
4 slices American cheese
Butter for cooking

- Split lobster tails in half. Remove meat from shell.
- Chop meat and mushrooms. Mix with Parmesan cheese.
- Divide into 4 equal parts and stuff into lobster shells.
- Top with melted butter.
- Bake at 400° until well heated, approximately 10 minutes.
- Top each tail with slice of cheese. Return to oven until cheese melts.

 Thaw fish in milk — it draws out frozen taste and provides a fresh-caught flavor.

Carla's Linguine and Oysters

Serves 4

8 ounces linguine, cooked
   and drained
7 slices thick bacon, diced
½ cup whipping cream
1 egg
1 pint oysters
3-4 tablespoons parsley,
   chopped
2-3 leaves fresh basil or ½
   teaspoon dried
Pepper to taste

- Fry chopped bacon until brown. Drain away most of grease.
- In small amount of remaining grease over medium heat slowly add whipping cream.
- Add beaten egg and continue stirring until mixture begins to thicken (small amount of cornstarch may be added, if needed).
- Add oysters and liquid, stirring constantly.
- Add seasonings and bacon.
- Remove from heat and toss with cooked linguine.

Oysters Mosca

Serves 4-6

6 green onions, sliced
4 tablespoons olive oil
3 cloves garlic, chopped or
   crushed
¼ teaspoon oregano
1 pint oysters (2 dozen) plus
   liquid
Salt, pepper and red pepper
   (optional)
Worcestershire sauce
   (optional)
Bread crumbs
4-6 ounces fresh grated
   Parmesan cheese
Lemon juice

- Saute' green onions in olive oil. Add garlic and oregano. Saute' for a few more minutes.
- Add oysters and liquid. Cook only until mixture begins to boil.
- If needed, add a little water.
- Add salt, peppers and Worcestershire sauce.
- Add bread crumbs until mixture is thick but moist as in stuffing. Put into casserole or individual ramekins.
- Sprinkle abundantly with Parmesan cheese and squeeze lemon juice over top.
- Bake at 375° for 15 minutes.

Oysters Bienville

from Chef Norbert

Serves 4

2 dozen unshucked oysters
Dry white wine
2 slices bacon, minced
1 cup mushrooms, canned or
    fresh, drained and minced
4 green onions, minced
1 tablespoon butter
2½ tablespoons flour
½ cup milk
¼ pound shrimp, cooked,
    peeled, deveined and
    minced
1 tablespoon lemon juice
1 tablespoon sherry
1 tablespoon chopped parsley
½ slice American cheese,
    diced
Hot sauce to taste
Salt to taste
Yellow food coloring
2 cups rock salt

*Hint: Oysters (and clams)
will be simple to open if
washed thoroughly, then
placed in plastic bags. Freeze
for 1 hour.*

- Wash and rinse oysters thoroughly in cold water.
- Shuck oysters, reserving deep half of shell and 5 tablespoons liquid.
- Place oysters in a saucepan and cover with wine. Simmer about 1 minute or until edges curl. Remove from heat.
- Using slotted spoon remove from wine and arrange oysters in shells. Set aside.
- Fry bacon until browned. Add mushrooms and onion.
- Saute' until onion is wilted.
- Add butter, stirring until melted. Blend in flour until smooth.
- Cook 5 minutes, stirring constantly. (Do not allow flour to brown.)
- Add milk, stirring constantly. Add shrimp, reserved oyster liquid, lemon juice, sherry and parsley.
- Cook sauce 2-3 minutes, stirring.
- Add cheese, hot sauce, salt and a few drops food coloring.
- Cook until thickened and smooth, stirring constantly.
- Spoon about 1 tablespoon sauce over each oyster.
- Place shells filled with oysters and sauce on a bed of rock salt in a shallow baking pan and broil until sauce is bubbly and begins to brown.

Oysters Rockefeller: Antoine's

Serves 6

36 freshly opened oysters on
  half shell
6 tablespoons butter
6 tablespoons finely minced raw
  spinach
3 tablespoons minced onion
3 tablespoons minced parsley
3 tablespoons minced celery
5 tablespoons bread crumbs
Tabasco sauce
½ teaspoon absinthe
½ teaspoon salt
Garnish with rock salt

- Melt butter in saucepan. Add remianing ingredients except oysters and rock salt.
- Cook 15 minutes, stirring constantly.
- Press through sieve or food mill.
- Cool.
- Place rock salt in pie tins. Set oysters on half shell on top. Put spoonful of sauce on each oyster.
- Broil until sauce begins to brown.
- Serve immediately.

Note: Absinthe is a liqueur with a flavor somewhat like anisette or Pernod.

Saffron Oyster Kabobs

Serves 6

1 pint shucked oysters
Sliced bacon, cut in 1-inch
  pieces
18 mushroom caps
Melted butter

- Preheat broiler and broiler pan. Drain oysters well.
- Thread oysters, bacon and mushrooms, alternately on 6 skewers.
- Brush with butter. Broil until bacon is crisp.
- Serve on saffron rice (see below).

Saffron Rice
3 cups water
1½ teaspoons salt
1½ cups rice
¼ teaspoon saffron
¼ cup butter

- Place water in 2-quart pan.
- Add salt and heat to boil. Gradually stir in rice. Add saffron and stir.
- Cover and cook on low until rice is tender and liquid absorbed.
- Add butter. Toss with fork to mix.

Scalloped Oysters

Serves 4-6

2 cups cracker crumbs
½ teaspoon salt
⅛ teaspoon pepper
½ cup melted butter
1 pint standard size oysters, drained
¼ teaspoon Worcestershire sauce
1 cup milk

- Combine cracker crumbs, salt, pepper and butter.
- Sprinkle 1/3 of this mixture into a buttered 2-quart casserole dish and cover with a layer of oysters. Repeat layers.
- Add Worcestershire sauce to milk. Pour over oysters.
- Sprinkle remaining crumbs over top.
- Bake at 350° for 30 minutes or until crumbs are brown.

Baked Salmon Croquettes

Serves 4-6

1 (15½-ounce) can pink salmon
Milk
¼ cup margarine
2 tablespoons chopped onion
5-6 tablespoons flour
½ teaspoon salt
¼ teaspoon pepper
1 tablespoon lemon juice
1 cup crushed corn flake crumbs

- Drain salmon, reserving liquid. Add enough milk to liquid to make 1 cup. Set aside.
- Melt margarine. Add onions and cook until tender.
- Add flour and cook while stirring 1 minute.
- Gradually add milk mixture.
- Cook over medium heat until thick.
- Add salt and pepper. Set aside.
- Remove skin and bones from salmon. Flake. Add lemon juice, ½ cup corn flakes and sauce. Stir well. Refrigerate until chilled.
- Shape into croquettes then roll in remaining corn flakes.
- Place on greased baking sheet and bake at 400° for 30 minutes.

Salmon Steaks in Lemon Sauce

Serves 4

½ cup dry white wine
½ cup water
¼ teaspoon dill weed
½ teaspoon mustard seed
1 thinly sliced lemon
1 tablespoon butter
4 fresh salmon steaks
2 teaspoons cornstarch
1 tablespoon water

- In large skillet, combine wine, water, dill, mustard, lemon and butter. Heat until boiling.
- Add salmon steaks. Cover and simmer until fish flakes easily with a fork, about 15 minutes.
- Remove fish.
- Stir cornstarch with 1 tablespoon water and mix with pan juices over low heat until sauce thickens.
- Spoon over fish.

Company Casserole

Serves 4-6

½ pound scallops
½ pound fresh mushrooms, sliced
½ pound raw shrimp, peeled and deveined
¼ cup butter
½ cup heavy cream
2 tablespoons brandy
2 tablespoons finely chopped chives or parsley
Salt and pepper to taste
Bread crumbs

- Sauté scallops, shrimp and mushrooms in butter until barely cooked.
- Put everything except bread crumbs in baking dish.
- Sprinkle top with bread crumbs.
- Dot with butter and bake at 350° for 25 minutes.

Coquilles St. Jacques

Serves 6

1½ pounds scallops
2 cups white wine
¼ cup water
1 bay leaf
1 tablespoon chopped parsley
¼ teaspoon thyme
½ pound fresh mushrooms
1 small onion, chopped
6 tablespoons butter
3 tablespoons flour
1 egg yolk
4 tablespoons heavy cream
Juice of 1 lemon
Dash of cayenne
Salt and pepper to taste
Buttered bread crumbs

- Cut scallops into bite-sized pieces. Drop into hot white wine.
- Add water, parsley, bay leaf and thyme. Simmer 2 minutes.
- Drain scallops, saving liquid.
- Remove bay leaf. Set aside.
- Slice mushrooms. Sauté with onion in scallop liquid for 5 minutes, until moisture is reduced. Set aside.
- Melt butter. Gradually add flour with wire whisk. Blend well, adding scallop liquid. Cook 5 minutes.
- Add egg yolk to heavy cream. Blend in lemon juice. Combine with scallops. Blend well.
- Add mushrooms and onion mixture, cayenne, salt and pepper to taste.
- Fill 6 baking shells. Sprinkle generously with buttered crumbs.
- Bake at 350° for 10 minutes, until bubbly.

Boiled Shrimp

Serves 8

4 pounds large shrimp
1 can beer
2 cans water
1 onion, chopped
3 stalks celery, sliced
½ teaspoon salt
Pepper to taste
2-3 teaspoons shrimp seasoning

- Put all ingredients, except shrimp, in 5-quart pot. Bring to a boil.
- Add shrimp and bring to a second boil.
- Reduce heat and cook 5-8 minutes. Do not over cook.

Broiled Shrimp in Bacon

Serves 4

8-12 slices bacon, halved
Hot spicy mustard
16-24 medium-sized raw
   shrimp, shelled and
   deveined

- Preheat broiler.
- Place bacon on waxed paper and brush generously with mustard.
- Wrap bacon around each shrimp, mustard side facing shrimp and secure each roll with a toothpick.
- Broil on broiling pan until bacon is crisp, turning once.

Cajun Shrimp

Serves 4-6

1 cup diagonally sliced celery
1 medium onion, chopped
½ cup chopped green pepper
¼ cup butter or margarine
¼ cup flour
1½ teaspoons salt
1 (1-pound) can stewed
   tomatoes
1 pound shrimp, cooked,
   peeled and deveined
¼ cup sherry
1½ cups grated cheddar cheese
4 hard-boiled eggs, sliced

- Saute' celery, onion and green pepper in butter.
- Stir in flour and salt.
- Add tomatoes, shrimp, sherry and cheese.
- Place in casserole dish and carefully fold in eggs.
- Bake at 350° for 30 minutes.
- Serve over rice.

Shrimp à la Lille

Serves 4-6

3 pounds shrimp, cleaned and
   par-boiled 1 minute,
   drained
1½ cups crushed cheese
   cracker crumbs
¾ cup melted butter
1 teaspoon garlic juice
2 tablespoons lemon juice
2 tablespoons white wine

- Arrange shrimp in a single layer in a shallow casserole.
- Sprinkle with crumbs.
- Combine next 4 ingredients. Spoon over shrimp combination.
- Bake at 375° for 20 minutes.

Shrimp and Artichoke Casserole

Serves 8

1 (14-ounce) can artichoke
   hearts
2 pounds shrimp, shelled
2 tablespoons butter
3 tablespoons flour
½ teaspoon paprika
¼ teaspoon cayenne pepper
1 teaspoon salt
1 pint half and half
1 tablespoon catsup
1 tablespoon Worcestershire
   sauce
1 tablespoon lemon juice
3 tablespoons sherry
1 cup grated sharp cheese

- Layer artichokes and shrimp in 1½-quart casserole.
- To prepare sauce, melt butter and stir in flour until mixture is lightly browned. Add paprika, cayenne pepper, salt and half and half.
- Heat until bubbling, stirring constantly.
- Remove from heat and add remaining ingredients, except for cheese.
- Pour sauce over shrimp and artichokes.
- Cover with cheese.
- Bake at 350° for 45 minutes. Serve with rice.

Shrimp and Pea Pods

Serves 4

12 ounces shrimp, shelled
2 tablespoons salad oil
2 cups pea pods
2 tablespoons green onions,
  thinly sliced (use tops also)
2 teaspoons fresh ginger root,
  shredded or ½ teaspoon
  ground ginger
1 clove garlic, minced
1 teaspoon cornstarch
½ teaspoon sugar
½ teaspoon salt
¼ cup chicken broth
1 teaspoon soy sauce
¼ cup chopped celery
  (optional)
1 (4-ounce) can chopped
  water chestnuts (optional)

- Heat oil in skillet. Add shrimp and cook quickly 3-5 minutes until pink.
- Add pea pods, onion, ginger and garlic. Cook over high heat for 1 minute.
- Combine cornstarch, sugar, salt and broth.
- Add soy sauce and 2 teaspoons cold water. Mix until smooth.
- Pour over shrimp mixture. Toss and cook until thickened and clear, about 1 minute.
- If more sauce is desired, add more broth and cornstarch.

Shrimp and Mushrooms

Serves 4-6

½ cup olive oil
2 teaspoons minced garlic
Salt and pepper to taste
2 pounds shrimp, peeled
2 (4-ounce) cans mushrooms
Juice of 1 lemon
½ cup sherry
Parsley, chopped
Parmesan cheese

- Heat oil in skillet. Add garlic, salt and pepper.
- Add shrimp, stirring until pink.
- Add mushrooms, lemon juice and sherry.
- Steam for 6-8 minutes.
- Arrange in individual ramekins.
- Top with chopped parsley, then Parmesan cheese.
- Place under broiler or put in microwave for several minutes until heated and cheese melts.

Shrimp Creole

Serves 6-8

½ cup flour
½ cup bacon drippings
1½ cup chopped green onion
1½ cup chopped onions
1 cup chopped celery
1 cup chopped green pepper
3 cloves garlic, crushed
1 tablespoon dried parsley
1 (6-ounce) can tomato paste
1 (16-ounce) can chopped
   tomatoes with liquid or
   tomato purée
1 (8-ounce) can tomato sauce
½ cup red wine and ½ cup
   water or 1 cup water
4 teaspoons salt
¾ teaspoon black pepper
¼-½ teaspoon red pepper
   (optional)
Tabasco sauce, to taste
1 teaspoon sugar
1 tablespoon lemon juice
3 bay leaves
¼ teaspoon dried basil
½ teaspoon dried thyme
3-4 pounds peeled, deveined
   raw shrimp

- Make a dark brown roux of flour and bacon drippings. This takes about 15 minutes but it's the most important part in most creole recipes. Simply cook and stir flour and bacon grease over medium heat until mixture is a dark brown - not burned.
- Add onions, celery, bell pepper, garlic and parsley.
- Saute' until soft, 15-20 minutes.
- Add tomato paste and mix well.
- Add remaining ingredients and spices, except shrimp.
- Simmer over very low heat for 1 hour, stirring occasionally.
- Add shrimp and cook only until shrimp is done, 5-15 minutes. Do not overcook shrimp.

Hint: This is best made the day before or at least long enough for shrimp to absorb the flavors of the sauce. Reheat before serving, but do not boil.

For sweet, juicy-tasting rock shrimp, submerge shrimp in boiling water for only 25 seconds. Overcooking toughens the meat and destroys the taste. The shells hold heat, and the shrimp will continue to cook after they are removed from the boiling water.

Shrimp Scampi

Serves 6

2 pounds large raw shrimp
1 cup melted butter
½ cup olive oil
½ cup vermouth
1 tablespoons finely minced
  garlic
1 teaspoon salt
½ teaspoon white pepper
1 tablespoon M.S.G.
Juice of 2 lemons
4 tablespoons chopped fresh
  parsley
¼ cup chopped scallions,
  including tops
1 tablespoon chopped capers
¼ cup fresh grated Parmesan
  cheese

- Wash, shell and devein shrimp, leaving tails intact.
- Combine next 9 ingredients in blender. Blend on high speed for 10 seconds.
- Arrange shrimp in large flame-proof shallow serving dish.
- Pour marinade over shrimp and let stand at room temperature 1 hour.
- Sprinkle scallions, cheese and capers over shrimp.
- Place shrimp in preheated broiler 3-4 inches from heat for 5 minutes or until browned. Turn over and broil 1-2 minutes, until brown and firm to touch.

Shrimps de Jonghe

Serves 6

2 pounds raw shrimp, unshelled
¼ cup lemon juice
1 stalk celery, chopped
1 small onion, chopped
2 bay leaves
¼ cup sour cream
½ cup butter or margarine,
  softened
1 cup bread crumbs
¼ cup chopped parsley
2 cloves garlic, minced
1 teaspoon Worcestershire
  sauce
1 teaspoon bottled steak sauce
1 teaspoon salt
Dash fresh ground black pepper

- Place unshelled shrimp in 6 cups boiling water. Add 2 tablespoons lemon juice, celery, onion and bay leaves. Cover. Bring to boil.
- Reduce heat and simmer gently until shrimp turn pink, about 5-6 minutes. Remove from heat and let cool in cooking liquid.
- Cream softened butter with remaining ingredients.
- Drain, peel and clean shrimp.
- Place in 6 individual baking dishes. Cover with butter mixture.
- Bake at 400° until shrimp are heated through, about 15 minutes.

Shrimp Rosemary

Serves 4-6

½ cup olive oil
1 teaspoon rosemary
½ teaspoon oregano
6 garlic cloves, minced
Salt and pepper to taste
2 pounds raw shrimp, peeled
1 cup sherry

- Heat olive oil in frying pan.
- Add rosemary, oregano, garlic, salt and pepper.
- Put shrimp in hot pan and fry until pink, stirring constantly.
- Add sherry. Stir.
- Cover and steam on low for 6-8 minutes.

Shrimp Thermidor

Serves 4

¾-1 pound shrimp
½ cup sliced mushrooms
¼ cup melted butter
¼ cup flour
1 teaspoon salt
¼ teaspoon dry mustard
Dash cayenne
2 cups milk
Paprika
Grated Parmesan cheese

Variation: May substitute scallops for shrimp.

- Cook and clean shrimp.
- Cook mushrooms in butter for 5 minutes.
- Blend in flour and seasonings.
- Add milk gradually, stirring constantly until very thick.
- Stir in shrimp and pour into greased individual dishes or baking shells.
- Sprinkle cheese and paprika on top.
- Bake at 400° for 10 minutes until brown.

Shrimp Verde

Serves 4

1 pound raw shrimp
Salt and freshly ground
  pepper
2 tablespoons plus 4
  teaspoons flour
¼ cup olive oil
¼ cup chopped green onions
1 tablespoon finely chopped
  garlic
¾ cup fish broth or clam juice
  (bottled clam juice may be
  used)
½ cup dry white wine
¼ teaspoon dried red pepper
  flakes
½ cup finely chopped parsley
½ cup green peas, preferably
  fresh, cooked briefly in
  boiling salted water and
  drained

- Peel and devein shrimp, leaving last tail segment intact.
- Sprinkle with salt and pepper to taste. Coat on all sides with 2 tablespoons flour.
- Shake off any excess flour.
- Heat oil in a skillet large enough to hold the shrimp in 1 layer.
- Add shrimp and cook about 45 seconds on each side.
- Quickly transfer shrimp to another skillet.
- Leave oil in the original skillet.
- To oil in skillet add the remaining flour, stirring with a whisk.
- Add chopped green onions and garlic while stirring.
- Add fish broth and wine. Stir.
- Cook over moderately high heat, stirring often, for about 1 minute. Add pepper flakes.
- Add the parsley and stir to blend.
- Spoon sauce over the shrimp and add the peas. Stir.
- Bring to a boil and simmer about 2 minutes.
- Serve piping hot with rice.

 To get rid of "canned" taste of canned shrimp, soak them in a little sherry and 2 tablespoons of vinegar for 15 minutes.

Space Coast Shrimp Curry

Serves 4

5 tablespoons butter
3 tablespoons flour
1-2 teaspoons curry powder
½ teaspoon salt
¼ teaspoon paprika
Dash nutmeg
2 cups half and half
3 cups cleaned, cooked
　　shrimp
1 teaspoon ginger
1 tablespoon lemon juice
1 teaspoon sherry
1 teaspoon grated onion
Dash Worcestershire sauce

- In a saucepan or skillet, melt butter. Blend in next 5 ingredients.
- Gradually stir in cream. Cook and stir until mixture thickens and bubbles.
- Add remaining ingredients. Heat through.
- Pour into casserole appropriate for serving.
- Bake at 400° for 10 minutes or until top is lightly brown.
- Serve with curry condiments: chutney, grated orange peel, flaked coconut and chopped peanuts.
- May also be served with rice cooked with orange juice instead of water.

Tasty Shrimp

Serves 6

2 pounds fresh medium
　　shrimp
½ cup butter
1 clove garlic, minced
¾ teaspoon salt
⅛ teaspoon pepper
½ cup minced parsley

- Peel and devein shrimp. Wash and dry.
- Melt butter in skillet over medium heat. Add garlic and salt. Brown and stir.
- Add shrimp. Cook until underside turns pink. Turn and cook other side for about 5 minutes.
- Add pepper and additional salt, if desired.
- Sprinkle with minced parsley.
- Cook 1 minute longer.

Leghorn Seafood Stew

¼ cup olive oil
¼ cup finely chopped onion
1 teaspoon finely chopped garlic
½ teaspoon crumbled sage leaves
½ cup dry white wine
2 tablespoons tomato paste, dissolved in 1 cup water
½ cup fresh or bottled clam juice
2 bay leaves
1 teaspoon salt
½ pound squid, cut in ½-inch strips (optional)
2 (1-pound) lobsters, cut up
½ pound each of 2 kinds fine white fish (bass, snapper, haddock, flounder) cut into 2-inch pieces
½ pound sliced sea scallops
2 tablespoons finely chopped fresh parsley
1 freshly grated lemon peel

- Heat olive oil in a heavy 4-6-quart saucepan or flameproof casserole.
- Add onion and cook over moderate heat, stirring frequently, for 8-10 minutes, until lightly colored.
- Add garlic and sage. Cook, stirring for 1 minute longer.
- Pour in wine and boil briskly over high heat, stirring constantly, until reduced to about ¼ cup.
- Add tomato paste and water, clam juice, bay leaves and salt.
- Reduce heat and simmer sauce, partially covered, for 10 minutes.
- Drop squid into the sauce. Cover and cook for 10 minutes. Add lobster. Cover and cook another 5 minutes.
- Add the white fish. Cover and cook for 5 minutes.
- Finally, add scallops and cook, covered, for 5 minutes longer.
- With large slotted spoon, carefully transfer cooked fish and seafood to a heated serving platter, arranging them as attractively as possible (a lobster shell may be reserved to decorate center of tray).
- Simmer sauce for a moment. Taste seasoning. Spoon sauce over fish and seafood. Sprinkle with chopped parsley and grated lemon peel.
- Arrange slices of garlic toast around the platter.

 If soup or stew is too salty, add cut raw potatoes and discard once they have cooked and absorbed the salt.

Reggae Ragoût

Serves 6

1½ cups Uncle Ben's wild rice
    mix, cooked
1 green pepper, chopped
1 cup chopped celery
1 onion, diced
1 pound mushrooms,
    chopped and sautéed
1 pound lobster, cut up
½ pound crabmeat, cleaned
½ pound shrimp, shelled
1 teaspoon curry
1 teaspoon Worcestershire
1½ cups mayonnaise
Bread crumbs and butter

- Mix ingredients together (except bread crumbs and butter) in an ungreased casserole.
- Put buttered crumbs on top.
- Bake 45 minutes at 350°

Grouper Margarite
from the Mango Tree, Cocoa Beach

Serves 4

4 grouper fillets
salt and pepper to taste
½ cup water
½ cup fresh lemon juice
12 ounces peeled shrimp
12 ounces scallops
4 tablespoons butter
1 finely minced garlic clove
Hollandaise sauce

- Place fish in baking dish. Salt and pepper to taste.
- Pour mixture of water and lemon juice over fish.
- Bake 10-12 minutes at 350° until water evaporates.
- While fish is baking, sauté shrimp and scallops in butter with garlic for 3-4 minutes.
- Drain away butter. Spoon shrimp and scallops over each fillet.
- Top with hollandaise sauce. Place under broiler until brown.

Adriatic Style Fish

From the Mango Tree, Cocoa Beach

Serves 6

6 (7-ounce) fillets, grouper or
  snapper

Sauce
2 cups olive oil (extra virgin)
3-4 cloves freshly chopped
  garlic
1 cup fresh lemon juice
3 tablespoons chopped
  parsley
2 tablespoons chopped
  dillweed
2 tablespoons salt

- Mix sauce ingredients. Oil will separate and rise to top.
- Dip fillets in oil. Cook 3-4 minutes on each side in cast iron skillet or on griddle until done.
- Warm remaining sauce. Stir and pour over fish before serving.

Cold Lobster in Dill Sauce

from the Phoenix, Satellite Beach

Serves 2

½ onion
½ lemon
2 bay leaves
4 garlic cloves
2 teaspoons salt
1 tablespoon vinegar
1 medium-sized live lobster
lettuce

Sauce
1½ cups mayonnaise
1½ tablespoons finely
  chopped fresh dillweed
½ cup heavy cream
½ teaspoon salt
½ teaspoon white pepper
1 teaspoon lemon juice
brandy to taste

- In large pot of boiling water add first 6 ingredients.
- Drop in lobster. Simmer 20 minutes. Remove lobster and let cool.
- Split lobster in half. Rinse to clean.
- Remove meat from shell and cut into slices.
- Clean shells and line with shredded lettuce. Lay lobster slices over top.
- Mix sauce ingredients thoroughly.
- Pour sauce over lobster.
- Serve with garnishes of boiled eggs, black olives, tomatoes, white asparagus spears.

VEGETABLES

Manatee Pair, By Charles Velek. Original Watercolor, 30x48.

Vegetables

Seminole Saute'

Serves 10

1 large spaghetti squash
4 large zucchini
1 head cauliflower
1 large bunch broccoli
2 large onions
3 carrots, grated
2 ounces butter
Garlic powder to taste
Salt and pepper to taste
Parmesan cheese

- Pierce squash in several places and bake 1½ hours at 350°.
- Cut in half and remove seeds.
- Rake with fork to make spaghetti.
- Slice all vegetables into small pieces.
- Heat butter and seasonings in large skillet or Dutch oven. Sauté vegetables until very soft.
- Serve vegetables over squash and sprinkle with cheese.

Artichoke Bottoms with Hollandaise

Serves 8

3 egg yolks
¼ cup lemon juice
½ cup firm butter
2 (14-ounce) cans artichoke bottoms, chilled
Paprika

- Stir egg yolks and lemon juice briskly with wooden spoon in small saucepan.
- Add half the butter. Stir over very low heat, until butter is melted. Add and melt remaining butter, stirring briskly until sauce thickens. (Melt butter very slowly to allow eggs to cook and thicken sauce without curdling.) Cool slightly.
- Cover and refrigerate 1 hour.
- Drain artichoke bottoms.
- Arrange on serving platter. Spoon about 1 tablespoon sauce into each artichoke bottom.
- Sprinkle with paprika.
- Garnish with watercress, if desired.

Heart's Delight

Serves 6-8

2 (10-ounce) boxes frozen
  chopped spinach
½ cup butter
6 ounces cream cheese
1 (8½-ounce) jar marinated
  artichoke hearts, drained
  and chopped
¼ teaspoon pepper
1 tablespoon lemon juice
1 tablespoon Parmesan
  cheese
1 tablespoon seasoned bread
  crumbs

- Cook spinach and drain well.
- Combine butter and cheese.
  Heat until butter melts.
- Combine these and all other
  ingredients, except Parmesan
  cheese and bread crumbs.
- Put in greased 1½-quart
  casserole.
- Top with bread crumbs and
  Parmesan cheese.
- Bake at 350° for 30 minutes.

Asparagus and Company

Serves 6

2 (10-ounce) packages frozen,
  cut asparagus
1 can cream of onion soup
½ cup sour cream
¼ cup shredded carrot
½ teaspoon instant minced
  onion
⅛ teaspoon black pepper
½ cup herb-seasoned stuffing
  mix
1 tablespoon melted
  margarine

*Hint: If made ahead and
  refrigerated, increase baking
  time to 40-45 minutes.*

- Cook asparagus according to
  package instructions.
- Drain well.
- Combine asparagus, onion soup,
  sour cream, carrot, onion and
  pepper.
- Pour into ungreased 1-quart
  casserole.
- Combine stuffing mix with
  margarine. Sprinkle around edge
  of casserole.
- Bake uncovered at 350° for 30-35
  minutes.

Crunchy Creamy Casserole

Serves 8

2 cans green beans, drained
1 pint sour cream
8-ounce package Swiss
  cheese, grated
2 tablespoons melted butter
2 teaspoons flour
1 teaspoon salt
¼ teaspoon pepper
2 tablespoons sugar
4 teaspoons grated onion

Topping
6 teaspoons melted butter
2 cups crushed corn flakes

- Combine beans, sour cream and cheese.
- Stir in all other ingredients, except topping. Place in buttered casserole.
- Melt 6 teaspoons butter and add 2 cups crushed corn flakes.
- Sprinkle mixture over top of casserole.
- Bake at 350° for 30 minutes.

Howard Twilley's Green Beans

Serves 8

2 packages frozen French cut
  green beans
½ teaspoon summer savory
¼ teaspoon oregano
¼ teaspoon basil
¼ teaspoon garlic salt
2 tablespoons butter, melted

- Cook beans according to directions on package.
- Drain.
- Add butter and seasonings, toss and serve.

This was the Twilley contribution to all Miami Dolphin team gatherings during the perfect season in 1972 — 17 wins, no losses, and World Champions!

Fancy Green Beans

Serves 6-8

2 (9-ounce) packages frozen
  French-style green beans
6 slices bacon, diced
½ cup diced onion
¼ cup all-purpose flour
2 chicken bouillon cubes in
  1½ cups water or 1½ cups
  fresh chicken stock
⅛ teaspoon pepper
½ cup shredded cheddar
  cheese
Chopped water chestnuts
  (optional)

- Cook green beans according to directions. Drain.
- Preheat oven to 350°.
- Cook diced bacon and onion until browned.
- Stir in flour. When blended, gradually add liquid and pepper.
- Cook, stirring constantly until thickened (very thick).
- Add beans and chestnuts. Stir until blended.
- Pour in 1½-quart casserole. Cover with grated cheese and bake for 30 minutes.

Ranch House Beans

Serves 8-10

1 pound dried pinto beans
½ pound slab bacon, cut into
  1-inch pieces
Salt
3-4 cloves garlic, chopped
2 onions, chopped
1 green pepper, chopped
1 (32-ounce) can tomatoes
Dried hot pepper, to taste

- Cook beans with bacon and salt until tender, about 3 hours.
- Add onions, green pepper and garlic.
- Put tomatoes in bottom of large roaster. Pour beans over top.
- Cover and bake at 325° for 1 hour.

256

Banquet Broccoli

Serves 4-6

1 (10-ounce) package frozen
  chopped broccoli
3 carrots, sliced
1 (14-ounce) can artichoke
  hearts, drained and
  quartered
¾ can cream of mushroom
  soup, undiluted
½ cup mayonnaise
2 eggs, slightly beaten
1 teaspoon lemon juice
1 teaspoon Worcestershire
  sauce
1 cup shredded sharp
  cheddar cheese
Bread crumbs
¼ cup melted butter or
  margarine
Garlic salt

- Cook broccoli until tender. Drain and set aside.
- Cook carrots until tender. Drain and set aside.
- Place artichokes in a buttered 9-inch shallow casserole.
- Combine soup, mayonnaise, eggs, lemon juice and Worcestershire sauce. Mix well.
- Combine soup mixture, broccoli and carrots. Pour over artichokes.
- Sprinkle with cheese and bread crumbs and pour melted butter over top.
- Sprinkle with garlic salt.
- Bake at 350° for 25 minutes.

Stir-fry Broccoli

1 bunch fresh broccoli
3 tablespoons oil
2 cups chopped celery
3 tablespoons soy sauce
½ teaspoon ginger

- Slice broccoli into ½-inch thick slices.
- Heat oil in wok or a large frying pan over medium-high heat.
- Stir in broccoli and celery.
- Cook until wilted.
- Add soy sauce and ginger.
- Cover and steam 5-8 minutes until crisply tender.

Marinated Broccoli and Cauliflower

Serves 8

1 bunch fresh broccoli
1 head fresh cauliflower
½ cup white vinegar
½ cup cider vinegar
½ cup vegetable oil
1 tablespoon dillweed
1 tablespoon M.S.G.
1 teaspoon salt
1 teaspoon pepper
1 teaspoon garlic salt

- Break broccoli and cauliflower into florets.
- Place uncooked into glass dish.
- Mix remaining ingredients and pour over.
- Let marinate at least 6 hours or overnight.

Brussels Sprouts in Mustard Herb Sauce

Serves 4-6

1¼ pound Brussels sprouts
1 teaspoon prepared mustard
1 teaspoon Worcestershire sauce
1 teaspoon sugar
1 teaspoon salt
½ teaspoon dry basil
¼ teaspoon thyme
¼ teaspoon pepper
¼ cup red wine vinegar
1 cup salad oil
½ cup thinly sliced green onion
2 cups cherry tomatoes

- Clean sprouts and cut in half lengthwise.
- Cook in salted boiling water about 7-10 minutes until just crisp tender. Drain well.
- Combine all other ingredients, except cherry tomatoes.
- Transfer warm Brussels sprouts to bowl and pour over mustard dressing, mixing to coat.
- Cover and chill at least 4 hours, stirring occasionally.
- Just before serving, stir in cherry tomatoes, cut in half lengthwise.

Creole Cabbage

Serves 6-8

2-4 slices bacon, cut up
1 large onion, chopped
1 green pepper, chopped
1 (28-ounce) can tomatoes,
chopped (save juice)
1 head cabbage, coarsely
chopped
2 teaspoons salt
½ teaspoon pepper
Dash Tabasco
Dash cayenne pepper
1 clove garlic, minced

- Saute' bacon, onion and pepper.
- Add tomatoes, juice and cabbage. Stir well.
- Add all other ingredients. Stir well.
- Bring to a boil and cover.
- Simmer for 30 minutes.

Marna's Swamp Cabbage

Serves 20

5 pounds swamp cabbage,
diced
1½ pounds smoked ham,
diced
1 tablespoon salt
2 teaspoons pepper
1 tablespoon M.S.G.
Water to cover cabbage

- Place all ingredients in large pot. Bring to a boil.
- Cook on medium heat until done, about 20 minutes. Adjust salt and pepper to taste.

Hint: Immediately upon removing heart of palm from palm tree, cover with water. Cabbage will turn black when exposed to air.

 Big Mama Sellars says a pinch of soda when cooking vegetables will reduce the chance of indigestion.

Scalloped Carrots

Serves 8

12 carrots, sliced
¼ cup butter
1 small onion, minced
¼ cup flour
1 teaspoon salt
¼ teaspoon dry mustard
2 cups milk
⅛ teaspoon pepper
⅛ teaspoon celery salt
½ pound sliced cheddar
   cheese
3 cups buttered bread
   crumbs

- Cook and drain carrots.
- Saute' onion in butter.
- Stir in flour, salt and dry
  mustard.
- Add milk. Stir until smooth.
- Add pepper and celery salt.
- In casserole dish, alternate layers
  of cheese, carrots and sauce.
- Top with buttered bread crumbs.
- Bake for 25 minutes at 350°.

Zesty Carrots

Serves 6-8

6-8 carrots, scraped and cut
   lengthwise into 4 pieces
¼ cup water
1-2 tablespoons grated onion,
   or to taste
1-2 tablespoons horseradish,
   or to taste
½ cup mayonnaise
½ teaspoon salt
¼ teaspoon pepper
¼ cup cracker crumbs
1 teaspoon butter

- Cook carrots in ½ cup water
  until fork tender. Drain.
- Toss with other ingredients,
  except crumbs and butter.
- Spoon into baking dish and top
  with crumbs and butter.
- Garnish with paprika.
- Bake at 375° for 15-20 minutes.

Celery Cypress Gardens

Serves 6

4 cups 1-inch celery slices
5-ounce can water chestnuts,
  drained and sliced
1 can cream of chicken soup
¼ cup diced pimiento
½ cup soft bread crumbs
¼ cup toasted slivered
  almonds
2 tablespoons melted butter

- Cook celery slices in a small amount of salted, boiling water until crisp-done, about 8 minutes. Drain.
- Mix celery, water chestnuts, cream of chicken soup and pimiento in a 1-quart casserole.
- Toss bread crumbs with toasted slivered almonds and butter. Sprinkle over casserole.
- Bake in 350° oven for 35 minutes.

Eggplant Americano

Serves 6-8

1 large eggplant
Butter
1 onion, chopped
2 large fresh tomatoes, sliced
½ small green pepper,
  chopped
¼ pound American cheese,
  grated

- Peel and slice eggplant ½-inch thick.
- Cut slices in half and brown in butter.
- Place in buttered casserole in layers: eggplant, onion, tomatoes, pepper and small amount of cheese.
- Withhold top layer of cheese.
- Cover and bake at 375° for 45 minutes.
- Remove and sprinkle remainder of cheese. Return to oven until cheese melts.

Deep-fried Eggplant

Serves 4-6

2 ripe firm eggplants, unpared
Flour, as needed
1¼ cups milk
3 eggs
Salt and pepper
1 cup cracker crumbs

- Cut eggplant top to bottom, then cut into strips.
- Dip in flour.
- Dip into mixture of milk and eggs.
- Add salt and pepper.
- Coat with cracker crumbs.
- Fry in heavy pan with hot oil.
- Cook until golden brown.

Fluffy Eggplant Casserole

Serves 4-6

1 large eggplant, peeled and
**   cut into 1-inch cubes**
½ cup cream of mushroom
**   soup**
5-6 tablespoons mayonnaise
1 egg
⅛ teaspoon onion juice
¾ cup saltine cracker crumbs
3 tablespoons margarine,
**   melted**
1 cup sharp cheddar cheese,
**   grated**
Salt to taste

- Cook eggplant in boiling salted water for 8-10 minutes. Drain.
- Mix all ingredients, except ¼ cup of cracker crumbs.
- Spoon into greased 1-quart dish.
- Top with remaining cracker crumbs.
- Bake at 350° for 30 minutes.

 Celery keeps longer stored in paper bags instead of plastic ones. Do not remove outside leaves or stalks until ready to use.

Layered Vegetable and Cheese Bake

Serves 6-8

1 tablespoon vegetable oil
1 large onion, coarsely
 chopped
1 large green pepper, cut into
 1-inch squares
1 small eggplant, pared and
 cut into 1-inch squares
½ pound mushrooms, sliced
1 large tomato, chopped
1 teaspoon salt
½ teaspoon thyme
Dash pepper
1 cup packaged herb-
 seasoned stuffing mix
2 cups shredded Swiss
 cheese, divided

- In a large skillet, heat oil over medium heat. Sauté onion and green pepper 3 minutes.
- Add eggplant and mushrooms. Sauté 3 minutes. Stir constantly.
- Add tomato, salt, thyme and pepper. Cook 1 minute.
- Spread stuffing mix over bottom of buttered 9 x 13 x 2-inch baking dish.
- Layer half of vegetable mixture and 1 cup cheese over stuffing.
- Top with remaining vegetables.
- Bake, covered, at 350° for 30 minutes.
- Sprinkle with remaining cheese and bake, uncovered, for 10 minutes more until cheese melts.

Mushrooms au Gratin

Serves 4

3 tablespoons butter
1 pound fresh mushrooms,
 halved
¼ cup chopped onion
Salt and pepper
1 cup sour cream
1 tablespoon flour
Grated Parmesan cheese
Dry bread crumbs

- Melt butter in a large skillet. Add mushrooms, onion, salt and pepper.
- Cover and simmer over medium-low heat for 7-10 minutes or until tender. Drain.
- Spoon mushrooms into a lightly greased shallow 1½-quart baking dish.
- Mix sour cream and flour well. Spread over mushrooms.
- Sprinkle with cheese and bread crumbs. Broil 3-5 minutes or until lightly browned.

Mushroom Business

Serves 6-8

1 pound mushrooms
8 slices bread
½ cup chopped green pepper
½ cup chopped onion
½ cup chopped celery
3 tablespoons butter
½ cup mayonnaise
¾ teaspoon salt
¼ teaspoon pepper
2 eggs
1½ cups milk
1 (10¾-ounce) can cream of
  mushroom soup
¼ pound cheddar cheese

- Wash and coarsely chop mushrooms.
- Butter and cube bread. Separate into 3 portions.
- Place 1 portion in 2-quart casserole.
- Sauté mushrooms, green pepper, onions and celery in butter for 5 minutes over low heat.
- Add mayonnaise, salt and pepper. Place on bread cubes.
- Add another portion of bread cubes.
- Mix eggs and milk and pour over top of casserole.
- Refrigerate at least 1 hour.
- Spoon on mushroom soup.
- Add last portion of bread cubes.
- Bake at 300° for 1 hour.
- Sprinkle with cheese. Return to oven until cheese melts.

Down Home Okra and Tomatoes

Serves 6

1 large onion, chopped
2 stalks celery, chopped
1 tablespoon bacon grease
1 pound fresh okra, sliced
1¼ teaspoon salt
½ teaspoon paprika
2½ cups fresh tomatoes or 1
  (16-ounce) can tomatoes
  with liquid
¼ teaspoon curry powder
2 teaspoons brown sugar

- Saute' onion and celery in bacon grease.
- Add okra and cook for 5 minutes.
- Add remaining ingredients. Cover and cook until tender, about 30 minutes.

Gourmet Onions

Serves 6

5 medium-sized onions, sliced
½ teaspoon M.S.G.
½ teaspoon sugar
½ teaspoon salt
½ teaspoon pepper
½ cup sherry
5-6 tablespoons margarine or
butter
2 tablespoons grated
Parmesan cheese

- Season onions with M.S.G., sugar, salt and pepper.
- Melt butter and cook onions for 5-8 minutes or until onions are barely tender.
- Stir to separate rings.
- Add sherry and cook an additional 3 minutes.
- Sprinkle with cheese and serve hot.

Beer Batter Onion Rings

Serves 6-8

1½ cups flour
1 teaspoon salt
1½ cups beer
3 large onions, cut into ½-
inch slices
Oil
Salt

Hint: For extra-crisp rings, soak onions in ice-cold milk (add cubes as necessary) for 1 hour.

- Combine flour and salt.
- Stir in beer and beat.
- Let stand 3 hours.
- Separate onion slices into rings. Dip in batter and fry in 2-inches very hot oil on both sides, 3-5 minutes.
- Sprinkle with salt and keep warm in 200° oven.

Bahamian Pigeon Peas and Rice
from Grand Bahama Island Hotel

Serves 4-6

1 small onion, finely chopped
1 stalk celery, finely chopped
1 heaping tablespoon tomato
  paste
1 (8-ounce) can pigeon peas,
  drained
2½ cups water
2 cups white rice
Salt to taste
Pepper to taste
Pinch thyme
Dash Tabasco, to taste

*Note: If using dried pigeon peas,
  cook according to package
  directions. May substitute
  black-eyed peas.*

- Sauté onion and celery in small
  amount of cooking oil until tender.
- Add tomato paste and peas
  stirring constantly to prevent
  sticking.
- Set aside.
- Place water in a pot and bring to
  a boil. Add rice and vegetable
  mixture with seasonings.
- Leave pot uncovered until
  bubbling again.
- Stir rice mixture, cover and
  lower heat.
- Cook until rice is well cooked.
  Stir and serve.

Creole Peas

Serves 8-10

1 cup diced celery
1 cup diced green pepper
1 cup diced onion
2 hot peppers, chopped
½ cup salad oil
2 (16-ounce) cans stewed
  tomatoes
6 cups cooked (or canned)
  black-eyed peas
1 pound okra, sliced and
  sautéed separately
2 teaspoons salt

- Saute' celery, green pepper,
  onion and hot pepper in oil until
  tender, stirring frequently. Set
  aside.
- Coarsely chop tomatoes and add
  with juice to sauteed vegetables.
- Stir in peas, okra and salt.
- Bring to a boil. Lower heat and
  simmer until okra is tender.

Hoppin' John

Serves 4-6

2 cups dried black-eyed peas
¼ pound lean salt pork,
  cubed
2 cups cooked rice
Salt and pepper, to taste
Cayenne pepper, to taste

- Wash peas and soak overnight.
- Drain, add salt pork and cover with water. Add salt and pepper.
- Cook 40-50 minutes, or until tender. Check liquid. Do not let boil dry.
- Stir in cooked rice. Adjust seasoning. Add cayenne. Blend well.
- Cover, place over low heat.
- Serve immediately.

Peas Epicurean

Serves 8

4 strips bacon
½ large Bermuda onion,
  chopped
1 cup sliced mushroom caps
1 cup heavy cream or half
  and half
1 tablespoon flour
¼ cup sherry
Dash Worcestershire sauce
Salt and pepper to taste
1 (16-ounce) can English peas

- Chop raw bacon into pieces and sauté with onion and mushrooms until brown.
- Add flour and cream. Stir constantly on low heat until thickened.
- Add sherry and seasonings.
- Fold peas in gently.

 Southern cooks know the secret of flavorful leafy vegetables and legumes is adding at least 2 tablespoons of bacon drippings and 2 tablespoons of sugar while cooking.

Pea Pods with Almonds

Serves 3-4

½ cup water
1 tablespoon soy sauce
1½ teaspoons cornstarch
1 teaspoon instant chicken
  bouillon granules
2 tablespoons butter or
  margarine
2 tablespoons slivered
  almonds
1 (6-ounce) package frozen
  pea pods
1 (4-ounce) can sliced
  mushrooms, drained

- Combine water, soy sauce, corn-starch and bouillon granules. Set aside.
- Melt butter or margarine in a 10-inch skillet.
- Add almonds. Stir-fry 2 minutes or until lightly browned.
- Add pea pods. Stir-fry 2 minutes and stir in mushrooms.
- Stir cornstarch mixture into above and stir until thickened and bubbly. Let cook for 2 minutes and serve.

New Potatoes with Basil

Serves 6

6 cups new potatoes,
  unpeeled
3-4 tablespoons olive oil (or ½
  olive oil and ½ butter)
1 cup chicken broth
Salt to taste
Pepper to taste
¼ cup fresh basil, chopped

*Hint: Herbs other than basil
  may be used. If dried herbs
  are substituted, use about 1/3
  the quantity and rub them
  between your palms to
  release the flavor.*

- Scrub and slice potatoes ¼-inch thick.
- In a large skillet, quickly saute' potatoes in oil until they begin to brown.
- Add just enough broth to cover.
- Reduce heat and cook, covered, until liquid is absorbed, about 15 minutes.
- Allow potatoes to brown slightly.
- Add salt, pepper and basil.

Potato Pancakes

Yields 8-12 pancakes

2 cups raw potatoes - finely
   grated or finely chopped in
   food processor
2 eggs
2 teaspoons salt
1 tablespoon flour
Grated onion (optional)

- Mix all ingredients.
- Pour ¼ cup mixture in ½-¾ inch hot oil. Spread evenly in circles.
- Fry until brown, turn and brown on other side. Drain on paper towel. Serve with applesauce or sour cream.

Sour Cream Potato Casserole

Serves 10

6 medium potatoes
2 cups shredded cheddar
   cheese
½ stick butter
2 cups sour cream
¼ cup chopped green onions
Salt and pepper to taste
2 tablespoons butter

- Boil potatoes until almost tender. Do not overcook. Peel.
- Grate cheese and potatoes.
- Combine all remaining ingredients in large bowl. Mix well and pour into greased casserole.
- Dot with remaining butter.
- Bake at 350° for 25 minutes.

 Overcooked potatoes can get soggy when the milk is added. Sprinkle with dry powdered milk for the fluffiest mashed potatoes ever.

Yam Good Potatoes

Serves 8

½ cup brown sugar, divided in half
½ cup orange juice, divided in half
6 tablespoons butter or margarine, melted and halved
2 (16-ounce) cans sweet potatoes, drained
2 eggs
1 teaspoon salt
¼ teaspoon ground cloves
1 teaspoon ground cinnamon
1 cup chopped pecans
Marshmallows

- Glaze: Combine ½ brown sugar, ½ orange juice and ½ butter. Mix and set aside.
- Whip potatoes until smooth.
- Beat in eggs. Add remaining sugar, juice and butter.
- Add salt, cloves and cinnamon.
- Mix well and pour into 1½-quart casserole. Sprinkle pecans on top. Pour glaze over pecans.
- Bake 350° for 40 minutes.
- Top with marshmallows and place under broiler until marshmallows are light brown.

Variation: For a different topping, mix together the following: ½ cup crushed cornflakes, ¼ cup brown sugar, ¼ cup butter or margarine, ½ cup coconut and ¼ cup chopped nuts (omitting nuts in potato mixture). Instead of glaze, bake casserole at 400° for 20-25 minutes. Spread topping over potato mixture and return to oven for 15 minutes.

 Did you know? To remove corn silk presto, dampen a paper towel and brush downward on the cob. Every strand will come off!

Spinach Ring

Serves 6-8

2 pounds fresh spinach or 2
    (10-ounce) packages
    frozen, chopped spinach
Grated Parmesan cheese
4 tablespoons butter or
    margarine
½ cup chopped onion
1 cup light cream
1 teaspoon salt
½ teaspoon sugar
Dash pepper
Dash nutmeg
4 eggs
½ cup fresh bread crumbs
½ cup grated Swiss or
    Gruyère cheese

- Wash spinach. Remove and discard large stems.
- Place in large kettle with just the water clinging to leaves.
- Cook, covered, for 5 minutes or until just tender. Toss with fork once or twice.
- Drain very well.
- Chop coarsely.
- If using frozen spinach, cook according to package directions and drain very well.
- Grease 4½ cup ring mold and dust with grated Parmesan cheese.
- Melt butter in large saucepan. Add onion and saute' until tender. Add spinach, cream, salt, sugar, pepper and nutmeg. Heat just to boiling. Remove from heat.
- In large bowl, beat eggs slightly.
- Add bread crumbs and cheese. Gradually stir in spinach mixture.
- Turn into prepared mold.
- Set mold in baking pan on oven rack. Pour boiling water into pan to depth of 1½ inches.
- Place a piece of waxed paper over top of mold.
- Bake at 350° 30-35 minutes or until knife inserted in center of spinach mixture comes out clean.
- Loosen mold around edge with a small spatula. Invert onto heated serving plate.

Spinach with Sour Cream

Serves 4-5

1 bag fresh spinach
2 tablespoons water
2 eggs
1 tablespoon chopped onion
½ cup sour cream
1 cup Parmesan cream
1 tablespoon flour
2 tablespoons butter
Dash salt
Dash pepper to taste

- Rinse spinach in cold water and place in pan with 2 tablespoons water.
- Steam spinach until leaves are limp, then drain well.
- Beat eggs and mix with rest of ingredients.
- Combine spinach and egg mixture.
- Bake in greased casserole for 25-30 minutes at 350° or until center is set.
- Do not overcook, as it may separate.

Spinach Souffle'

Serves 8-10

3 tablespoons butter
3 tablespoons flour
1 cup milk
½ teaspoon chopped onion
Salt and pepper to taste
½ pound grated American
  cheese
1 cup cooked spinach or 2
  cartons frozen chopped
  spinach, cooked and
  thoroughly drained
3 eggs, separated

- In a small saucepan over low heat, make sauce of butter, flour and milk.
- Add seasonings, onion and grated cheese, stirring until cheese is melted.
- Remove from heat. Add spinach that has been thoroughly drained.
- Add beaten egg yolks and mix well.
- Fold in beaten egg whites.
- Pour in buttered 2-quart casserole.
- Set casserole in a pan of hot water and bake at 350° until center is firm, approximately 40 minutes.

Party Squash

Serves 8

1 pound sliced yellow squash
1 teaspoon sugar
½ cup mayonnaise
½ cup minced onion
¼ cup finely chopped green
   pepper
½ cup chopped pecans
1 egg, slightly beaten
½ cup grated cheddar cheese
Salt and pepper to taste
Bread or cracker crumbs
½ stick butter or margarine

- Boil squash until tender.
- Drain and mash.
- Add other ingredients, except
  butter and crumbs.
- Mix and place in a 2-quart
  casserole dish.
- Top with crumbs.
- Dot with butter.
- Bake 35-40 minutes at 350°.

Skillet Squash

Serves 6

2 tablespoons olive oil
2 tablespoons butter or
   margarine
3 cups sliced zucchini
3 cups sliced yellow squash
1½ teaspoons chopped fresh
   parsley
1½ teaspoons chopped fresh
   chives
¼ teaspoon dried whole
   tarragon
¼ teaspoon dried whole basil
¼ teaspoon dried dillweed
1½ cloves garlic, minced
¼ teaspoon salt
½ teaspoon pepper
3 tablespoons Parmesan
   cheese, grated

- Heat oil and butter in a large
  skillet. Add remaining
  ingredients, except for Parmesan
  cheese, and sauté 10-15 minutes,
  or until squash is crisp-tender.
- Stir in Parmesan cheese. Serve.

Stuffed Crookneck Squash

Serves 6

6 yellow squash
Boiling, salted water
1 small onion, minced
2 tablespoons butter or
  margarine
Salt and pepper to taste
½ cup bread crumbs
¼ cup shredded cheese
6 slices cooked bacon,
  crumbled

- Cook squash 7-10 minutes in boiling, salted water until barely tender. Cool.
- Cut in half lengthwise and scoop out pulp, leaving shells about ¼ inch thick, reserving pulp.
- Cook onion in butter until tender.
- Add scooped out squash pulp, salt, pepper and bread crumbs.
- Mix well and stuff into shells.
- Top with cheese and bacon.
- Bake at 400° for 15 minutes or until lightly browned.

Zucchini Boats

Serves 4

4 large zucchini
Small onion, chopped
2 tablespoons margarine
1 cup wild rice, cooked
1 cup chopped fresh
  mushrooms
6 ounces shredded Swiss
  cheese
Salt and pepper to taste

- Boil squash in water until skin is cooked (8-10 minutes).
- Cut in half lengthwise and scoop out center, reserving pulp.
- Sauté onion and squash pulp in margarine.
- Add wild rice and mushrooms. Continue stirring.
- Add Swiss cheese and mix well.
- Stuff mixture into zucchini shells.
- Bake 10-15 minutes at 350° until heated through.

Corny Zucchini Bake

Serves 6-8

1 pound zucchini, cut into ½-
inch slices
¼ cup chopped onion
1 tablespoon butter
2 cups cooked corn
2 beaten eggs
1 cup grated Swiss cheese
¼-½ teaspoon salt
¼ cup Italian bread crumbs
2 tablespoons grated
Parmesan cheese
1 tablespoon melted butter

- Cook zucchini in small amount of water until tender. Drain and mash.
- Saute' onion in butter until tender.
- Mix with zucchini, corn, eggs, Swiss cheese and salt.
- Pour into a greased baking dish.
- Combine bread crumbs, Parmesan cheese and melted butter.
- Sprinkle over zucchini mixture.
- Bake at 350° for 40 minutes.

Zucchini Neopolitan

Serves 6

1½ pound zucchini, scrubbed
well and cut crosswise into
¼-inch slices
¼ cup all purpose flour
1½ teaspoon salt
1½ teaspoon dried oregano
¼ teaspoon pepper
¼ cup olive or salad oil
2 medium tomatoes, sliced
1 cup sour cream
½ cup grated Parmesan
cheese

- Preheat oven to 350°.
- In medium bowl combine flour with ½ teaspoon salt, ½ teaspoon oregano and ⅛ teaspoon pepper. Toss zucchini slices in flour to coat well.
- Slowly heat oil in large heavy skillet. Saute' zucchini until golden brown, about 4 minutes on each side. Drain.
- Cover bottom of lightly greased 8 x 8 x 2-inch baking dish with zucchini. Top with tomato slices.
- Combine sour cream, rest of salt, oregano and pepper.
- Spread evenly over tomato slices. Sprinkle with cheese.
- Bake 30-35 minutes or until cheese is melted.

Tomatoes Rockefeller

Serves 6

6 large tomatoes
4 tablespoons butter or
  margarine
½ cup finely chopped onion
2 (10-ounce) packages frozen,
  chopped spinach, cooked
  and drained
1 tablespoon M.S.G.
½ teaspoon thyme
1 teaspoon salt
½ cup seasoned herb
  dressing
1 tablespoon Worcestershire
  sauce
1 clove garlic, crushed
6 drops Tabasco
2 eggs, slightly beaten
¼ cup Parmesan cheese

- Cut tops off tomatoes. Scoop out seeds.
- Turn upside down on paper towels to drain.
- Melt butter. Add onion and cook until tender.
- Add cooked spinach, seasonings and herb dressing. Mix well.
- Add eggs and cook, stirring until well mixed.
- Stuff tomatoes with mixture. Sprinkle cheese over top and dot with additional butter.
- Bake at 350° for 10 minutes or until brown and heated.

Tomatoes Tampa Bay

Serves 4

2 large tomatoes
2 dashes Crazy Jane salt
2 dashes Italian seasoning
4 tablespoons Parmesan cheese
Parsley

- Slice tomatoes in half.
- Sprinkle with salt and seasoning.
- Top with cheese. Bake in ovenproof dish for 30 minutes at 350°.

DESSERTS

Wood Storks, By Charles Velek. Original Watercolor, 24x30.

Desserts

Florida Orange Cake

2 cups strained orange juice
2 cups granulated sugar
1 teaspoon grated orange
  peel
1 cup butter
2 cups sugar
2 teaspoons vanilla
½ teaspoon salt
6 whole eggs
3 cups sifted flour
2 teaspoons baking powder
1 cup milk

- Stir juice, sugar and orange peel until sugar dissolves. Set aside.
- Cream butter, sugar, vanilla and salt.
- Add eggs to creamed mixture. Mix well.
- Sift flour and baking powder together. Add to creamed mixture alternately with milk. Beat only on low speed.
- Bake in a greased and floured 9 x 13-inch pan or three 8-inch pans for 25-35 minutes at 350°.
- While cake is hot, puncture with toothpick and pour juice mixture over top, using back of wooden spoon to spread.

Key Lime Cake

Serves 12-16

Cake
1½ cups sugar
2 cups flour
½ teaspoon salt
1 teaspoon baking powder
½ teaspoon baking soda
1 (3-ounce) package lime gelatin
5 eggs
1¼ cups cooking oil
¾ cup orange juice
½ teaspoon vanilla
1 teaspoon lemon extract

Glaze
3 tablespoons Key lime juice
5 tablespoons powdered sugar
Whipped cream and lime slices
  for garnish

Cake
- Mix all dry ingredients.
- Add liquids and blend well.
- Cook cake in 9 x 13 x 2-inch pan at 350° for 25-30 minutes.
- Cool for 15 minutes.
- Prick holes all over cake with fork.

Glaze
- Mix lime juice and powdered sugar. Drizzle over cake.
- Cover cake and refrigerate in pan.
- To serve, cut in squares and top with whipped cream and thin lime slices.

279

Ambrosia Cake

Serves 12

1 package yellow cake mix

Ambrosia Filling
1 orange, unpeeled, cut in chunks, seeds removed
1½ cups sugar
3 tablespoons cornstarch
¼ teaspoon salt
¼ cup butter
1 cup water
1 (3½-ounce) can flaked coconut

1 can prepared creamy white frosting

To assemble: Split cooled cake layers, making 4 in all. Spread layers (cut side down) and top cake with filling. Spread creamy frosting on sides.

- Prepare cake mix according to package directions.
- Pour into 2 paper-lined 1½ x 8-inch round pans.
- Bake according to instructions.
- Cool 5 minutes. Remove from pans. Cool on racks.
- Blend orange chunks in blender on low until almost smooth to make ¾ cup ground orange.
- Combine sugar, cornstarch, and salt. Add butter, water and orange.
- Cook and stir to boiling point. Cook 2 minutes.
- Cool. Stir in coconut.

Fresh Apple Cake

2 cups sugar
1½ cups vegetable oil
½ teaspoon lemon juice
2 teaspoons vanilla
2 eggs
1 teaspoon salt
3 cups flour
1¼ teaspoon baking soda
½ teaspoon cinnamon
1 cup chopped pecans
3 cups chopped apples, pared

Glaze
1 stick butter
½ cup brown sugar
2 tablespoons milk

- Combine sugar, oil, lemon, vanilla, eggs and salt. Beat well.
- Add all other ingredients, apples last.
- Bake in a tube pan at 350° for 1½ hours.
- Mix butter, brown sugar and milk together in saucepan.
- Bring to a hard boil.
- Drizzle over cake.
- Store in a covered container.

Hint: Best served warm.

Bourbon Cake

1 pound candied red cherries, cut in half
½ pound light raisins, cut in half
1 pint bourbon
3 sticks butter
2 cups granulated sugar
1 cup brown sugar
6 eggs, separated
5 cups sifted all purpose flour
1 teaspoon baking powder
2 teaspoons ground nutmeg
4 cups pecans

- Soak fruit in whiskey overnight.
- Cream butter and sugars until fluffy. Beat in egg yolks.
- Add fruit with remaining whiskey.
- Reserve a small amount of flour for dredging nuts. Sift remaining flour, baking powder and nutmeg. Add to creamed mixture.
- Beat egg whites and fold in.
- Add pecans dredged with flour.
- Bake in large greased tube pan or two 4 x 8 x 2-inch loaf pans. Line bottom of pans with greased paper. Bake at 300° for 3-4 hours, depending on pan size.

Calamondin Supreme Cake

Serves 12-18

1 package lemon-flavored cake mix
1 (3-ounce) package lemon gelatin
5 tablespoons milk
½ cup calamondin purée
4 large eggs
¾ cup cooking oil
1 teaspoon lemon extract

Glaze
2 cups sifted powdered sugar
2 tablespoons cooking oil
5 tablespoons calamondin purée
2 tablespoons water or purée, for desired consistency
Whipped topping for garnish

- To make purée, cut fruit in quarters and process in blender. Freeze in 1-cup portions.
- Thoroughly mix cake mix, gelatin, milk and calamondin purée.
- Beat eggs, oil and lemon extract and add to first mixture. Mix well.
- Pour into greased and floured 9 x 13-inch pan.
- Bake at 350° until cake springs to touch or sharp knife inserted at center comes out clean.
- Stir together glaze ingredients. Do not cook.
- Prick top of hot cake with fork. Leave in pan and pour glaze over top.
- Serve with whipped topping.

Cassata alla Siciliano

Serves 10

Large frozen pound cake
1 pound ricotta cheese
2 tablespoons heavy cream or
milk
¼ cup sugar
3 tablespoons orange liqueur
or Amaretto
3 tablespoons chopped
cherries, fruit, or citron
2 or more ounces semisweet
chocolate minichips

Frosting
12 ounces semisweet
chocolate minichips
¾ cup coffee, ground or
instant
2 sticks unsalted butter,
thoroughly chilled and cut
into chunks

- Slice off ends of cake. If desired, level off, too. Cut horizontally in four ½-¾-inch slabs.
- Sieve ricotta. Beat until smooth. Stir in cream, sugar and liqueur.
- Fold in cherries and chocolate.
- Fill slabs a layer at a time. Try to keep ends and sides even. End with a plain top.
- Gently compress. May be wobbly. (Do not scrape excess from sides.)
- Chill 2-3 hours until ricotta is firm. Remove excess and return to refrigerator.
- In heavy saucepan melt chocolate and coffee. Stir until dissolved and remove from heat.
- Beat in chilled butter, a piece at a time, until fully smooth.
- Chill until thick enough to spread.
- Frost cake with metal spatula.
- Leave overnight in refrigerator.
- Slice like bread for serving.

Orange Blossom Special

Yields 6 dozen cupcakes

1 box lemon cake mix
Grated rind from 3 oranges
Juice from 3 oranges
Juice from 3 lemons
1½ boxes powdered sugar

- Mix rind, juices and sugar. Allow to sit at least 8 hours.
- Prepare cake mix according to directions on box. Bake in mini-sized cupcake pans.
- While cupcakes are still warm, dunk into juice mixture. Place on waxed paper.

Chocolate Espresso Cheesecake

3 (8-ounce) packages cream cheese
26 chocolate wafers, crushed (1½ cups)
2 tablespoons sugar
¼ cup melted butter
2 (6-ounce) packages semi-sweet chocolate pieces
2 tablespoons instant espresso (may substitute 2 tablespoons plus 2 teaspoons instant coffee)
2 tablespoons hot water
1 cup sugar
3 tablespoons flour
3 eggs
2 egg yolks
1 cup heavy cream (unwhipped)

To serve: Loosen cake around edge with metal spatula. Remove side of spring form pan. Serve at room temperature. Keep unused cake in refrigerator. Garnish with whipped cream, chocolate curls, strawberries or bing cherries.

- Let cream cheese soften to room temperature.
- Blend the chocolate crumbs, sugar and melted butter in medium size bowl.
- Press firmly over the bottom and half way up the sides of a lightly buttered 9-inch spring-form pan.
- Chill briefly before filling.
- Melt chocolate in double boiler.
- Dissolve espresso in hot water.
- Beat cream cheese with electric mixer at medium speed until smooth.
- Add sugar gradually, beating until light and fluffy.
- Sprinkle flour over mixture. Blend thoroughly.
- Add eggs and egg yolks, 1 at a time, beating well after each addition.
- Beat in melted chocolate, espresso and unwhipped cream at low speed.
- Pour into prepared pan.
- Bake at 350° for 1 hour.
- Turn off oven and let cake remain in oven with door closed for 40 minutes.
- Remove cake from oven. Let cool completely on wire rack.
- Refrigerate several hours or overnight.

Deli Cheese Cake

Serves 10

1 pound cream cheese,
  softened
1 pound ricotta cheese
1½ cups sugar
4 large eggs, room
  temperature
¼ cup butter
3 tablespoons flour
3 tablespoons cornstarch
2½ teaspoons vanilla
2 cups sour cream

*Hint: Serve plain or topped with
a sprinkling of ground coffee
or fruit.*

- In large bowl, cream together cream cheese, ricotta and sugar. Beat in eggs, 1 at a time, beating well after each addition.
- Add melted and cooled butter, flour, cornstarch and vanilla. Beat well. Fold in sour cream.
- Pour batter into an ungreased 9-inch springform pan. Bake, in center of oven, 325° for 1 hour. The cake will be soft in center.
- Turn off heat. DO NOT open oven door. Leave for 2 hours.
- Let cake cool completely. Loosely cover. Chill at least 2 hours.
- Remove from pan to serving plate. Keep refrigerated.

Mini-Cheesecake Cups

Yields 4 dozen

3 (8-ounce) packages cream
  cheese, softened
5 eggs
1 cup sugar
½ teaspoon vanilla

Topping
1 cup sour cream
¼ cup sugar
¼ teaspoon vanilla

- Cream cheese well and add eggs. Beat well.
- Mix in sugar and vanilla.
- Fill paper-lined mini-muffin tins 2/3 full.
- Bake at 325° for 25 minutes.
- Cool 5 minutes.
- While cooking, mix topping ingredients together.
- Frost cakes with topping and bake 5 additional minutes.
- Refrigerate before serving.

Italian Cream Cake

Serves 16-20

1 stick margarine
½ cup shortening
2 cups sugar
5 eggs, separated
2 cups flour
1 teaspoon soda
1 cup buttermilk
1 teaspoon vanilla
1 cup coconut
1 cup chopped pecans

Icing
1 (8-ounce) package cream
  cheese
½ stick margarine
1 box powdered sugar, sifted
1 teaspoon vanilla

- Cream margarine, shortening and sugar.
- Add egg yolks 1 at a time.
- Sift flour and soda.
- Add with buttermilk, vanilla, coconut and pecans.
- Beat egg whites and fold in.
- Bake in three 9-inch pans at 325° for 18-20 minutes.
- Cool completely before icing.
- Beat cream cheese and margarine together until fluffy.
- Add sugar and vanilla.
- Beat well.
- Spread between layers and on top.
- Sprinkle with nuts.

Piña Colada Cake

1 package white cake mix
1 (3¾-ounce) box coconut
  instant pudding
4 eggs
½ cup water
5 tablespoons rum
¼ cup oil

Frosting
1 (3¾-ounce) box coconut
  instant pudding
1 (8-ounce) can crushed
  pineapple
5 tablespoons rum
1 (13-ounce) container
  whipped topping, thawed
1 cup flaked coconut

- Blend cake mix, pudding, eggs, water, rum and oil. Beat 4 minutes at medium speed.
- Pour into 2 greased and floured 9-inch layer cake pans.
- Bake at 350° for 25-30 minutes.
- Cool in pans for 15 minutes. Remove and let cool completely before frosting.
- Combine pineapple with juice, pudding and rum. Blend well.
- Fold in whipped topping.
- Fill and frost cake.
- Sprinkle coconut on top and sides. Refrigerate.

Oatmeal Cake

Serves 12 or more

1½ cups boiling water
1 cup oats (uncooked)
1½ cups flour
1 teaspoon cinnamon
1 teaspoon soda
½ teaspoon salt
1 cup brown sugar
1 cup white sugar
½ cup oil
2 eggs

Topping
1 stick butter
1 cup brown sugar
½ cup milk
½ cup chopped nuts
1 can coconut

- Pour boiling water over oats.
- Sift dry ingredients together.
- Add sugars, oil and eggs to oats. Stir in dry ingredients.
- Pour into greased and floured 9 x 13-inch pan.
- Bake at 350° for 35 minutes or until top springs back when touched.
- Mix butter, sugar and milk. Bring to rolling boil.
- Add nuts and coconut.
- Pour over cake while still in pan.
- Cool before cutting.

Regal Raspberry Almond Cake

Serves 10-12

¾ cup sugar
½ cup unsalted butter
8 ounces almond paste
3 eggs
1 tablespoon kirsch
¼ teaspoon almond extract
¼ cup flour
½ teaspoon baking powder
Powdered sugar

Sauce
2 cups fresh raspberries or 1 (12-ounce) frozen package, thawed and drained
Sugar to taste

- Combine sugar, butter and almond paste. Blend well.
- Beat in eggs, liqueur and almond extract. Add flour and baking powder, beating until just mixed.
- Bake in well buttered and floured 8-inch cake pan at 350° for 40-50 minutes or until tester inserted in center comes out clean.
- Cool. Invert onto serving plate; dust lightly with powdered sugar.
- Puree raspberries and sugar in blender. May press sauce through fine sieve to remove seeds. Serve on cake slices.

Old-fashioned Chocolate Cake

Serves 10-12

2 cups sifted cake flour
2 cups sugar
1 teaspoon cinnamon
½ teaspoon salt
1 teaspoon instant coffee
½ cup butter
½ cup shortening
1½ squares unsweetened
   chocolate
1 cup cold water
3 eggs, beaten
1 teaspoon vanilla
½ cup buttermilk
1 teaspoon baking soda

Frosting
½ cup butter
1½ squares unsweetened
   chocolate
5 tablespoons half and half or
   milk
¼ teaspoon salt
1 pound sifted powdered sugar
1½ teaspoons vanilla
½ cup finely chopped nuts

- Sift together first 4 ingredients.
- Stir in instant coffee.
- Combine butter, shortening, chocolate and water in small, heavy saucepan.
- Bring to simmer, stirring until chocolate melts.
- Pour chocolate mixture over dry ingredients, blending thoroughly.
- Stir in eggs and vanilla.
- Mix together buttermilk and baking soda. Stir into chocolate mixture, blending thoroughly.
- Pour into greased and floured 9 x 13-inch pan.
- Bake at 350° for 35 minutes.
- Cool and frost in pan.
- Combine first 4 frosting ingredients in heavy saucepan, stirring until melted and smooth.
- Remove from heat. Stir in sugar and vanilla, beating until smooth.
- Fold in nuts.
- Spread cake with warm frosting.

 Use cocoa rather than flour to dust pans for chocolate cakes.

Chocolate Pound Cake

Serves 20

½ pound butter
½ cup shortening
3 cups sugar
5 eggs
1 teaspoon baking powder
½ teaspoon salt
½ cup cocoa
3 cups flour
1 tablespoon vanilla
1 cup milk

Frosting
1 box powdered sugar
½ cup cocoa
1 stick butter, softened
¼ cup evaporated milk

- Cream together butter and shortening.
- Add sugar and eggs.
- Sift dry ingredients.
- Add vanilla and dry ingredients alternately with milk to creamed mixture.
- Bake in 10-inch tube pan for 1 hour and 20 minutes at 350°.
- Mix together in bowl sugar and cocoa.
- Add butter and milk. More milk may be needed for desired consistency.
- Spread in cooled cake.

One-Bowl Pound Cake

Serves 10-16

2 cups sugar
2 sticks butter or margarine
4 eggs
1 teaspoon vanilla
½ teaspoon soda
1 teaspoon salt
2¼ cups flour
1 (8-ounce) container sour cream or yogurt
Fruit topping or ice cream for garnish

- Cream sugar and margarine.
- Add eggs, vanilla, soda and salt.
- Pour in flour.
- Blend sour cream. Mix well.
- Pour in Bundt pan or 2 loaf pans.
- Bake at 350° for 60-65 minutes for Bundt pan; for loaf pans, bake 30-40 minutes.
- Cool and remove from pan.
- Serve with fruit topping or ice cream.

Swedish Pound Cake

Serves 10

1 cup margarine
2 cups sugar
5 eggs
2 cups flour
1 teaspoon vanilla
1 cup coconut
1 cup pecans

Glaze
¾ cup sugar
¾ cup water
1 stick margarine
1 teaspoon almond extract

- Cream margarine and sugar.
- Add eggs, 1 at a time. Beat well.
- Stir in flour until well blended.
- Add vanilla, coconut and nuts. Mix well.
- Bake in greased and floured tube pan at 350° for 1 hour.
- Combine sugar and water in pan and boil for 3 minutes.
- Remove from heat and add margarine and almond extract. Stir.
- With a long bamboo skewer, poke holes in warm cake. Pour glaze over while it's still warm.

Sherbet Cake

Serves 16-20

1 gallon vanilla ice cream, 3 flavors sherbet (½ gallon each)
1 large chocolate bar
2 cups chopped pecans

- Melt vanilla ice cream and pour 1 inch into bottom of angel food cake pan.
- Put in freezer to harden.
- When frozen fill half-way with different colored sherbet, scooped into balls. Leave space around balls and at top of pan.
- Pour more ice cream over this to fill spaces. Re-freeze.
- Make ½-inch layer of shaved chocolate and nuts.
- Repeat process of sherbet balls to top.
- Cover with remaining ice cream.
- Freeze until time to serve. Unmold and serve immediately.

Sunshine State Cake

Serves 8-12

1 cup sugar
1½ cups butter
1 teaspoon soda
2 eggs
5-6 tablespoons sour milk
2 cups flour
1 orange
1 cup raisins

Icing
½ cup white sugar
Juice of 1 orange

- Mix sugar and butter together.
- Add soda, eggs and milk.
- Add flour and mix.
- Juice the orange and save it.
- Grind the orange rind, pulp and raisins.
- Add to the above mixture. Mix well.
- Bake in a 9 x 13-inch pan.
- Bake at 350° for 30 minutes.
- Mix sugar with orange juice and spread on cake while hot.

Vanilla Wafer Cake

1 (12-ounce) box vanilla wafers
2 sticks butter or margarine, melted
2 cups sugar
2 cups shredded coconut
6 eggs
2 cups chopped pecans
½ cup milk or cream
½ pound glazed pineapple
½ pound glazed cherries

- Place cookies in heavy grocery bag and crush with rolling pin.
- Mix all ingredients together.
- Grease angel food pan and line bottom with waxed paper.
- Pour in batter and bake at 275° 1½ hours or until done.

Hint: Best to let this sit for a day to allow the flavors to blend.

Wine Fruitcake

Must prepare ahead

½ pound softened butter
1½ cups sugar
3 eggs
3 cups flour
½ teaspoon salt
¾ teaspoon each cinnamon,
  cloves, allspice
1 (8-ounce) package dates,
  chopped
½ pound candied red
  cherries, chopped
½ pound candied mixed fruit,
  chopped
½ cup red wine
½ cup applesauce
Additional red wine
1½ cups chopped pecans or
  walnuts

- Cream butter and sugar until light and fluffy.
- Add eggs, 1 at a time, beating well after each addition.
- Combine flour, salt and spices. Set aside.
- Combine fruit and pecans in a large bowl. Add ¾ cup flour mixture and toss to coat fruit.
- Add remaining flour mixture to creamed mixture alternately with wine and applesauce, mixing well after each addition.
- Fold in fruit and pecans.
- Spoon batter into a greased and waxed paper-lined 10-inch tube pan and bake at 250° for 3 hours or until done.
- Cool. Wrap tightly in foil or wine-soaked cheesecloth (after drizzling with ¼ cup wine).
- Store in refrigerator and drizzle with ¼ cup wine every 4-5 days.

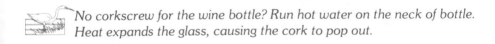

No corkscrew for the wine bottle? Run hot water on the neck of bottle. Heat expands the glass, causing the cork to pop out.

Caramel Chews

Yields 2 dozen

36 vanilla caramels
3 tablespoons light cream or
  milk
1 cup crisp rice cereal
1 cup flaked or shredded
  coconut
1 cup corn flakes
1 cup chopped pecans

- Place caramels and cream in top of double boiler and heat until caramels melt.
- Mix other ingredients and add to caramel mixture. Mix well.
- With buttered hands, roll into small walnut-sized balls and place on waxed paper.
- Store in airtight container.

Caramel Corn

Yields 5 quarts

2 cups packed light brown
  sugar
½ cup light corn syrup
½ pound butter or margarine
¼ teaspoon cream of tartar
1 teaspoon salt
1 teaspoon baking soda
5 quarts freshly popped corn

- In saucepan combine brown sugar, corn syrup, butter, cream of tartar and salt.
- Heat to boiling, stirring, over medium-high heat. Boil rapidly to hard-ball stage, stirring continuously.
- Remove from heat. Stir in baking soda quickly but thoroughly and pour at once over popcorn in a large roasting or baking pan. Stir until well coated.
- Bake at 200° for 1 hour, stirring 2-3 times during baking.
- Turn out on waxed paper. Spread apart and allow to cool. Break apart and store in tightly covered container.

Clara's Chocolate-Covered Cherries

1 stick unsalted butter,
softened
1 box powdered sugar, sifted
1 teaspoon vanilla
1-2 teaspoons heavy cream
1 (16-ounce) jar maraschino
cherries
8 ounces semi-sweet
chocolate
2 ounces parafin

*Hint: These taste best if made in
advance. They freeze well.*

- Cut butter into sugar until well blended.
- Add vanilla and enough heavy cream (1 teaspoon at a time) to form a stiff dough.
- Drain cherries and blot with a paper towel.
- Roll small amount of dough around each cherry.
- Place on cookie sheet and chill.
- Melt chocolate and wax in top of double boiler.
- Place toothpicks in top of each cherry, working with 20 at a time, and dip into chocolate mixture.
- Place on waxed paper to set.
- After all cherries have been dipped, spoon a drop or two of chocolate mixture on top of each cherry to cover hole made by toothpick.
- Refrigerate after making.

French Chocolates

Yields 5 dozen

1 (12-ounce) package semi-
sweet chocolate pieces
1 cup chopped walnuts or
pecans
¾ cup sweetened condensed
milk
1 teaspoon vanilla
¼ teaspoon salt
1 cup chocolate sprinkles

- In top of double boiler, melt chocolate pieces.
- Stir in nuts and other ingredients, reserving sprinkles.
- Cool mixture about 5 minutes or until easy to shape.
- With buttered hands, shape into 1-inch balls. Roll each immediately in chocolate sprinkles.
- Put in small bon-bon cups for storage.

Coconut Chews

Yields 2 dozen

2 grated coconuts
2 egg yolks
2½ cups sugar
1 can sweetened condensed
   milk
1 tablespoon vanilla
3 tablespoons margarine

- Mix ingredients and cook in heavy iron skillet until dry and sticky. Stir often.
- Form into small balls.
- Roll in plain or colored sugar.

Date Delights

Yields 30-40

2 sticks butter
2 cups dark brown sugar
1 (8-ounce) package dates,
   chopped
1 cup coconut
1 cup nuts, chopped fine
4 cups crisp rice cereal
1 teaspoon almond extract
½ cup powdered sugar

- Mix first 4 ingredients and heat slowly to bubbling point. Cook 5 minutes longer on low heat.
- Cool slightly. Fold in nuts, cereal and almond extract. Let cool.
- Roll into balls size of thumb then roll in powdered sugar.

Pralines

Yields 3 dozen

1½ cups sugar
¾ cup light brown sugar,
   packed
½ cup milk
¾ stick butter
1½ cups pecans

- Combine all ingredients.
- Bring to soft-ball stage (238-240°).
- Remove from heat. Stir until mixture cools and thickens.
- Spoon onto buttered waxed paper.
- When hardened, store in air-tight container.

Divine Divinity

Yields 32 pieces

2 cups sugar
6 tablespoons white corn
  syrup
½ cup water
Pinch salt
2 stiffly beaten egg whites
1 teaspoon vanilla
1 cup chopped nuts

*Hint: Do not attempt on a
humid or rainy day. Candy
will not reach hard-ball stage.
DO NOT DOUBLE — too
hard to work with.*

- Bring first 4 ingredients to boil until temperature reaches 210° or hard-ball stage.
- Remove from heat and slowly pour over stiffly beaten egg whites, beating entire time.
- When mixture begins to thicken and lose its gloss, discontinue beating. Add vanilla and nuts.
- Quickly drop by teaspoons onto waxed paper.

Peanut Brittle

2 cups sugar
1 cup corn syrup
½ cup water
1 teaspoon salt
2 cups shelled raw peanuts
1 teaspoon butter
1 teaspoon vanilla
1½ teaspoons baking soda

- Combine sugar, corn syrup, water and salt in pan. Bring to boil.
- Add peanuts. Cook until nuts become brittle and syrup turns amber.
- Add butter and vanilla.
- Cook slowly to 300° on candy thermometer, stirring occasionally.
- Remove from heat.
- Add soda. Stir well.
- Pour onto buttered cookie sheet or slab.
- Cool and pull thin. Break into pieces.

Cinnamon-Sugared Pecans

Yields 4 cups

1 cup sugar
¼ cup water
1 teaspoon cinnamon
½ teaspoon ginger
4 cups pecan halves

- Boil sugar and water until it reaches soft-ball stage.
- Add cinnamon and ginger.
- Pour over nuts and stir until all nuts are evenly coated.
- Cool.

Toffee Butter Crunch

Yields 1 pound

1 cup butter (do not use
  margarine)
1¼ cups sugar
3 tablespoons water
1 tablespoon light corn syrup
1 cup coarsely chopped
  blanched almonds, toasted
1 (8-ounce) milk chocolate
  bar
1 cup finely chopped
  blanched almonds, toasted

- Grease well a 9 x 13 x 2-inch baking pan.
- In large saucepan, melt butter.
- Add sugar, water and corn syrup.
- Cook over medium heat, stirring occasionally, to hard crack stage (300°).
- Quickly stir in coarsely chopped almonds and spread in prepared pan.
- Cool thoroughly.
- Turn out on waxed paper.
- Melt milk chocolate and spread over mixture.
- Sprinkle with finely chopped almonds.
- Chill to firm chocolate. Break into pieces.

 To shell Brazil nuts easily, bake at 350° for 15 minutes. Crack and shell.

Almond Crescents

Yields 8 dozen

2 cups soft butter
1 cup granulated sugar
½ teaspoon salt
3 teaspoons almond extract
4 cups sifted flour
1 cup finely chopped nuts
Powdered sugar

- Mix butter with sugar until light and fluffy.
- Add salt and extract.
- Add flour a little at a time. Mix well.
- Add nuts. Stir well.
- Refrigerate until easy to handle, about 1 hour.
- Shape dough into crescents.
- Place on ungreased cookie sheet.
- Bake at 350°, 12-15 minutes or until light brown.
- While still warm, roll in powdered sugar.
- Store in tight container.

Frosted Apricot Jewels

Yields 3 dozen cookies

1½ cups flour
¼ cup sugar
1½ teaspoons baking powder
¼ teaspoon salt
½ cup butter
1 (3-ounce) package cream cheese
½ cup flaked coconut
½ cup apricot preserves
Pecan halves

Frosting
1 cup sifted powdered sugar
1 tablespoon butter
¼ cup apricot preserves

- Combine flour, sugar, baking powder and salt.
- Cut in butter and cream cheese until mixture resembles coarse meal.
- Add coconut and preserves, mixing well.
- Drop by teaspoon onto ungreased cookie sheets.
- Bake at 350° for 15-18 minutes.
- Cool completely on a wire rack.
- Combine all frosting ingredients and beat until smooth.
- Spread each cookie with frosting and top with pecan half.

Baklava

Yields approximately 80 pieces

1 pound chopped walnuts
½ cup sugar
1 teaspoon cinnamon
5-6 sticks melted butter
1 pound box filo dough or
    struedel leaves

Syrup
3 cups sugar
2 cups water
1-2 teaspoons lemon juice

- Combine nuts, sugar and cinnamon. Set aside.
- Take defrosted filo dough out of box just before using. Cut whole package of dough in half to make two 9 x 12-inch sections.
- Melt butter.
- Using two 9 x 12-inch pans, brush butter on bottom of each pan.
- Lay 1 sheet of dough in pan and brush with butter.
- Repeat with 6 more layers, buttering each layer.
- Sprinkle 1-1½ cups nut mixture on dough.
- Add 7 more layers as the first 7 are done.
- Add 1-1½ cups more nut mixture.
- Add rest of dough, buttering each layer.
- Chill 30 minutes before cutting.
- Cut with sharp knife before baking, using a diagonal cut across vertical cuts.
- Bake at 300° for 1 hour, until light golden brown.
- Watch carefully, as burns easily.
- Bring all syrup ingredients to a boil. Reduce and simmer 15 minutes. Looks like water and tastes like honey.
- Pour hot syrup on cooled baklava using half on each pan.
- Let sit in refrigerator or at room temperature overnight to soak up juice.

Chewy Bran Bars

Yields 16 bars

2 tablespoons butter
¼ cup peanut butter
¼ cup brown sugar
½ cup honey
1½ cups chopped walnuts
2 teaspoons cinnamon
1 teaspoon vanilla
⅛ teaspoon salt
½ cup raisins, prunes or
   dates, chopped
2 cups whole bran cereal

- In heavy 3-quart pan, combine butter, peanut butter, brown sugar and honey.
- Cook over low heat, stirring constantly, until mixture begins to boil.
- Remove from heat.
- Add walnuts, cinnamon, vanilla and salt. Stir until blended.
- Stir in raisins and bran cereal.
- Mix until well coated.
- Turn mixture into a well-buttered 8 or 9-inch square pan.
- With a buttered spatula firmly press mixture into an even layer.
- Let cool until mixture begins to firm up, about 5 minutes.
- Cut into bars and let cool.
- Store airtight at room temperature.

Senate Brownies
from Senator Paula Hawkins

2 sticks margarine
4 squares unsweetened
   chocolate
2 cups sugar
3 eggs
1 teaspoon vanilla
1 cup flour
1½ cups walnuts
1 (6-ounce) package
   chocolate chips

- Melt margarine and chocolate in saucepan. Remove from heat.
- Stir in sugar until combined.
- Add eggs, 1 at a time.
- Stir in vanilla, flour and 1 cup walnuts.
- Spread in greased 9 x 13-inch baking pan.
- Top with ½ cup walnuts and chocolate chips.
- Bake at 350° for 35 minutes.

Anne's Cheesecake Cookies

¾ cup butter
¾ cup firmly packed brown
    sugar
2 cups flour
1 cup finely chopped pecans
1½ cups granulated sugar
3 (8-ounce) packages cream
    cheese
3 eggs
5 tablespoons milk
3 tablespoons lemon juice
1½ teaspoons vanilla

- Cream butter and brown sugar. Add flour and nuts.
- Using fingers, press all but 1½ cups for topping, in bottom of 9 x 13-inch pan.
- Bake at 350° for 12-15 minutes until lightly browned.
- Blend granulated sugar and cream cheese until smooth.
- Add eggs, milk, lemon juice and vanilla.
- Pour on top of baked crust and sprinkle with reserved crumbs.
- Bake at 350° for 25 minutes.
- Cool and cut into desired size squares.
- Refrigerate. Keeps 5-7 days in refrigerator.

Ginger Snaps

Yields 5 dozen

1½ cups shortening or
    margarine
2 cups sugar
2 eggs
½ cup molasses
4 cups sifted flour
2 teaspoons baking soda
2 teaspoons cinnamon
2 teaspoons cloves
2 teaspoons ginger

- Cream shortening and sugar.
- Beat in eggs. Add molasses and dry ingredients.
- Roll into 1-inch balls. Dip in granulated sugar.
- Place on greased cookie sheet 2 inches apart.
- Bake at 375° 15-18 minutes. Do not overbake.

Lunch Box Squares

Yields 25 bars or 1 cake

½ cup margarine
½ cup oil
1¾ cups sugar
2 eggs
1 teaspoon vanilla
½ cup buttermilk
2½ cups flour
1 teaspoon soda
½ teaspoon baking powder
½ teaspoon salt
¼ cup cocoa
1 teaspoon cinnamon
2 cups grated raw zucchini,
   drained and not peeled

- Cream margarine, oil and sugar.
- Add eggs 1 at a time. Blend in vanilla and milk.
- Add dry ingredients. Stir in zucchini.
- Spread in a greased 9 x 13-inch pan for a cake, or an 11 x 16-inch jelly roll pan for bars.
- Bake at 350° for 45 minutes for the cake or 10-20 minutes for the bars.

Orange Macaroons

Yields 4 dozen

1 (12-ounce) package vanilla
   wafers, crushed
½ cup frozen orange juice
   concentrate, thawed
¾ cup sifted powdered sugar
¾ cup shredded coconut
½ cup chopped pecans

- Combine all ingredients.
- Use hands to make a smooth mixture. Shape into 1-inch balls.
- Roll balls in additional powdered sugar.
- Store in covered container in the refrigerator.

Mocha Squares

Yields 24 squares

1 angel food cake
1 stick butter
1 box sifted powdered sugar
½ teaspoon vanilla
1 tablespoon instant coffee,
  dissolved in 2 tablespoons
  boiling water
1 large can salted peanuts,
  chopped

- Bake angel food cake according to mix directions or buy prepared cake. Cut into 1-1½ inch squares.
- Cream butter and sugar. Gradually add vanilla and cooled coffee.
- Spread frosting on cake squares and roll in crushed peanuts.

Monte Carlos

Yields 2 dozen

1 cup butter, room
  temperature
½ cup sugar
1 egg
1½ teaspoons vanilla
2 cups flour
1½ teaspoons baking powder
½ teaspoon salt
½ cup flaked coconut
¾ cup powdered sugar
2 teaspoons milk
½ cup raspberry preserves

- Combine ¾ cup butter, sugar, egg and 1 teaspoon vanilla. Beat on high speed until fluffy.
- Mix together flour, baking powder and salt.
- Add flour mixture and coconut to butter mixture. Mix well.
- Shape 1 teaspoon of dough into balls and place on greased cookie sheet. Flatten with a fork.
- Bake at 350° for 12-15 minutes until lightly browned.
- Remove from pan and cool.
- Beat remaining butter and powdered sugar together. Add milk and remaining vanilla. Mix well.
- Spread small amount of sugar mixture over smooth side of cookie then 1 teaspoon pre-serves. Top with second cookie, rough side up. Press together.

Oatmeal Lace Cookies

from Barbara Bush, wife of the President

Yields 4 dozen

½ cup flour
¼ teaspoon baking powder
½ cup sugar
½ cup quick cooking oats
2 tablespoons whipping
  cream
5 tablespoons melted butter
1 tablespoon vanilla
2 tablespoons white corn
  syrup

- Sift together into a bowl, the flour, baking powder and sugar.
- Add oats, cream, butter, vanilla and corn syrup.
- Mix until well blended.
- Preheat oven to 375°.
- Drop by slightly heaped ¼ teaspoon 4 inches apart onto ungreased baking sheet.
- Bake 4-6 minutes until lightly browned.
- Let stand a few seconds before removing from pan.

"The One" Cookie

Yields 8-9 dozen

1 cup margarine
1 cup granulated sugar
1 cup brown sugar (lightly
  packed)
1 large egg
1 cup oil
1 teaspoon vanilla
3½ cups flour
1 teaspoon salt
1 teaspoon baking soda
1 teaspoon cream of tartar
1 cup rolled oats
1 cup flaked coconut
1 cup crisp rice cereal
Granulated sugar

- Cream margarine and sugars.
- Beat in egg. Stir in oil and vanilla.
- Add salt, baking soda and cream of tartar to flour.
- Stir flour mixture into egg mixture until well blended. Stir in oats, coconut and cereal. (Dough will be very soft. Chill overnight in refrigerator.)
- Using a spoon, scoop up dough and form into 1-inch balls with hands.
- Place balls on ungreased cookie sheet. Flatten with bottom of glass dipped in sugar.
- Bake in a 350° oven for about 12 minutes.

Sharon's Caramel Pecan Bars

Yields 20-30 bars

¾ cup margarine
½ cup packed dark brown
 sugar
1½ cups flour
28 caramels
½ cup water
¼ cup margarine
2 eggs
¼ cup granulated sugar
½ teaspoon vanilla
¼ teaspoon salt
1 cup chopped pecans

- Cream margarine and brown sugar until light and fluffy.
- Add flour and mix well.
- Press dough into bottom of 9 x 13-inch baking pan.
- Bake at 375° for 15 minutes.
- Melt caramels with water and ¼ cup margarine over low heat. Stir occasionally until smooth.
- Combine eggs, granulated sugar, vanilla and salt. Gradually add caramel sauce. Mix well.
- Stir in pecans. Pour over crust.
- Continue baking 15 minutes.
- Cool. Cut into bars.

Pumpkin Bars

Yields 5 dozen bars

2 cups sugar
½ cup vegetable oil
1 (16-ounce) can pumpkin
4 eggs, beaten
2 cups buttermilk baking mix
2 teaspoons ground cinnamon
½ cup raisins

Frosting
1 (3-ounce) package cream
 cheese, softened
5-6 tablespoons margarine or
 butter, softened
1 tablespoon milk
1 teaspoon vanilla
2 cups powdered sugar

- Beat sugar, oil, pumpkin and eggs in large bowl on medium speed, scraping bowl occasionally, for 1 minute.
- Stir in baking mix, cinnamon and raisins.
- Pour into greased 10½ x 15½ x 1-inch jelly roll pan.
- Bake until wooden pick inserted in center comes out clean, 25-30 minutes. Cool.
- Beat cream cheese, margarine, milk and vanilla until creamy.
- Stir in powdered sugar until smooth and of desired consistency.
- Frost. Cut into 1 x 2 inch bars.

Lemon Pecan Squares

Yields 3 dozen bars

½ cup butter
¼ cup sugar
1 egg
1¼ cup sifted flour
⅛ teaspoon salt
½ teaspoon vanilla

Filling
2 eggs, beaten
1½ cups brown sugar
1½ chopped pecans
2 tablespoons flour
½ teaspoon baking powder
½ teaspoon salt
1 teaspoon vanilla

Icing
1½ cups powdered sugar,
    thinned with lemon juice

- Cream butter and sugar until well blended.
- Beat in 1 egg.
- Combine flour and salt. Add to creamed mixture. Blend well.
- Work in ½ teaspoon vanilla.
- Pat dough evenly into a 9 x 13-inch pan.
- Bake at 350° for 15 minutes.
- Mix filling ingredients and spread on top.
- Bake an additional 15 minutes.
- When cool, ice with powdered sugar mixture.

Potato Chip Cookies

1 pound butter
1¼ cups sugar
3½ cups flour
2 tablespoons vanilla
1½ cups crushed potato chips
Powdered sugar

Grandpa Foster won a blue ribbon at the Melbourne Beach Community Chapel social hour when the men prepared the refreshments one Sunday. He made potato chip cookies!

- Blend butter, sugar and vanilla. Cream well.
- Mix in flour and potato chips.
- Drop by teaspoon on ungreased cookie sheets.
- Bake at 350° for 12-15 minutes.
- While warm, sprinkle with powdered sugar.

Queen's Biscuits

Yields 6 dozen

4 cups sifted flour
1 cup sugar
1 tablespoon baking powder
¼ teaspoon salt
1 cup shortening
2 eggs, slightly beaten
½ cup milk
¼ pound (½-¾ cup) sesame
   seeds

- Sift together flour, sugar, salt and baking powder.
- Cut in shortening with a pastry blender or 2 knives until the pieces are size of small peas.
- Stir in eggs and milk to make a soft dough. Mix thoroughly.
- Break dough into small pieces and roll each piece between palms of hands to form rolls about 1½ inches long.
- Flatten slightly and roll in sesame seeds.
- Place on lightly greased cookie sheets ¾ inches apart.
- Bake at 375° for 12-15 minutes or until cookies are lightly browned. Cool completely before serving.

Ice Box Cookies

Yields 150 cookies

1 cup margarine
3 cups brown sugar
1 teaspoon almond or maple
   extract
1 cup chopped pecans
1 (7-ounce) package dry
   coconut
1 teaspoon soda
1 teaspoon baking powder
4 cups flour
2 eggs, well beaten

- Cream margarine and sugar.
- Add remaining ingredients. Dough will be quite stiff.
- Form into 2 rolls.
- Wrap in foil and store in refrigerator.
- When ready to bake, thinly slice dough.
- Bake on cookie sheet at 350° until light brown.
- Store baked cookies in air tight container.

Turtle Cookies

Yields 3 dozen

¾ cup butter or margarine
¾ cup powdered sugar
1 teaspoon vanilla
1¼ cups flour
¾ cup Quaker Oats, quick or
　old-fashioned, uncooked

Topping
25 caramels
2 tablespoons water
1 (6 ounce) package semi-
　sweet chocolate pieces
1 tablespoon oil

- Beat butter and sugar until light and fluffy. Blend in vanilla.
- Add remaining ingredients. Mix well.
- Shape into 1-inch balls.
- Bake on ungreased sheet at 325° for approximately 20 minutes until edges are light brown.
- Cool completely on wire rack.
- Melt caramels with water in small saucepan over low heat, stirring frequently.
- Spread or drizzle 1 teaspoon caramel sauce over each cookie.
- Melt chocolate with oil in small, heavy saucepan over low heat.
- Spoon over each cookie.
- Refrigerate to set chocolate.
- Store in tightly covered container at room temperature.

Peanut Butter Brownies

Serves 12-14

½ cup creamy peanut butter
5 tablespoons butter
1 cup sugar
¼ cup firmly packed brown
　sugar
2 eggs
1 teaspoon vanilla
1 cup flour
1 teaspoon baking powder
¼ teaspoon salt
6 ounces semi-sweet
　chocolate

- Beat peanut butter and butter.
- Add sugars and mix.
- Add eggs, 1 at a time.
- Add vanilla.
- Mix remaining ingredients and add to creamed ingredients.
- Bake in 9-inch greased pan at 350° for 30 minutes.

Amelia Plantation Mud Pie

15-20 Oreo cookies
2 tablespoons butter
15 ounces chocolate ice
  cream
2 tablespoons ground coffee
2 tablespoons Sanka
2 tablespoons whipped cream
2 tablespoons brandy
2 tablespoons Kahlúa
Kraft fudge topping

- Mix finely crushed cookies with melted butter.
- Press into 9-inch pie pan and place in freezer.
- Whip chocolate ice cream with ground coffee, Sanka, brandy and Kahlúa.
- Fold in whipped cream and pour mixture into cookie shell.
- Return to freezer until firm.
- Cover surface with fudge topping and garnish with whipped cream and a cherry.

Unique Apple Pie

Serves 6-7

1 cup sour cream
¾ cup sugar
2 tablespoons flour
½ teaspoon salt
1 teaspoon vanilla
1 egg
2 cups tart apples, peeled and
  diced

Topping
½ cup brown sugar
¼ cup flour
¼ cup butter
9-inch pie shell

- Mix first 6 ingredients. Add apples and stir.
- Pour into pie shell and bake at 400° for 25 minutes.
- Toss together topping ingredients until crumbly.
- Sprinkle over pie and return to oven for 20 minutes.

Whoopie Pies

Yields 3 dozen

1 cup sugar
2 cups flour
1 teaspoon baking powder
½ teaspoon salt
1 teaspoon soda
½ cup shortening
2 egg yolks
1 cup milk
5 tablespoons cocoa
1 teaspoon vanilla

Filling
2 egg whites
2 cups powdered sugar
1 teaspoon vanilla
¼ teaspoon salt
½ cup shortening

- Sift dry ingredients together.
- Add remaining ingredients and mix well.
- Drop by teaspoon on ungreased cookie sheet.
- Bake at 375° for 10-12 minutes until set but not crisp.
- When cool, put together sandwich style with filling.
- To make filling, combine all ingredients and beat until smooth.

Peanut Butter Blossoms

Yields 6 dozen

1 cup margarine
1 cup peanut butter
1 cup sugar
1 cup firmly packed brown sugar
2 eggs
1 teaspoon vanilla
2½ cups flour
1 teaspoon baking powder
1 teaspoon baking soda
1 teaspoon salt
Sugar
Nuts
Chocolate Kisses
Jam or jelly

- Using mixer at medium speed, beat first 6 ingredients until fluffy.
- At low speed, beat in next 4 ingredients.
- Shape into 1-inch balls. Roll in sugar.
- Place 2 inches apart on ungreased cookie sheets.
- Bake in 350° oven 12-15 minutes or until browned.
- Immediately press nuts or candies into cookies, or press with thumb and fill with jam.
- Cool. Store in airtight container.

Caramel Crunch Apple Pie

28 caramels
2 tablespoons water
4 cups peeled, sliced apples
½ teaspoon cinnamon
¾ cup flour
1/3 cup sugar
1/3 cup margarine or butter
½ cup chopped nuts
1 (9-inch) pie shell

- Melt caramels with water in top of double boiler, stirring occasionally until mixture is smooth.
- Layer apples and caramel sauce in pie shell.
- Combine cinnamon, flour and sugar.
- Cut in butter until mixture is crumbly. Stir in nuts.
- Sprinkle over top of pie and bake at 375° for 50-60 minutes or until apples are tender.

Chocolate Bavarian Velvet

Serves 10

1½ cups crushed Oreos
5-6 tablespoons melted margarine
8 ounces softened cream cheese
½ cup sugar, divided
1 teaspoon vanilla
2 egg yolks, beaten
1 (6-ounce) package semi-sweet chocolate chips, melted
2 egg whites
1 cup heavy cream
½ cup nuts

- Mix Oreos and melted margarine.
- Press into bottom of greased 9-inch spring-form pan.
- Bake 10 minutes at 325°. Cool.
- Blend cream cheese, ¼ cup sugar and vanilla.
- Add egg yolks and melted chocolate chips.
- Beat egg whites to soft peaks.
- Gradually add ¼ cup sugar.
- Fold into chocolate mixture.
- Beat heavy cream until stiff.
- Fold into chocolate mixture.
- Fold in nuts.
- Pour over crust and freeze.
- Thaw slightly before serving.

Chocolate Silk Pie

2 sticks butter, divided
2 cups coconut
1 cup chopped pecans
1½ cups sugar
4 squares unsweetened
    chocolate, melted
2 teaspoons vanilla
4 eggs
Whipping cream

- Melt ½ butter in skillet. Add coconut and brown lightly.
- Mix in pecans.
- Press mixture into a 9-inch pie pan, saving ¼ cup to sprinkle over top of pie.
- Cream remaining butter and sugar.
- Blend in melted chocolate and vanilla.
- Add eggs, 1 at a time, beating 5 minutes after each addition.
- Pour filling into crust and place in freezer for 1 hour before serving.
- Top with whipped cream and remaining crust mixture.

Coffee Ice Cream Pie

Serves 6

2 squares unsweetened
    chocolate
2 tablespoons butter
2 tablespoons hot milk
¾ cup powdered sugar
1½ cups unsweetened
    coconut
1 quart coffee ice cream

Variation: May substitute other flavors of ice cream.

- Melt chocolate, remove from heat.
- Add butter, hot milk, sugar and coconut. Mix well.
- Spread mixture evenly on bottom and sides of an 8 to 9-inch pie plate. Place in freezer until firm, about 30 minutes.
- Remove. Fill shell with ice cream and return to freezer until ready to serve.

Fudge Sundae Pie

Serves 8

¼ cup white corn syrup
2 tablespoons brown sugar
3 tablespoons butter
2½ cups crisp rice cereal
¼ cup peanut butter
¼ cup fudge sauce
3 tablespoons white corn syrup
1 quart vanilla ice cream

- Combine ¼ cup corn syrup, brown sugar and butter in saucepan.
- Cook over low heat until mixture begins to boil.
- Remove from heat.
- Add cereal, stirring until well coated. Press evenly into a 9-inch pie pan.
- Stir together peanut butter, fudge sauce and 3 tablespoons corn syrup.
- Spread half of mixture over crust. Freeze until firm.
- Spread softened ice cream into crust. Freeze until firm.
- Drizzle remainder of peanut butter mixture over top of ice cream.

Key Lime Pie

Serves 6-8

6 eggs (separated)
1 (15-ounce) can sweetened condensed milk
½ cup Key lime juice
3 tablespoons sugar
1 (9-inch) baked pie shell or crumb crust

- Beat egg yolks.
- Add condensed milk. Blend well.
- Add lime juice. Blend until smooth.
- Pour into baked pie shell or crumb crust.
- Beat egg whites. Gradually add sugar and beat until meringue stands in stiff peaks.
- Top pie filling with meringue.
- Bake 350° for 5-7 minutes, until meringue is a light golden brown.

Old-fashioned Peach Cobbler

Serves 6-8

1 stick margarine
1 cup sugar
1 cup milk
1 cup all purpose flour
2¼ teaspoons baking powder
¼ teaspoon salt
1 quart fresh sliced peaches
   or berries

- Melt margarine in 1½-2-quart glass dish in which pie is to be cooked.
- In medium mixing bowl, mix sugar, milk, flour, salt and baking powder. Beat until creamy.
- Pour into pan with melted margarine.
- Do not stir.
- Pour peaches or berries on top.
- Bake 1 hour at 350°.
- Serve with a scoop of ice cream or whipped cream.

Casbah Peanut Butter Pie
based on the original from "Pop's Casbah," Melbourne

1 (9-inch) baked pie shell
½ cup smooth peanut butter
Powdered sugar, to desired
   consistency
¾ cup granulated sugar
Dash salt
3 tablespoons cornstarch
2 cups milk
3 egg yolks, slightly beaten
2 tablespoons butter
1 teaspoon vanilla
Whipped cream or whipped
   topping

- Blend together peanut butter and powdered sugar until a crumbly streusel is formed. Set aside.
- In saucepan, combine sugar, salt and cornstarch. Gradually stir in milk and cook until mixture boils. Cook 2 more minutes; remove from heat.
- Stir small amount of hot mixture into yolks; return to hot mixture. Cook and stir 2 minutes. Remove from heat; add butter and vanilla. Cool to room temperature.
- Sprinkle enough streusel to cover bottom of pie shell.
- As you spread cooked filling into pastry shell, sprinkle streusel throughout. Do not stir.
- Top with sweetened whipped cream or topping.
- Chill.

Alberta's Pecan Pie

Yields 1 pie or 42 mini-pies

3 beaten eggs
1 cup white corn syrup
⅛ teaspoon salt
1 teaspoon vanilla
1 cup sugar
2 tablespoons melted butter
1 cup broken pecan pieces
1 baked pie crust

- Beat eggs with fork. Add syrup, salt, vanilla, sugar and butter.
- Mix and add nuts.
- Pour into prepared crust.
- Bake at 400° for 15 minutes.
- Reduce temperature to 350° and bake for 30 minutes or until set in center.
- If crust begins to brown too much, cover with foil and continue cooking.

Prohibition Pecan Pie

Serves 6-8

Pastry
1 cup flour
¼ teaspoon salt
6 tablespoons butter, chilled
3 tablespoons brandy, chilled

Filling
½ cup butter
½ cup sugar
¾ cup light corn syrup
¼ cup maple syrup
3 eggs, lightly beaten
3 tablespoons light rum
1½ cups whole pecans, divided

- Combine flour and salt.
- Cut in butter until mixture resembles cornmeal.
- Sprinkle brandy over mixture and stir until particles cling together when pressed gently.
- Shape dough into ball and chill 20 minutes.
- Roll out dough to fit 9-inch pie pan. Carefully place in pan and shape edges. Prick with fork.
- Bake in 425° oven for 12 minutes or until golden brown.
- Cream butter and sugar until light and fluffy.
- Add syrups, eggs and rum. Beat well. Stir in ¾ cup pecans.
- Pour filling into pastry and top with remaining pecans.
- Bake at 325° about 55 minutes.

Pumpkin Pecan Pie

from First Lady Nancy Reagan

4 eggs, slightly beaten
2 cups canned or mashed
   cooked pumpkin
1 cup sugar
½ cup dark corn syrup
1 teaspoon vanilla
½ teaspoon cinnamon
¼ teaspoon salt
1 (9-inch) unbaked pie shell
1 cup chopped pecans

- Combine ingredients, except pecans.
- Pour into pie shell. Top with pecans.
- Bake at 350° for 40 minutes, or until set.

Creamy Pumpkin Pie

Serves 8

2 cups canned pumpkin
14 ounces sweetened
   condensed milk
2 eggs
1 teaspoon cinnamon
½ teaspoon salt
½ teaspoon ginger
½ teaspoon nutmeg
1 (9-inch) pie shell baked until
   blistered and lightly
   browned

- Mix all ingredients. Blend well.
- Pour into baked pie shell and bake at 425° for 15 minutes.
- Turn oven down to 350° and bake 35-40 minutes. Chill.
- Serve with whipped cream or Cool Whip.

 Save butter or margarine wrappers, folded in half and stored in refrigerator. Use to grease cake pans before baking.

Key Lime Baked Alaska
from Marker 88, Florida Keys

Serves 12

4 egg yolks, beaten
1 can sweetened condensed
   milk
½ cup Key lime juice
½ gallon brick vanilla ice
   cream

Frosting
4 egg whites
½ teaspoon cream of tartar
½ cup sugar
Grated chocolate or toasted
   almonds

- Blend yolks in sweetened condensed milk. Add lime juice.
- Cut ice cream into 1-inch slices.
- Arrange half of the slices on bottom of loaf pan. Pour egg mixture over this. Top with layer of remaining ice cream.
- Freeze overnight.
- Unmold on brown paper and replace in freezer for 15 minutes.
- Beat egg whites with cream of tartar until very stiff.
- Gradually add sugar and continue beating.
- Frost ice cream mold with meringue about ½-inch thick.
- Sprinkle with chocolate or almonds.
- Place on bread board (so heat won't melt ice cream on bottom of mold).
- Bake in 500° oven 5 minutes, watching carefully.

Holiday Ambrosia

Serves 8

1 cup heavy cream, whipped
½ cup sour cream
1 tablespoon Grand Marnier
2 cups orange sections
1 cup grapefruit sections
1 cup grated fresh coconut
Marshmallows

- Whip cream. Fold in sour cream and liqueur.
- Add fruit sections, coconut and marshmallows.
- Must chill overnight.
- May garnish with green or red cherries for color.

316

Banana Split Dessert

Serves 12

Crust
2 cups chocolate cookies or
  graham cracker crumbs
1 stick butter, melted

Filling
3 sticks butter, softened
3 cups powdered sugar
3 eggs
1½ teaspoons vanilla

Topping
1 cup crushed pineapple, well
  drained
4 bananas, sliced
1 (8-ounce) container Cool Whip
Maraschino cherries
Walnuts or pecans, chopped

- Mix and spread crust ingredients in 9 x 13 x 2-inch pan.
- Mix and beat filling ingredients for 20 minutes with electric mixer. Thin with milk, if too thick. Spread over crust.
- Top with pineapple, bananas and Cool Whip. Garnish with maraschino cherries and nuts.
- Make ahead and refrigerate.

Frozen Chocolate Dessert
from Senator Paul Laxalt

Serves 10

6½ tablespoons margarine
2 cups powdered sugar
3 egg yolks, beaten
1 tablespoon vanilla
2 squares unsweetened
  chocolate, melted
1 cup nuts
Pinch salt
3 egg whites
1 package graham cracker
  crumbs
2 pints vanilla ice cream

- Mix first 7 ingredients.
- Fold in beaten egg whites.
- Butter a 9 x 9-inch (or 9 x 13-inch if recipe is doubled) pan.
- Put ½ the graham crackers in bottom of pan and add mixture.
- Freeze for 2 hours.
- Beat ice cream in mixer.
- Add to top of frozen mixture.
- Sprinkle top with remaining crumbs and freeze at least an hour or until ready to serve.

Bourbon on a Cloud

Serves 8

¾ cup sugar
1 envelope plain gelatin
3 egg yolks, beaten
¾ cup bourbon
3 egg whites
2 cups whipping cream
8 lady fingers

Hint: May be served in individual sherbet glasses.

- Combine half of sugar with gelatin in top of double boiler.
- Mix in egg yolks. Gradually add bourbon, stirring rapidly.
- Cook over hot, not boiling, water until slightly thick and mixture coats a metal spoon. Cool.
- Beat egg whites until stiff. Continue beating and gradually add remaining sugar.
- Gradually add the cooked mixture to egg whites.
- Chill until it begins to thicken.
- Fold in 1 cup of whipped cream.
- Arrange lady fingers in 2-quart mold. Pour mixture over top.
- Top with whipped cream.

Eclair Dessert

Serves 10-16

1 box graham crackers
2 (3-ounce) boxes instant French vanilla pudding
3½ cups milk
1 (9-ounce) container Cool Whip

Frosting
2 packages Redi-blend presoftened chocolate, unsweetened
2 teaspoons vanilla
3 tablespoons melted butter
1½ cups powdered sugar
3 tablespoons milk

- Cover bottom of 9 x 13-inch buttered pan with whole graham crackers.
- Mix pudding and milk, beat 2 minutes. Blend in Cool Whip.
- Pour ½ mixture over graham crackers.
- Add another layer of graham crackers.
- Cover with rest of pudding.
- Add third layer of crackers.
- Refrigerate 2 hours.
- Beat together frosting ingredients and spread on top of cake.

Gâteau Ganache

Serves 8

Cake

2 (4-ounce) packages ground
  almonds
4 egg whites
Pinch salt
⅛ teaspoon cream of tartar
1 teaspoon vanilla
1 cup sugar

Sauce

6 ounces sweet German
  chocolate
¾ cup sugar
1 cup water
1 tablespoon butter

Filling

2 cups whipping cream
1 teaspoon vanilla
1 teaspoon to 1 tablespoon
  rum

Cake
- Toast almonds to a golden brown at 350° for 8-10 minutes. Finely crush when cool.
- Beat egg whites to a firm snow with salt, cream of tartar and vanilla.
- Beat in sugar gradually.
- Fold nuts into the stiff egg whites very carefully.
- Turn the mixture into 2 cake pans 8 inches in diameter, greased and floured and lined with parchment paper.
- Bake at 350° for about 35 minutes.
- Turn out of cake tins and allow to cool.

Sauce
- Break up chocolate and put into a pan with the water.
- Stir over heat and allow chocolate to melt.
- Add the sugar and simmer uncovered for 10-15 minutes.
- Add 1 tablespoon butter.
- Cool.

Filling
- Whip cream and fold in 2-3 tablespoons of chocolate sauce, rum and vanilla.
- Spread this on 1 round. Cover with other round and frost the sides.
- Sprinkle top with powdered sugar and decorate with rosettes of whipped cream.
- This should sit several hours in the refrigerator before serving.
- Serve chilled with chocolate sauce.

Mazie's Miracle

Serves 20

Prepare day before serving

**4 dozen (10 ounces) Amaretti
(Italian Macaroons)**
1 cup bourbon
1 pound sweet butter
2 cups sugar
1 dozen eggs, separated
**4 squares unsweetened
chocolate, melted**
1 teaspoon vanilla
1 cup chopped pecans
2 dozen double ladyfingers
**1½ cups whipping cream,
whipped**

- Soak macaroons in bourbon.
- Cream butter and sugar together until light and fluffy.
- Beat egg yolks until light. Beat into creamed mixture.
- Beat chocolate into the butter mixture.
- Add vanilla and pecans.
- Beat egg whites until stiff but not dry. Fold into chocolate mixture.
- Line a 10-inch spring-form pan, around the sides and on the bottom with split ladyfingers.
- Alternate layers of soaked macaroons and chocolate mixture in lined pan.
- Chill overnight.
- Remove sides of pan and decorate the top with whipped cream.

Mango Cream

Serves 10

5 large ripe mangos
**Small amount of sugar to
taste**
**2 oranges, peeled and cut
into small pieces**
1 tablespoon lemon juice
**2 cups heavy cream, whipped
with sugar to taste**

- Purée mangos in food processor or blender.
- Add sugar and blend well.
- Remove from processor and place in another bowl.
- Add oranges and lemon juice. Blend well.
- Fold in whipped cream carefully and place in tall parfait glasses.
- Chill several hours.

Cheesecake Ice Cream

Serves 16

2 egg yolks
1 cup sugar
1 cup half and half
2 (8-ounce) packages cream
   cheese
½ teaspoon grated lemon rind
1 tablespoon fresh lemon
   juice
½ teaspoon vanilla
1 pint plain yogurt

- In a heavy saucepan beat egg yolks with ½ cup sugar. Blend in half and half.
- Cook over low heat, stirring constantly, just until thick enough to coat the back of a spoon. Do not boil.
- Remove from heat. Chill.
- Beat cream cheese until light. Add ½ cup sugar and remaining ingredients.
- Add chilled ingredients. Beat well.
- Freeze in ice cream freezer, using manufacturer's directions.

Fresh Grapefruit Sorbet

Yields 4 cups

3½ cups pink grapefruit juice
¾ cup sugar
1-2 tablespoons Kirsch
   (optional)

- Squeeze grapefruit, strain and stir in sugar until dissolved.
- Taste for sweetness.
- Add Kirsch and freeze.

 To increase amount of juice from citrus fruits, dip in hot water for 10 minutes or microwave for 15 seconds before squeezing. A longer time is required for larger fruits.

Ice Cream Crunch

Serves 8-12

1 stick margarine
½ cup oatmeal
½ cup brown sugar
1 cup flour
6 ounces chopped pecans
½ gallon natural vanilla ice
  cream, softened
Chocolate syrup
Whipped cream (optional)

- Melt margarine. Combine with oatmeal, brown sugar, flour and pecans.
- Place mixture on ungreased cookie sheet and brown for approximately 30 minutes at 350°.
- Stir frequently to prevent burning.
- Remove from oven and cool.
- Pat half of crunch mixture on bottom of 9 x 13-inch pan.
- Spread softened ice cream over this.
- Cover ice cream with chocolate syrup.
- Put remaining half of crunch mixture on top.
- Freeze until firm. May top with dollop of whipped cream before serving.

Mango Ice Cream

Serves 4

½ cup mango, crushed
½ teaspoon lemon juice
1 cup heavy cream
2 teaspoons crème de cocoa
4 egg whites
¼ cup sugar
Salt to taste

- Peel and mash mangos. Add lemon juice.
- Whip cream until stiff. Add crème de cocoa.
- Fold mangos into whipped cream.
- Beat egg whites and sugar gradually. Add salt.
- Fold into mango mixture. Freeze until firm.

Mango Sorbet

Yields 1½ quarts

1 cup sugar
3 cups water
5-6 ripe medium-sized
    mangos
¼ cup fresh lemon juice
¼ cup Cointreau or orange-
    flavored liqueur

- Combine sugar and water in saucepan, stirring constantly over low heat until sugar dissolves.
- Continue cooking until just boiling and reduce heat.
- Simmer 3-4 minutes. Remove from heat.
- Refrigerate covered until cold, usually 1-2 hours.
- Peel mangos, scraping all fruit from the pits.
- Puree fruit in 3-cup blender or processor.
- Blend mango puree, cold syrup, lemon juice and liqueur in bowl.
- Strain and freeze in metal pan.

Milky Way Ice Cream

Serves 8-10

8 Milky Way bars
2 cups milk
6 eggs
2 teaspoons vanilla
1½ cups sugar
2 large cans evaporated milk

- Melt candy with milk in double boiler.
- Let cool.
- While milk is cooling, beat eggs until frothy. Add sugar and vanilla. Beat well.
- Add evaporated milk.
- Fold in cooled Milky Way mixture. Mix well.
- Pour into 1-gallon ice cream freezer.
- Add additional milk as needed to fill to proper capacity according to freezer instructions.

Aunt Marg's Baked Apples

Serves 6

Sauce
2 cups sugar
2 cups water
¼ teaspoon cinnamon
¼ teaspoon nutmeg
¼ cup butter

Dumplings
¾ cup shortening
2 cups flour
1 teaspoon salt
2 teaspoons baking powder
½ cup milk

6 apples, pared and cored
Sugar
Cinnamon
Butter

Hint: For crispier pastry, bake 20 minutes before adding sauce.

- Make sauce by combining sugar, water, cinnamon and nutmeg.
- Cook 5 minutes. Add butter and set aside.
- Cream shortening.
- Mix together flour, salt and baking powder. Cut into shortening.
- Stir in milk and mix well.
- Roll pastry ¼-inch thick and cut into 5-inch squares.
- Place 1 apple in center of each square. Fill center of each apple with 1 tablespoon sugar, a dash of cinnamon and a dot of butter.
- Seal pastry on top of each apple.
- Place in greased baking pan. Pour sauce over apples.
- Bake at 375° for 35 minutes.

Bananas Foster

Serves 6

4 small firm bananas
Lemon juice
4 tablespoons packed brown sugar
6 tablespoons butter or margarine
Ground cinnamon
3 tablespoons banana liqueur or almond liqueur
3 tablespoons light rum
Vanilla ice cream, optional

- Peel bananas and cut in half crosswise and lengthwise. Brush with lemon juice.
- Melt brown sugar and butter in shallow chafing dish or skillet.
- Add bananas. Cook just until tender, 3-4 minutes, turning once.
- Sprinkle lightly with cinnamon.
- Drizzle liqueur over all.
- In a small saucepan heat rum over low heat just until warm. Ignite. Pour over bananas.
- Serve with vanilla ice cream, if desired.

Joe's Bread Pudding

from New Orleans School of Cooking

Serves 16-20

1 (16-ounce) loaf stale bread, broken into small pieces
4 cups milk
2 cups sugar
4 tablespoons melted butter
3 eggs
2 tablespoons vanilla
1 cup raisins, soaked in whiskey
1 cup coconut
1 cup chopped pecans
1 teaspoon cinnamon
1 teaspoon nutmeg

Whiskey Sauce
½ cup butter
1½ cups powdered sugar
1 egg
½ cup whiskey, to taste

- Combine all ingredients. Mixture should be very moist but not soupy.
- Pour into greased 2-quart shallow baking dish.
- Bake at 350° for 1 hour 15 minutes, until top is golden.
- Serve warm with sauce.
- Cream butter and sugar over medium heat until butter is melted.
- Remove from heat. Blend in egg.
- Pour in whiskey gradually, stirring. Sauce will thicken as it cools. Serve warm over bread pudding.

Hot Curried Fruit

Serves 8

¾ cup brown sugar
2 tablespoons cornstarch
1 tablespoon curry powder
1 (16-ounce) can pineapple chunks, undrained
1 (16-ounce) can sliced peaches, undrained
1 (16-ounce) can sliced pears, undrained
¾ cup maraschino cherries, drained
½ cup melted butter

- Butter a 2-quart casserole.
- Blend together brown sugar, cornstarch and curry powder.
- Place fruit and juice in casserole. Add melted butter.
- Blend in brown sugar mixture.
- Bake uncovered at 350° for 40 minutes.

Hint: Fresh fruit may be used.

Red Berry Pudding

Serves 4-6

2 (10-ounce) packages frozen
   raspberries, thawed
2 (10-ounce) packages frozen
   strawberries, thawed
¼ cup cornstarch
⅜ cup Amaretto
Granulated sugar
1 cup whipped cream
Blanched slivered almonds

- Bring berries to a boil in saucepan, stirring occasionally.
- Cool and purée in blender or processor.
- Combine cornstarch and liqueur into smooth paste.
- Return fruit to boiling. Add corn-starch mixture, stirring constantly.
- Cook 3 minutes; stir constantly.
- Pour into serving dish and sprinkle with sugar. Chill.
- Garnish with whipped cream and almonds.

Spanish Pudim Flan

Serves 6-8

2 cups sugar
4 eggs
4 egg yolks
1 pint milk
1 teaspoon vanilla extract

*Hint: When ready to serve,
  gently pass the blade of a
  knife around dish edges and
  carefully turn out.*

- Put 6 tablespoons of sugar into a small saucepan and heat until it browns, stirring carefully. Pour into a warmed soufflé dish, rotating it slowly to cover the bottom of the dish.
- In a large dish, lightly beat remaining sugar with eggs and yolks.
- Bring milk to a boil in a saucepan and gradually add to egg mixture, continuing to beat.
- Stir in vanilla.
- Pour mixture into soufflé dish and cover the top with foil.
- Place in a baking tin and pour enough boiling water in tin to reach half-way up sides of dish.
- Bake at 350° for 1-1½ hours. When set, remove from oven and cool. Chill.

INDEX

The Big Catch, By Nancy Vice. Photographed by Franko Photo.

"The orange tree, in our view, is the best worthy to represent the tree of life of any that grows on our earth. It is the fairest, the noblest, the most generous; it is the most upspringing and abundant of all trees which the Lord God caused to grow eastward in Eden."

Harriet Beecher Stowe

Index

331

335

NOTES

NOTES